D0247891

Exploring Play

for Early Childhood Studies

Mandy Andrews

WITHDRAWN FROM THE LIBRARY

UNIVERSITY OF WINCHESTER

KA 0381097 6

Exploring Play

for Early Childhood Studies

Mandy Andrews

UNIVERSITY OF WINCHESTER
LIBRARY

Learning Matters
An imprint of SAGE Publications Ltd
1 Oliver's Yard
55 City Road
London EC1Y 1SP

SAGE Publications Inc.
2455 Teller Road
Thousand Oaks, California 91320

SAGE Publications India Pvt Ltd
B1/I 1 Mohan Cooperative Industrial Area
Mathura Road
New Delhi 110 044

SAGE Asia-Pacific Pte Ltd
3 Church Street
#10-04 Samsung Hub
Singapore 049483

Editor: Amy Thornton
Development editor: Geoff Barker
Production controller: Chris Marke
Project management: Deer Park Productions,
Tavistock, Devon
Marketing manager: Catherine Slinn
Cover design: Wendy Scott
Typeset by: PDQ Typesetting Ltd
Printed and bound in Great Britain by: MPG
Books Group, Bodmin, Cornwall

© 2012 Mandy Andrews

First published in 2012

Apart from any fair dealing for the purposes of
research or private study, or criticism or review,
as permitted under the Copyright, Designs and
Patents Act, 1988, this publication may be
reproduced, stored or transmitted in any form,
or by any means, only with the prior
permission in writing of the publishers, or in
the case of reprographic reproduction, in
accordance with the terms of licences issued by
the Copyright Licensing Agency. Enquiries
concerning reproduction outside those terms
should be sent to the publishers.

Library of Congress Control Number:
2012936246

British Library Cataloguing in Publication data

A catalogue record for this book is available
from the British Library.

ISBN 978 0 85725 685 0 (pbk) and
978 0 85725 846 5 (hbk)

MIX
Paper from
responsible sources
FSC
www.fsc.org   FSC® C018575

UNIVERSITY OF WINCHESTER

Contents

Part 3: Children's rights and the ownership of play

The author

Mandy Andrews is a senior lecturer in Early Childhood at the University of Worcester on both undergraduate and postgraduate programmes. Formerly a Play Officer for a local authority she has a range of children's play experience from running an adventure playground and environmental play activities, through to community play projects and running a large Children's Centre in Cornwall before moving to the University of Worcester. Mandy has also been a playwork trainer for many years supporting programmes in Buckinghamshire, Berkshire, and Cornwall. She has undertaken research into children's play in early years settings, outdoors and at the Eden Project and continues to pursue a research interest in this area.

Acknowledgements

Every effort has been made to trace the copyright holders and to obtain their permission for use of copyright material. The publisher and author will gladly receive any instruction enabling them to rectify any error or omission in subsequent editions.

The author would like to thank all those who have helped her to source the information and images used in this book. Special thanks go to the following: Sian and Cassie Andrews; Jacob Cockle for the photograph of the play face in Chapter 1; Michelle, Josh and Jayden Dunkley for the use of the photograph in Chapter 5; Annie Vigar, Jeremy Vigar, Emma Waller and Mark Gregory for the use of the photograph of Poppy and Kitty Vigar with Zac Gregory in Chapter 6; Raymond Andrews and Laurent Depolla for the photograph of boys looking at the swan in Chapter 8.

Acknowledgement of thanks also to Bob Hughes for his permission to use his Taxonomy of Play Types (2002 and 2010 updated) in Chapter 2 and to Roger Hart for use of the Ladder of Participation diagram found in Chapter 9 extracted from the Unicef report 'Children's Participation: From Tokenism to Citizenship' Florence, Italy: UNICEF Innocenti Research Centre, 1992.

Introduction

When I was five I was allowed out to play in the woods opposite my house. I was not alone when I did so as I lived in the country with neighbours that little bit older than me. I thank my parents enormously for their desire to give me that opportunity to be part of a special 'child's world' in close contact with the environment – with the experiences and physical risks it contained. I thank my brothers and neighbours for the experiences of social negotiation, challenge and risk as we dropped in and out of friendships and power struggles.

In my adult working life I have worked with children at play in a range of contexts, from after school clubs to an adventure playground, nursery to youth group. Despite these later understandings, some of those very early experiences are so strongly ingrained in my memory that they are the influences that have shaped both who I am and the way in which I still approach the concept of play.

I can still easily recall the smell of the beech woods, rotten wood, charcoal burning and moss. I can see the prickly holly in which we made a den and memories leap back to me when the same scents arise in other contexts. I remember dragging stones and logs covered in moss to make seats; collecting the 'sowbugs' we found in cracks and nooks, watching ant trails across the footpaths as they cleared little highways with their traffic, as well as keeping 'pet snails'. I remember how the growing corn scratched and scraped my legs as we ran excitedly but nervously through the 'out of bounds' farmer's field and how my legs trembled as I was encouraged to leap into a redundant saw pit – a big dip in the ground.

When I was six, I moved house from living in the country with access to the woods, fields and neighbours to a town with a main road outside our front gate, a big garden and new play friends. My play opportunities changed as a result, but I did not stop playing. In this new context my play revolved around physical play with bicycles as we went round and round the house, racing and challenging, my brothers and I. We took things apart, regularly broke and fixed the bike chains, made 'milk' by crushing grass, and had fantasy 'Wacky Races', acting characters and combining games.

My parents were not 'tidy' and left lots of opportunity for exploratory play lying around. There were things that we could use to make ramps, potions, pathways and other constructions. Off-cuts of wood with hammer and nails allowed for 'building'. A shed afforded the opportunity for secrecy and hiding places, a tree house aided our climbing skills, cooking was always encouraged, and new neighbours with different cultural backgrounds helped our social skills and broadened our language and taste experiences.

My early memories of 'play' are surprisingly so much stronger than my memories of school. The few early school memories I have relate not to learning to read or write, or exciting play activities indoors, but to playing at break time; the way the steam rose from the hot black playground after a thunderstorm on an otherwise sunny day. So much stronger than my school experiences are the ones of the woods, or squirting crazy foam on the shed, and digging to Australia at the end of the garden. So there you have it – I am a bit of a romantic about play, believing that it really does lay the foundations for the future. Thanks to my early experiences I am not scared to fiddle and look at how things work. I know how to make things such as a den or a go-kart and value the smells and sounds of the natural environment.

I hope that I have offered my children the same opportunities for play, but that the interpretation of it will be entirely theirs, not mine. I job-shared with my husband, Tony, and we have run children's play activities and events since our children were small. The children came to work with us, saw children's theatre at open park events, took part in every craft you could imagine, had an adventure playground as their garden, and collected frog spawn each spring. They heard the woodpecker chicks in the tree, were 'done to' in terms of having their faces painted, but could in turn face paint with skill, and knew how to set up play days and bouncy castles. They were fetchers and carriers on the team; pickers in the allotment; and had water fights, water slides, a shed that could be an anything place, neighbours of a similar age, and a quiet street that was good for wheeled toys. Their generation, perhaps more restricted in free-ranging distance, had as many early play experiences as I had, but different ones.

I tell you all this to give you a taste of where I am coming from, and the range of experiences that I consider are play. There will be little mention of purposeful play for maths or structured phonics play for learning in this book. I draw on some of the ideas from the epistemology of school-aged play, ideas of compound flexibility, risk and resilience and *loose parts*; of being *playful* when not at play, but *in the flow zone* when you are. I write of energy release and that recalcitrance of being in a setting that is *not school*, nor preparation for school. My after-school and adventure playground work followed by children's centre management means that I am not tied to a simplistic view of play as a vehicle to couch learning in, but see that play crosses boundaries and creates challenges. It is a deep process that has a rhythm of integer space, flow and not-flow bordering on chaos.

This is an important time to be considering play. Neuroscience has shown us the importance of early experiences for brain development. Important new research is highlighting how such ideas move from conscious competence in the outer cortex to an unconscious repetitive ability using the primitive synapses in the core of the brain. Theorists are re-conceptualising education and play in recognition that dispositions are of increasing importance, and flexibility in applying understanding stems from play. The future is going to be more flexible than we can imagine, with very young children already displaying adaptive behaviour as they can use new electronic resources with greater skill than their parents. It is perhaps not yet clear just how important that range of early experiences we shall call play will be to a generation that will inherit a world of increasing invention, and risk. This book therefore intends to explore understandings of play and what play behaviour means for children.

There is a danger that, having played as children we take the term for granted such that we look no further than a surface understanding. How often do we stop to really consider what play looks like, what it isn't, and what other people have said about it? Knowing more about theories of play, taking time to look at children playing, and thinking about your roles in supporting play can help your practice in supporting children to become empowered now – and grow into the flexible creative thinkers of the future.

How to use this book

Each chapter begins with an indication of the main points within it and at the end of each there is a summary of the main points raised. Activities for individual reflection or group discussion should help the reader to engage with the ideas and their application to practice. A number of text boxes explain concepts raised and each chapter contains suggestions for further reading which are annotated to encourage further exploration. The timeline at the end of the book largely relates to Chapter 3 (the historical development of play and playful ideas).

Organised in three parts, it is intended that this book will unfold from initial consideration of what play is (how it looks, how it feels and how we support it) through an understanding of its value and impact to children (physically, socially and intellectually), before moving to a consideration of children's rights, the adult role and the importance of environment.

In the first section, observed *features of play* will be considered (play behaviours, the *play face*, and intrinsic motivation) before key theoretical *concepts* of play are raised in the second chapter. The third chapter will consider historical contributions to understandings of play from Plato's recognition of the link of play to social development and culture, through enlightenment philosophy to the modern eclectic mix of ideas that reflect an increasing awareness of the complexity of play. Stepping aside into practical activity, the fourth chapter will prompt consideration of observation of children at play to identify the many ways that play reveals itself in their behaviour.

The second section considers the perceived benefits of play from psychological, sociocultural and biological perspectives. Why are we concerned about play? Who has said what about its importance and impact? Here we will consider amongst others, Piaget and Inhelder (1969); Athey's (2004) interest in schemas; Vygotsky's (1933) zone of proximal development; Rogoff (2005) and Konner's (1991) social play in cultural contexts. Concepts of creativity and possibility thinking, and the value of risk will be introduced.

The third section will consider play from an adult perspective, further developing ideas of children's rights (United Nations Convention on the Rights of Children – UNCRC, 1989 – and the right to play), participation and ownership of play activity and a consideration of the adult role and pedagogy.

Part 1: What is play?

Chapter 1: Identifying features of play

This chapter will look at how we consider whether a child is playing or not. *Features of play* will be considered (such as observable play behaviours, the *play face*, indications of intrinsic motivation, free choice, social behaviour, excitement and fun).

Chapter 2: Understanding concepts of play

Readers will be introduced to some key theoretical *concepts* and perspectives, beginning with the need to classify play by outcome, or current behaviour. Play as preparation for the future, or being in the moment? Some concepts such as the terms 'ludic' and heuristic play (Goldschmied and Jackson, 1994); ludic and epistemic behaviours and games with rules (Hutt, 1976); classifications by Hughes (2001); concepts of *flow* (Bruce and Csickszentmihalyi, 1979) and involvement (Laevers, 1993/2000) will be outlined and explored.

Chapter 3: Historical perspectives and principles

This chapter considers the changing perspectives and concepts of play from ancient times to the present day. It contains prompts to consider the social environment, toys and resources; and the adult attitudes that have impacted on children's play experiences over time. One emphasis of this chapter is awareness of these historical influences on our current play understandings, from Greek cultural play, through Christian morality and the work ethic, to the modern mix of attitudes and values we see today.

Chapter 4: Observing play

In order to understand children's play, practitioners need to look and see what children are doing when they are considered to be *at play*. It is therefore important to just watch or reflect on interests and activities, social interaction and developmental intentions in children's play actions. Drawing on research writing relating to ethnographic observations of children, we will consider how you might observe children at play, what the issues are for practitioner 'researchers', and how you might analyse what you have seen to be better informed about a child's play activity.

Part 2: The benefits of play

Chapter 5: The value of play in child development

This chapter will look more closely at adult interpretations of play – what is play *for*? What impact does it have and why are we interested in play-based curricula? This initial chapter of this second section will also focus on the cognitive benefits of play.

Here we will consider among others, Piaget and Inhelder's (1969) stages and Athey's (2004) schemas, concept development and combinatorial flexibility (Hughes, 2001; Fraser-Brown, 2003).

Chapter 6: Play and social development

The perceived benefits of play from psychological and socio-cultural perspectives will be expressed and considered. This chapter will consider Vygotsky's view of the purpose of play and his zone of proximal development. We will also consider cultural influences on and purposes of play (drawing on Rogoff, 2003) and Konner's (1991) considerations of play in socio-cultural contexts). Issues of rough and tumble play, emotional containment and play as a means of exploring relationships will also be introduced.

Chapter 7: Play, creativity and risk

This chapter considers the emotional impacts of play (the desire for exhilaration) and the creative and risky aspects of it. The chapter will briefly introduce concepts of risk; (the *dizzy* aspect of play (Kalliala, 2006); creativity and possibility thinking; and links to relevant observed play behaviours.

Chapter 8: Contexts for play

Up until this point, the book has been considering what play is about. In this chapter we will look at where it happens: indoors, outdoors, the *theatrical space* or the environmental connection; play within boundaries, for a set period of time, or play unbounded; play in the street, or play in the living room. Prompts will be in place to consider the value and limitations of the contexts. Else's *imaginal theatre of their own construction* (Else, 2008, page 21), Nicholson's *loose parts* (Nicholson, 1971) and affordances of objects (Gibson, 1996) will be considered in this chapter.

Part 3: Children's rights and the ownership of play

Chapter 9: The ownership of play: Play space, play cues and play actions

Referring back to our original concepts of play and freedom of choice this chapter will further develop ideas of children's rights (UNCRC and the right to play) and ownership of play activity, even where adults are present. The ladder of participation (Hart, 1992) will be presented along with concepts of children *inviting* adults into their spaces. The play cycle will be introduced (Else and Sturrock, 2007; Else, 2009) and we will consider supportive action that does not take over the play process.

Chapter 10: Developing a pedagogy for play

The concept of pedagogy and a play-based curriculum is now re-introduced with some comparative ideas (Denmark, Reggio Emilia, New Zealand) to stimulate thought about adult facilitation of play. Pedagogic concepts will be outlined as a framework with an activity approach to student alignment of their perceptions of play facilitation within a spectrum. The role of play in delivering the EYFS and its greater importance in the Welsh curriculum is raised and considered. Readers are encouraged to explore their own developing understanding of play and its relevance to their practice or setting.

Chapter 11 Conclusion: Play is for life, not just for nursery

Finally I would like to leave readers with a chapter that considers whether adults play. This chapter will prompt reflective activity relating to being 'in the moment', and at 'flow' in contrast to managed output and outcome. In this chapter readers will be asked to consider whether they are playful in their approach. They will be reminded of some of the benefits of playful activity, for social involvement and idea generation, attitude and process rather than purpose and output. There will be prompts for playful reflective practice to maintain connection with the feelings and benefits of the topic and to stimulate further understanding of the need to advocate play for children and adults.

Part 1

What is play?

1 Identifying features of play

Through reading this chapter, you will:

- consider your own recollections of play and the difficulty of defining play in practice;
- reflect on the difference between 'play' and 'playfulness';
- explore potential visible indicators of play activity in children;
- consider whether we can see play, and if so what is it about the things we see that can be identified as common indicators of play.

This chapter also introduces some observable play behaviours such as the *play face*, and concepts of intrinsically and extrinsically motivated play behaviour.

Introduction: exploring the term 'play'

Play is such a common term that we all think we know exactly what it is. Our own childhood memories may be full of examples of playing: those long, hot summer days in the garden; playing with sand on the beach; or perhaps being indoors with small toys spread out on the floor in winter time. I recall my own children playing with my neighbour's children. They were a little 'gang of four' who created fantasy play adventures around a climbing frame; messed about with water in the summer; created a 'vets' in the shed to care for our many long-suffering guinea-pigs, and 'cooked perfume' with mud, flowers and grass. I remember their word-play as they marched around repeating loudly 'fish-bowl' for the strange sounds it made, and their games with specific rules that went on for weeks.

Perhaps your own memory of play is football in the garden, or playing computer games with your friends. Some people indicate that they have spent much of their later childhood 'playing about' with their peers, either on the streets, in parks and gardens or in more organised settings. Even small babies are seen to 'play' with keys, hanging objects, and their own feet!

ACTIVITY 1

Try to think back to your own childhood and remember both your earliest and best memories of play. What were you doing? Were you inside or outside, with friends or family, or playing alone? What made it memorable?

continued

ACTVITY 1 continued

My earliest play memory is:

My best play memory is:

Reflect again on these two experiences and consider what it was about these that mean you consider them to be 'play'.

Our use of the term 'play' is so familiar that we rarely stop and think about what it really is, or what we mean when we use the word. Yet we seem to recognise that there is a common, shared value in it. There is something about 'play' that we all relate to, but actually fail to define. Janet Moyles has stated that:

> *Grappling with the concept of play can be analogised to trying to seize bubbles, for every time there appears to be something to hold on to its ephemeral nature disallows it being grasped!*

(Moyles, 1994, page 5)

Play is therefore a concept that we consider we understand and see clearly, but that clarity seems to disappear when we try to define it, or control it. It is often ephemeral, or a passing moment. We should try to make more concrete this elusive and fleeting concept before we even begin to consider its impact on, or value to, children's development and learning.

The meaning of play

The word 'play' is more confusing than many in that it can be a noun (naming word), a verb (doing word) or an adjective (descriptive word). One dictionary definition given is that play is *to engage in games or other activities for enjoyment rather than for a serious or practical purpose* (*Concise Oxford English Dictionary (OED)*, 2001).

This gives us an understanding that play is frivolous, something we do to pass the time. It is often considered to be the opposite of work. We watch a play; musicians play their instruments; we can play board games and tricks on others. In literature we read of the wind *playing* with leaves and children are very often described as *playful*. If we delve a little more deeply we will find that the word 'play' has not come from a Latin word for meaningless activity, as we may think, but actually emerges from an old English word for *exercise*, or *brisk movement*. This understanding of *play* instantly gives a more positive interpretation to the term than much of its common usage today. There is indeed often energy, movement and activity in play. Just as light plays from reflective objects, or the wind plays with sand and dust, so a child is playing when they are spinning around with the energy of a five year old, experiencing the sheer delight of disorientation. Perhaps you have seen children jumping on the spot merely because they can? In line with this definition use of the word play has, over time, become synonymous with lightness, pleasure, and activity without time boundary.

ACTIVITY 2

Consider the following passage and the use of the word play.

The weather was extremely hot and the children had a piece of ice to play with. They broke it up with a hammer and each had some pieces. They put some into water and said 'oh that makes it a lot colder than the water out of the tap...'

(Isaacs, 1930, page 125)

Are these children playing or exploring, or experimenting?

If Susan Isaacs had not used the word *play* in the passage above would you have considered the children to be playing? Would you need additional information to decide whether they were really *playing* or doing something else such as *exploring* or *studying*?

For Janet Moyles, play is not an observable moment as in the passage above, *but a process, or series of processes, which in turn include a range of motivations, opportunities, practices, skills and understandings* (Moyles, 1994, page 5).

What makes something play is the child's approach, the underlying processes, not the observer's assumptions about the activity. It is therefore possible to be playful at one's work and work at one's play. As play involves a complex interaction of opportunity, motivation, disposition and skill, Moyles reminds us that children are not either *in play* or *out of play*, but that they can be *more or less* playing in different degrees.

Susan Isaacs, who wrote the above passage about the ice play, observed children for many hours in the 1920s and 1930s. It is her writing that first reminded us that *play is indeed the child's work* (Isaacs, 1929, page 9). Her intention in publishing her detailed records of children's activities was to capture what children do. This led to an understanding that play should be given respect for its impact on children's development, rather than being dismissed merely as a leisurely alternative to productive activity, hence a *child's work*. She astutely argued that play for children was *nature's means of individual education* (Isaacs, 1929, page 9). This is similar to our understanding that play can be a tool for differentiated learning today. What is important about Isaac's work is that she started with careful observation of what children were doing. It was from these observation notes that she began to identify the nature of play, and its impact on the physical, intellectual and social development of children.

The notion of play as work

The notion of play as *a child's work* has continued to be applied from Susan Isaac's words in 1930 to today. Many statements affirming this perspective can be currently seen on play-related websites and in early childhood textbooks. This adult interpretation of the serious value of play, whilst arising from the best intentions, has offered a view of children's play as a *tool* to be prompted by adults for development or learning. This interpretation has been applied to the extent that there is a danger we now write and talk about *purposeful play* and its alternative *free-play*. Many early childhood practitioners appear to readily accept a role of offering adult-initiated play to *move on* children's development, rather than taking time to consider what makes a child's action or involvement *play* in the first instance.

The UK Early Years Foundation Stage 2012 requires that:

> *Each area of learning and development must be implemented through planned, purposeful play and through a mix of adult-led and child-initiated activity. Play is essential for children's development, building their confidence as they learn to explore, to think about problems, and relate to others. Children learn by leading their own play, and by taking part in play which is guided by adults.*

(DfE, 2012a, page 11)

In this document practitioners are advised that play is essential in assisting children's learning and development. The now superseded document 'Birth to Three Matters' (DfES, 2005, page 7), which considered the development needs of very young children, also recognised the value of play and indicated the importance of children *becoming playfully engaged and involved* in their own development. In other education documents (Qualification and Curriculum Authority, or QCA, 2002) we are told that schools use play for learning but also that, in contrast to expected lesson time, children have play times or free play, in which they relax and let off steam.

Is play perhaps so many things gathered together under one heading, that a perceived shared understanding has emerged that in reality is not so shared? Is it a term that needs more 'unpacking' before we understand its real meaning? Perhaps we take it so much for granted as a term or word that we fail to acknowledge and explore its appearance (what it looks like to us) and essential qualities (what it feels like to a child)? How can we decide whether we should, and how we should, provide for *purposeful play* if we have not actually taken time to determine what play really is?

Elizabeth Wood has recently argued that we see play from two perspectives, *what play **does** for children* or *what play **means** for children* (Wood, 2010, page 11). When we look at what play *does*, we consider adult-framed outputs of creativity, children's development or physical growth. When we look at what play means, we consider the child's intentions in play, their social and emotional development, children's cultures and emergent child-led links. Neither of these approaches actually works to define play as an experience or action in the moment. Perhaps, like Susan Isaacs all those years ago, we should start with a consideration of what play *is* or what it looks like rather than what it does or what it means. We shall later in this book return to the consideration of what it does and how it feels to children.

Observing the signs of play

All early childhood practitioners should take time to observe children at play and consider how play and playful activity is seen through behaviours of children. This would mean beginning, not with theoretical definitions of play, or policy statements about the benefits of play for education, but with a careful consideration of what children are actually doing when we consider them to be *at play*. Undertaking your own observations and reflections at this point will help you to define what it is and also to consider your own values and position in relation to the term.

ACTIVITY 3

If you were asked to close your eyes and visualise children at play, what would you see?

Now think again about that image in your mind. What is it that the children are doing, saying or showing that makes you consider it is play?

Note down the things you saw in your mind.

Why not ask a colleague or friend to do the same thing and compare ideas?

Are your visualised understandings of play similar or different?

Through such reflections you are beginning to define play in your own way.

In the exercise above, did you perhaps visualise a playground, noisy, colourful, encouraging physical activity, with children running around? Perhaps you visualised a child creating something with junk in the corner, engrossed, tongue sticking to top lip, head tilted in concentration, showing great involvement? An alternative vision may be a seated baby exploring the items in a treasure basket exclaiming loudly with glee at the discovery of each new texture and action. The pleasure of that moment can be so strong for the child that their whole body moves in energy. There are many more scenarios of different ages and contexts that involve emotion and movement: children jumping for joy because they can; children involved with exploring nature, their bodies tense with concentration as they stretch to see; children exploring boundaries by play fighting. All of these things we call play have similarities in emotion and action, but they are each very different experiences.

ACTIVITY 4

Drawing on your visualisation of play in Activity 3, above, consider what it is that makes an activity play rather than, say, a learning activity, or taught lesson. Is it perhaps the place and the activity, the way the adult behaves, the attitude of the child, or something else?

What is it about the child that tells the observer they are playing? Make a list.

When I work through the above activity with my students, the same list of *indicators of play* come up time and time again:

- smiling faces;
- movement, physical activity, energy;

- clear enthusiasm for, and engagement in, what is going on – we assume children want to play, and that they show this desire, so they are not *forced* to play;

- observed acts of communication or narration – children talk to each other, to other adults, or even to themselves as they narrate their own activities;

- interaction with others or requests for affirmation from others – there often seems to be something social about play;

- a concentration that is sometimes so deep that there is an indication of a lack of awareness of others. We may term this 'involvement';

- an absence of adult intervention, no adult questions;

- evidence of challenge and emotional challenge, risk, chance and temporary fear.

Although this is a good list it is by no means comprehensive and you may find that you can add other ideas. Why not test your own understanding by taking time to observe some children *at play*.

ACTIVITY 5

Sit and watch some children you consider to be at play for a short period of time (10–15 minutes will be sufficient). This can be indoors or outdoors.

Jot down what they are doing – note only the behaviours you can see (please don't make any assumptions about learning or development at this point).

Does your list of their behaviours look similar to the one above? Can you add to this list?

The play face

If we seek to merely *see* what indicates to us a child is playing or *being playful*, we could be said to be taking a *structural approach* to children's play. This approach attempts to identify and describe what behaviours occur in play, rather than consider-ing the purpose or benefit of play. Smith, Cowie and Blades (2003) remind us that one key example of a behaviour that only occurs in play – and indicates to those around that the child is playing – is the *play face*. Usually in children this takes the form of an open mouth and broad smile, the child's eyes will signal *playfulness*. Look carefully at the children in your setting. A play face to an adult will give a cue or invitation to join in the play (Else, 2009). A play face during rough and tumble play signals to the other child that no malice is intended.

More signs of play

Not all play is indicated by such clear signals as the *play face*. Often a child's play is made up of behaviours that are familiar to us in other contexts. Play can involve

Figure 1.1 The play face – with open mouth and broad smile, eyes indicating *playfulness* and inviting communication

running, jumping, moving objects around or gathering sociably in a corner. It can be done alone, or in groups. Look and see if a child playing alone shows a *play face* or whether that is only used in a social context? Usual behaviours are seen as *playful* if they are exaggerated, re-ordered or repeated. A child running up a slope may be going somewhere and is therefore not *at play*, they are moving with a purpose. A child running up a slope and then down the slope several times without reaching a planned destination shows repetition of an activity which can be seen as play. A child walking up the slope with giant steps, or jumping is exaggerating 'normal' behaviour and this can be seen to be *play*. Children also re-order activities when they are playing, they try things out differently, and so a child might try to slide up the slope on his or her bottom and then run down it when the top is reached.

This exaggeration and re-ordering behaviour can sometimes be considered to be *poor behaviour* by practitioners wanting compliance to usual ways of behaving and it is perhaps this that gives our understandings of play a tension. Play is some-how accepted as the work of the child, but is also *outside of the norm*, by its nature being challenging and testing. There can be a tension in practice between acknowledging that play is vital to a child's development, and the desire to control the testing behaviours that are involved in play.

Play as a social activity

Some practitioners and researchers have identified through observations of children that play is a social activity (Lewis, 1979) and would therefore involve interaction between two or more people (the mother and child, child to child, play worker and child, or many children for example). So you might look for communication with others, spoken and visual as an indicator of play. It is true that the lone observing child is unlikely to be playing, whilst the noisy group sharing an activity are likely to be playing. However, not all interactions between people are play, nor are all play activities social or noisy. Think of the raised voices and challenging postures of arguments that are clearly not play, or the quiet enjoyment of a board game played by two people which may be considered as play. This understanding is also confused by the pretence of play. You may see children pretending to argue. As practitioners we will need to draw on our careful observation skills to identify whether actions are indicators of play exaggerations or real feelings. Children may show the *play face* whilst pretending to argue, or offer an altered pitch of voice pretending to be someone else. You may also hear them testing out phrases heard from others.

Signs of play as interaction

Some observers of children have found that play is not an ongoing social activity, but rather is stimulated by interaction with other people or things which sets a train of thought, an involvement with materials, or exploration of their physical capabilities. Here the child may be a lone player or explorer. Other people, materials or environment, rather than direct social interaction or adult involvement, may provide the initial stimulus for a play response. A parent gives a child a treasure basket for example and this stimulates the play activity of exploration in the child. The play element is shown in the child's choice to participate, their involvement and behaviour responsive to the materials. The parent may well not *play* with the child, but merely sit and observe the infant's *play* with these new stimulating materials as the infant is sufficiently stimulated by them.

Play as a feeling?

Play may be considered to be a *disposition* or a way of being (McCall, 1979; Else and Sturrock, 2007; Tovey, 2010). It is not the outward involvement in the activity that you can see that is play, but the way that the child feels about the activity. More sophisticated observation skills will be needed to identify the indicators as we are not here merely looking for signs of play, but for signs of the child's emotions that we consider may indicate a playful attitude. Some children can therefore be seen playing in a class lesson at school; they have the open mouth, the smiling face, the bright eyes, offering signs of involvement and challenge response. Other children perhaps do not treat that lesson the same way and are more serious in their response to the teacher's planned activity. They may be concentrating and doing as instructed but are not, in terms of disposition at that moment, *at play*.

ACTIVITY 6

Consider the following descriptions of behaviour. Would you consider these to be play?

1. *A child's nappy is being changed and the mother blows raspberries with her mouth on her baby's feet. The sensation makes the baby laugh, and the mother laughs too. She blows on the feet again, the baby laughs again, and moves her feet more. Then the mother tickles the baby's stomach. They giggle together.*

2. *A toddler has found a bunch of keys and a tin. She puts the keys in the tin, then takes them out of the tin, then puts them in the tin again and shakes it. They make a loud noise. She looks around and makes eye contact with her carer. Then puts the keys in the tin again, shaking it around and saying 'vrooom vroom'. She takes the keys out of the tin and puts one into a crack in the door. 'Open,' she says. The carer says, 'Open the door. What is through the door?' 'Spiders' the toddler says, and the carer pretends to be frightened – 'Oh no,' she cries. The toddler laughs and moves her body rhythmically.*

3. *Children aged between five and seven are den building. The parents are sitting some distance away, half watching, half distracted. The children go to the resources. There are so many bits and pieces to choose from. A boy picks up a piece of corrugated piping and swings it around in a big circle. It makes a noise and he runs off to tell his friend, who is carrying a big piece of bamboo. Another child is carrying several bits of rubber tubing, and is also struggling with a big wooden frame. He is asked if he needs help and declines this, turning his face away, wishing to continue the struggle himself. The other children smile at him and indicate that he can follow them. He does so and together they make a 'den'. They keep returning to swing the pipe around to make a noise, they are smiling and animated, chatting excitedly about how they are going to build a den in Africa, by the river, to keep them safe from lions and other dangerous animals. There is a great deal of transporting back and forth of ma-terials. They finally wrap the tarpaulin over their makeshift frame and crawl inside. 'We're safe now,' they exclaim. The game goes no further. They seem bored, the play faces are gone, and shortly after they run off to their respective parents on the bank. There is no 'goodbye' and the ethereal moment of play is over.*

4. *In the pre-school classroom, children are seated on carpet squares listening to a story. They are instructed by the adult to sit quietly on their own mat and she be-gins the story of The Very Hungry Caterpillar (Carle, 2003). Two boys have heard*

continued

---

this many times before and begin to make eye contact with each other. They make caterpillar movements with their hands – wiggling their fingers along the arms and backs of each other. Their faces are smiling and they become engrossed in their play behaviour. One of the boys then pretends to eat a cake and rubs his stomach. The other laughs out loud – he can't help it. The teacher temporarily stops the story and asks them to 'behave please'. They lunge at each other and roll on the floor, laughing in silence. They are conspirators together, fighting the teacher's will. She again stops the story and tells them they must sit still and show 'good listening'. They take this seriously, smile at each other, making eye contact again as if to acknowledge the end of the game, and then sit facing the teacher who continues with the story.

All of these could be considered to be play or *playful behaviour*. The first and third clearly show the social element, while the fourth demonstrates the challenge and alteration of the norm. All indicate a disposition to play. Some of this activity is productive in adult terms, but some may be considered destructive in terms of group behaviour. The children were indicating they were *at play* by their outward signs. This balance of outward response and inward inclination to playfulness is an interesting concept to explore further and can be seen in some of the many definitions of play.

Play is motivated from within

Many writers have attempted to define play, but Catherine Garvey recognised the difficulty of the balance between play and not-play and the reliance of one upon the other. She identified five key characteristics of play and elements of Catherine Garvey's five-point definition (Garvey, 1991, page 4), given below, are commonly found in many current definitions of play:

1) Play is pleasurable and enjoyable. Even when not actually accompanied by signs of mirth it is still positively valued by the player.
2) Play has no extrinsic goals. Its motivations are intrinsic and serve no other objectives. In fact it is more an enjoyment of means than an effort devoted to some particular end.
3) Play is spontaneous and voluntary. It is not obligatory but is freely chosen by the player.
4) Play involves some active engagement on the part of the player.
5) Play has certain systematic relations to what is not play.

These five points can clearly be seen in the following definition in which play is:

...freely chosen, personally directed behaviour, motivated from within. It is through play that the child explores the world and his or her relationship with it, elaborating all the while a flexible range of responses to the challenges she or he encounters.

(SPRITO, 1992)

So play was here considered to be a child's elaborate response to a challenge, the exaggerated and altered behaviours we have already discussed that lead to greater knowledge. Another definition highlights that play is shown by:

> ...*behaviour that is freely chosen, personally directed and intrinsically motivated. The value of play derives from the play process itself, not from any extrinsic goal, reward or end product. Play is often spontaneous and unpredictable. Through play children experience their world and their relationship with it.*
>
> (Joint National Committee on Training for Playwork, JNCTP, 2002)

This latter definition has highlighted that play is spontaneous and unpredictable, it is process driven, and does not relate to an end product. These definitions tell us that play is challenging, flexible and personal. It is prompted from within the person playing, in other words it is *intrinsically motivated*.

THEORY FOCUS

Intrinsic and extrinsic motivation

Intrinsic motivation is when the prompt or desire to do something comes from inside a person. The individual child wants to take part in the play activity, or feels the need to explore their own abilities or emotions without being prompted by someone else to do so. The children listening to the circle time story above were intrinsically motivated (against the adult's wishes) to *play* with each other. A child is intrinsically motivated to play when they choose how and when to play, and what they are going to play with. The impulse to play comes from the child and they seek opportunities to pursue their individual interests.

Extrinsic motivation is the motivation, or the pressure to do something, that comes from outside a person. The teacher in the storytelling example was providing extrinsic motivation for listening, and visualising during a circle story time by her expectations and potential discipline. Under extrinsic motivation a child is encouraged by another person, perhaps their teacher or play worker, to take part in an activity. An extrinsic, or external, motivator is reward, such as praise, a sticker, extra responsibility or a prize. Extrinsically motivated children may enjoy the activity, and may approach the activity *playfully* and with enthusiasm, but are perhaps not as deeply engaged in play as they would be if they had chosen it themselves.

Some people consider that an extrinsically motivated activity is not *play*, as children are not in control of when or how it happens. Wood, for example, reminds us that *truly free play is open-ended and unpredictable, and is controlled and directed by the players* (Wood, 2010a, page 13).

A range of perspectives

I work with a range of colleagues who have experience of working with children aged 0–5 in different settings or contexts. When we teach together on play modules it becomes clear that we all have our own particular understandings of what play is. A teacher who has successfully used play in the classroom will perhaps consider that play is a positive activity that can be harnessed to encourage involvement in learning and is prompted by an adult through the provision of interesting resources and environments. It is a way of being, a feeling, a challenge, an exciting, engrossing moment in which time and product have no meaning (for the moment, or until it is time to end the activity). However, a play worker will perhaps consider that such an engineered situation cannot be play as it has been initiated by the adult for a particular and planned outcome and therefore removes the power from the child. Play for the latter is about children's rights and the opportunity to control experiences – adults are only involved in the play activity when invited by the child.

The majority of early childhood workers now recognise the value of play as a vehicle for development and learning, but sometimes express confused ideas about who is in control of the play activity, and the management of attitude and behaviour in a child challenging boundaries. This confusion is evident but not addressed in government documents. We are told that play can be *child initiated* or *adult initiated* (EYFS, DfE, 2012a) and the Tickell review of the Early Years Foundation Stage (DfE, 2011, page 28) *supports the use of play-based approaches combined with instructional yet playful teaching.* These ideas of play-based approaches and instruction that is also playful can be confusing so we should here consider whether, and how, play can be both child initiated and adult initiated, instructional and playful. The theory box below gives a little more definition to these concepts.

THEORY FOCUS

Who initiates play?

Child-initiated play is a situation in which the child begins to show play activity behaviour that is not prompted by adult. In essence the child is doing something that they choose to do. An example of child-initiated play may be where a child sees a pile of leaves and spontaneously rushes over to them to throw and kick them into the air. They may then *transport* the leaves around the playground or look in the pile for spiders and bugs and so develop their own ideas at their own pace. No adult has planned this activity.

Adult-initiated play is a situation in which the adult plans and stimulates playful or play-like activity in children. Usually this requires creation of an environment that will stimulate creative thinking, perhaps by offering space within an activity for individual freedom of thought. The child may well respond with playful behaviours seen by indicators such as involvement and the play face. However, an adult-initiated play activity is likely to be designed to meet adult-defined outcomes, such as addressing a particular area of learning within the curriculum.

THEORY FOCUS *continued*

Using the same example as above, an adult may spot the pile of leaves and decide to arrange some play activities around the theme of autumn. They may encourage the children to find the different colours of brown in the pile, to build a collage of leaves for an autumn tree, or even to sweep up the leaves so that they learn responsibility. Children may enjoy the experience that the adult has promoted and may show indicators of playfulness such as laughter and energy in movement. The adult may allow space for engagement and freedom of exploration.

Is this really play? There is no easy answer to this question. Perhaps, as we shall see in Chapter 8, it will depend on how the children perceive the activity that they are not in control of.

Being playful

I use the term 'playful' to denote behaviour that is similar to play, but within situations not entirely owned by the child and therefore being not *free play*. The Oxford English Dictionary considers that to be *playful* is to be *light-hearted* and giving or having amusement and pleasure. Being playful is in this definition as much about attitude as it is about the ownership of the activity which may be called play. Children listening to a story can be *playful* within an organised *adult-led* activity that does not have the full freedom of a *play* activity owned by the child. Children measuring water for a science activity can *playfully engage*, but are not necessarily engaged in play in its most pure definition. These are concepts we will explore further throughout this book.

SUMMARY

In this chapter, we have started to explore the concept of play and attempted to begin to define something of its nature. It is clear that there is not a neat distinction between play and not play, or play and learning as is often supposed. It is important to begin by considering what play looks like (rather than what it 'does'). Such observations throw up a range of indicators that point us to an understanding of a child's actions being play. The play face and experimental or exaggerated behaviours are a few such indicators. You are encouraged to continue to reflect on the concept of play and develop your own individual understanding and informed approach to practice.

Play is purposeful, not merely recreational. Children are doing something quite deeply exploratory whilst playing and this can be seen in outward behaviours shown by the child although they may not be able to articulate the purpose. This intensity of involvement in a process is strengthened if the child is intrinsically motivated rather than prompted by rewards. However, children at play may not always be doing things that adults consider are productive because of that element of challenge and risk. As an early

continued

SUMMARY *continued*

childhood practitioner you will need to find a balance of understanding and support that works in your context. It is possible to support children's learning through a play-based curriculum approach. To help you in this we will, in the next chapter, consider some of the theory that informs our current understanding of play and its benefits for children's development and learning.

FURTHER READING

Brock, A, Dodds, S, Jarvis, P and Olusoga, Y (2009) *Perspectives on Play: Learning for Life.* Harlow: Pearson Education.

This is a very useful reference book. The first chapter offers three 'Perspectives on Play' and there are definitions of play throughout the book.

Canning, N (2011) *Play and Practice in the Early Years Foundation Stage.* London: Sage.

This book argues that play should be at the forefront of, and is fundamental to, early years practice. The first chapter considers the unique qualities of play and also explores why play is so difficult to define.

National Playing Fields Association (NPFA) (2000) *Best Play: What Play Provision Should Do For Children.* London: NPFA.

A classic booklet on play that contains some very convincing definitions of play and key ideas about play activity shown by children.

Smidt, S (2011) *Playing to Learn: The Role of Play in the Early Years.* London: Routledge.

Sandra Smidt argues that all play is purposeful and supports the view that an action can only truly be considered to be play if the child is able to choose what, where and how to do it. The first chapter explores 'What is this thing called play?'.

2 Understanding concepts of play

In reading this chapter you will be encouraged to consider:

- the difference between perspectives on and theoretical concepts of play;
- some key perspectives relating to children and play;
- a range of common theoretical concepts used to categorise, explore and understand play behaviours;
- the terms 'involvement', 'flow' and 'free-flow' as applied to play.

You are asked to consider throughout how you use theory to support your practice.

Introduction

This chapter aims to introduce and explore some common theoretical concepts relating to play. We begin with a consideration of what we can see when children are at play and how we can categorise this into types to help our analysis and understanding. We will consider children's exploratory play and symbolic behaviour and finally progress to a consideration of emotional well-being, the idea of *flow* and the deep involvement of children at play. The theoretical ideas presented may help you to reflect on your own practice and understand a little more about the meaning of play.

There is a key secondary theme introduced in this chapter. You are prompted to consider both how you use theory, and where theory has come from. Behind any concept or framework presented is a series of views or opinions that will make up an author's *perspective*. It is important to consider such perspectives when reading material presented by an author or theorist, as their perspectives are likely to reflect the culture and thinking of the time of writing, or perhaps a particular approach to a subject. Authors writing about play in a time of strict religious influence on society, for example, may emphasise the moral, or immoral, aspects of play. In contrast, authors writing in a time of new research into the subconscious aspects of the mind may emphasise the psychological or therapeutic aspects of play. You are encouraged, as you read, to reflect on the theories presented and determine which perspective you consider most closely aligns to your own views about the value of play.

THEORY FOCUS

Perspective or concept?

A *perspective* is a viewpoint, or philosophical position we take in relation to something. A politician's *perspective* on play may be one which relates to ideas about creating future citizens, diverting young people from trouble. This may be very different to an adventure playground worker's perspective, which both promotes risk and advocates for children's voices as citizens now, able to create their own play spaces. Both perspectives are focused on improvement for the child, but with different outcomes in mind.

A *concept* on the other hand is a specific idea, an experimental model, or a plan which is often researched. Play is therefore a *concept* (an idea) that we are here trying to explore and define. A play-based curriculum is also a *concept* (being a plan for learning through play activities), and the notion of play as a way of learning presented by a researcher is also a *concept* (in the form of an experimental model).

Why should we consider theories of play and development?

There is much to learn from past and current theorists. Their ideas and experiments can help us to think differently, drawing on a range of ideas to aid our understanding of how we can best support children's play. An initial reading of a new theory may inform our practice through offering new ideas that we then try to apply. Re-visiting theories over time may help to further shape our practice and clarify our understanding by bringing new challenges to old ideas. Theories and concepts can also strengthen our arguments for play as we can articulate, analyse and justify its benefits. As we come across more theories we are able to question the ideas we read before, and so we build more complex personal understandings helping us to adjust and refine our practice again. Theory and practice coming together in this reflective way is often called *praxis* (Siraj-Blatchford, 1994; Freire, 1996), and helps us to develop our own particular ways of working that are informed by both theory and our own values and experiences.

THEORY FOCUS

Theory, praxis and practice

Theory	Praxis	Practice
A practitioner operating at a theoretical level without an emphasis on practice may restrict development of her practical and interpretative skills. She knows how to do things *in theory*, but has not developed her practical skills and may be afraid of adaptation.	The practitioner who draws on theory and brings this to reflection on practice as a result is most likely to improve her way of working for the better.	A practitioner operating at a practice level, without ever considering the reasons behind actions may be uninformed and fail to update, adapt or improve. She may be perceived as a technician, able to do as instructed, but there is a lack of understanding of what she is doing and so limited adaptation to context and individual need.

Table 2.1 The theory and practice continuum

Using theory

We probably use theory every day in various forms. We often seek to understand a subject *in theory* by researching it online or in books before we do something in practice. We may then link our *research* from our reading to practical experiences in real life. Here is a simple example. Imagine you are looking for the theory of *how to make play dough* by looking up a recipe before making play dough for real. Once you have found a recipe, you will probably have a go at making the dough according to the recipe. You will then probably adapt the theory (the recipe) to align with your own understanding of how the experience went, and what outcome was achieved. It takes some courage to let go of the recipe book and amend the quantities, operating in a new way, but you may need to do so as you experience things that are not quite like the recipe writer's initial experiment. Perhaps your cooker is different, or you want to adapt the dough by adding colour. If things do not quite work as expected, you have to adjust your approach and adapt the recipe. You have not left the theory behind, but the theory and your practical experience of making play dough in your context have come together in a new way to ensure success that is relevant to you. Over time you are able to leave the recipe book behind as the recipe gradually becomes accommodated into your memory and common practice such that eventually you may even forget where it has come from.

You are encouraged to consider and use the play theories and concepts given in this book in a similar way to the example of the play dough recipe above, as researched understandings or experiments that you can draw on to inform you and give you ideas to support appropriate adaptation for improvement in your practice. If you did not ever refresh your approach with new theory and ideas, your practice would soon become stale and limited. If you only read theory and never put it into practice, on the other hand, you may become detached from the hands-on experience that also informs your skills development in work with children (see Figure 2.1 above).

ACTIVITY 1

Take a little time here to reflect on the theories you have recently considered in relation to your practice:

- *Perhaps you have been on a training course, or a colleague has talked to you about something they have read in an early years magazine.*

- *Perhaps you have had to look up something in relation to a child's particular needs or interests.*

- *Perhaps you have recently heard from a colleague about theories of heuristic play and treasure baskets.*

Once you have identified the theories that you have been exposed to recently, think about whether you adopted a particular perspective or viewpoint in relation to these.

---

continued

ACTIVITY *1 continued*

Did you agree with the author's viewpoint?

What perspective did the author present? Try to identify their main position. Positions of education or care are often quite distinct, for example.

* *How did you respond to these newly learnt theories in relation to your practice?*
* *Do you interpret a little?*
* *Did you stick rigidly to the rules?*
* *Do you adopt different approaches at different times?*
* *Have you questioned the theory you learnt?*

Finally, can you articulate the new theory clearly to others?
It is also important for you to be able to explain to others (colleagues and parents or carers for example) why you do the things you do. Explanation to others will both stimulate greater clarity in your own approach and reassure others.

Different perspectives on play

Many people have researched and written about play: what it is, and what it does. They have attempted to define it, examine its parts, and determine how it can impact on children's development. There is, in the United Kingdom, common use of the term play and a broad acceptance of the principle of supporting play for learning. However, individual perceptions of what it actually is, or how it will support learning, will vary. Our individual beliefs, values, understanding and experiences combine to create our own personal perspective on play. Our personal perspectives often draw on our own early childhood experiences and the society in which we have grown up; our deep-rooted values, principles and aspirations.

The child as a blank sheet

Two early perspectives that still influence our understandings of education and play today are those of John Locke and Jean Jacques Rousseau. John Locke lived in the seventeenth century and is often cited as an early supporter of play. In 1699 he wrote that parents and tutors should study their children, work with their dispositions, their likes and dislikes, and allow children to play to learn:

> *...for a child will learn three times as much when he is in tune, as he will with double the time and pains, when he goes awkwardly, or is dragged unwillingly to it. If this were minded as it should, children might be permitted to weary themselves with play, and yet have time enough to learn what is suited to the capacity of each age.*
>
> (Locke, 1699, page 74)

In other words, children learn so much more through play that it should be given more time than formal learning. Locke had observed children closely and drew on this in developing his position. He considered that learning came from experience, and that a child's mind was a blank sheet or *tabula rasa* waiting to be filled with knowledge acquired through experiences. This is a perspective we can still hear today in the writings of some authors who argue the importance of the adult role to pass knowledge on to the developing child.

Locke was influenced by the culture and philosophy of the period in which he lived and wrote. This culture in turn drew on the work of classical scholars from ancient Greece and Rome. He knew, for example, that the Greek philosopher Plato had also supported children's play for learning. Locke was a puritan and the influence of religion also played a part in forming his concepts. He emphasised the need for moral instruction, and argued that although they could learn through play, children should be guided and protected from evil by an informed adult *whose care it should be to fashion them aright, and keep them from all ill, especially the infection of bad company* (Locke, 1699, page 90).

Drawing on the influences of his lifetime, Locke both recognised play as a vehicle for learning and promoted the adult role in providing strong direction to these playful activities. In so doing he revealed the tension between the freedom and anarchy of play, and concern for creation of future moral citizens. This tension of freedom and control still exists today.

The child as noble savage

Locke's position, which promotes the acquisition of knowledge from experience (but with morality and direction offered by a more experienced and respected adult), is a very different perspective to that held by the followers of another philosopher who mentioned play some 50 years later. Jean Jacques Rousseau was influenced by the growing interest in studying the *natural sciences* (biology and the study of plants) that were becoming popular in his lifetime. These studies emphasised natural maturation and intrinsic motivations for action. Just as plants and animals are programmed to grow in appropriate conditions, so he considered children would also grow. Rousseau did not see the child as a blank sheet to be filled with knowledge and spared from evil. In contrast, he argued that children were naturally inclined to be active explorers and social beings, instinctively learning (through play) for future survival. For Rousseau, a child's innocence was spoiled by the rules and constraints of society: *The lessons scholars learn from one another in the playground are worth a hundredfold more than what they learn in the classroom* (Rousseau, 1762/1964).

Rousseau goes on to indicate a child's learning is like a cat's exploration, an instinctive desire to know the environment.

> *Watch a cat when she comes into a room for the first time. She goes from place to place, she sniffs about and examines everything. She is never still for a moment. She is suspicious of everything until she has examined it and*

found out what it is. It is the same with a child when he begins to walk and enters, so to speak, the room of the world around him. The only difference is that, while both use sight, the child uses his hands and the cat the subtle sense of smell which nature has bestowed upon it. It is this instinct, rightly or wrongly educated, which makes children skilful or clumsy, quick or slow, wise or foolish.

(Rousseau, 1762/1964)

Rousseau's ideas of the child underpin much of our *child-centred* approach to early childhood education today. He considered that children are intrinsically motivated to play and to learn from interaction with their environment. He also raised the idea that children develop in stages, just as animals and plants do, but that humans are programmed to develop socially and work in groups. Rousseau lived in a time of political awareness that was questioning the way society operated, and he is sometimes attributed with influencing the French Revolution through his writing.

THEORY FOCUS

Comparing Locke and Rousseau

Today we draw on the perspectives of both of these philosophers in our consideration of childhood, play and learning.

John Locke	Jean Jacques Rousseau
Children learn through the senses and experiences, through play.	Children learn through interaction with their environment.
Children's minds are a 'blank sheet', or *tabula rasa*, waiting to be filled with knowledge from experience.	Children have an innate (pre-programmed) drive to explore and learn that is unique to the individual: *every mind has its own form* and children have a *natural liveliness* to explore and experiment.
Play supports learning as children learn best when they are enjoying themselves.	
Children do not know good from bad, and need adult support and guidance to prevent them from going down the wrong moral pathway.	A child will play as a *young savage* seeking to develop physical skill and resilience to challenge through play.
Good health (but not comfort) is essential to support learning and development. (Locke advocated that children should have daily baths to keep their feet cool and sharpen their minds!)	Rather than being *taught*, people should have the freedom to draw on experience and work out their own conclusions, including social ones.
	Children will seek out different sorts of knowledge and understanding as they mature through stages of development.
	Children are generally *good* and their experience and learning is often corrupted by adult involvement.

Table 2.2 Comparisons between theories of Locke and Rousseau

ACTIVITY 2

We have considered two perspectives in relation to children and play. Have you ever considered what your own perspective (or viewpoint) relating to children and play might be? Your own perspective is likely to have developed since your own childhood, and will have been influenced by your experience of children, work experiences, training, reading and visits to other settings. It may be influenced by observations of children you have worked with, or the practice of a colleague.

One way to identify your own perspective is to step back and reflect on why you are doing the things you are. Think about the following questions.

- *What is play for? What do I think its purpose is?*
- *What am I trying to do when I support children's play?*
- *Which perspective do I prefer: that of Locke or Rousseau?*
- *Is there an outcome I expect to see as a result of my efforts (filling the blank sheet), or do I believe play is free of outcome (the child develops their own direction)?*
- *What do I think the adult's role is in supporting children's play?*

Then think a little further about the influences on your ideas.

- *Where have my ideas come from?*

One person may answer to the above activities that play is what children do, but that it has a range of purposes or planned outcomes. The person may consider that he is trying to ensure that children learn through play with an expected outcome encouraged by carefully adult-structured purposeful activity directed towards gaining the right knowledge. This perspective would align more with Locke that play is essential as part of the child's developmental process, and that they will learn through such activity, but that the adult has a strong role giving boundaries and controlling direction.

In contrast, another person may consider that children can give direction to their own play and development. This second perspective may consider that children will freely play and learn if the environment is right. She will take care in setting things out to be attractive, encouraging exploration and social interaction. The adult does not model or steer children's learning, rather she steps back to let children play and make their own way socially and cognitively. This perspective aligns with that of Rousseau, who saw limitations to Locke's systematic approach.

In asking these questions of yourself you will be able to acknowledge and refine your personal understanding of childhood and play in relation to learning and direction.

Looking at some recent perspectives on play

Both Locke and Rousseau were influenced by the thinking of their time and adopted particular perspectives as a result.

Recent authors Else and Sturrock (2007) recognise a range of influences and consider there to be four key perspectives on play. They are the:

- *physiological and biological perspective*, in which the role of children's play is to develop their body and physical skills;

- *psychological perspective*, in which play is a way of dealing with trauma, and a tool to explore emotions and anxieties. In this perspective children may use toys to express anger or grief; to act out conversations or arguments so that they can work through them to a more balanced state;

- *cognitive and developmental perspective*, in which play is important for intellectual development, the development of thinking and understanding. Children use toys to explore theoretical ideas in a practical way;

- *socio-cultural perspective*, in which play performs the role of skills development and role practice for later life in a particular cultural context. So children may role-play laying the table and making tea, to practise skills they may later need in restaurants or the home.

Else and Sturrock further add that:

> *All of these can find evidence... all of them are true from a given point of view. But how can all of these theories claim to be representative of the phenomenon that is play? Which one is the true theory?*
>
> (Else and Sturrock, 2007, page 145)

The answer, of course, is that there is not one *true theory* but that there will be many theoretical perspectives that influence what we see as play, its benefits, purpose or impact. Else and Sturrock are arguing that all of these perspectives indicate different purposes for play, and all may apply at different times. The *true* theory is perhaps the one that aligns most with our own viewpoint and intentions at the time of use.

Introducing some theories of play

Let us now move on from the perspectives to concepts and theoretical understandings of play. Theoretical approaches to play largely fall into three main categories:

- what play is;

- what play does;

- what play means to children.

These are helpful pointers to aid our exploration of play. Garvey (1991) clearly indicates we should give a primary importance to an initial consideration of what play is and how first we must *describe the aspects of young children's play before offering speculations about its causes or its functions in the course of development* (1991, page 4).

She is arguing the importance of first identifying the range of behaviours that are considered to be play before we begin to explore what it can do.

ACTIVITY 3

Take time to observe a child or children at play. Note down any behaviours that you see and consider as either play *or* playful.

Use this list of behaviours to refer to, and make comparison with, whilst reading the following paragraphs.

Considering types of play

Theorists who research the *types* of play that exist, explore what play is by observing and then categorising the range of activities seen when children are considered to be *at play*. Such breaking down of the broad concept of play to a range of parts helps us to analyse what play is about.

The earliest and simplest categorising of play *types* concentrated on whether an activity was or was not play. However, in 1991 Garvey reminded us that many play behaviours may be *borrowed* from non-play activity and this realisation led Garvey to have concerns about categorising *play* and *not play*. Although we should bear Garvey's warning in mind, *taxonomies* of play (or lists of observed play activity) are helpful in prompting a deeper consideration of what children are doing when they play. Where such lists become regularly used, they can also offer a common terminology to describe and discuss play's appearance and nature.

Hughes' taxonomy of play

Bob Hughes, for example, has categorised play into 16 *types* from symbolic play through to recapitulative play, or the repetition of previous experiences for greater understanding (Hughes 2002). His 'Taxonomy of Play Types' is now widely accepted by those working in children's play in the UK as an informative list.

Prior to his carefully compiled list, many play workers used the acronym SPICE to think of the types of play activity found in the domains of social, physical, intellectual, creative and emotional development activity in children.

- *Social Play* = Playing with others, developing social skills.

- *Physical Play* = Play that helps to develop muscular control and strength.

- *Intellectual Play* = Play that stimulates problem solving, or involves puzzles and cognitive development.

- *Creative Play* = The generation of new ideas or things.

- *Emotional Play* = The release of emotions, therapeutic activity, exploring emotional responses and control.

Practitioners began to realise that many play activities crossed the boundaries of this simple framework. Playing a board game could be both intellectual and social, for example.

Hughes' analysis greatly extends such a limited approach and raises some interesting conceptual ideas about play as an observed behaviour. His perspective draws on ecological and social understandings, concerned with the child in context. He also offers a perspective in which play has an important role in prompting adaptation and adjustment for the evolution of human beings into the future. He argues that the word 'play' tells us little about what is happening when children play, or indeed why it may be happening. Rather his observations offer a brief classification and exploration of the different way play *presents itself* in what children do.

THEORY FOCUS

Hughes' Taxonomy of play (National Playing Fields Association, NPFA, 2000)

Play type	Hughes' comment
Symbolic	Play which allows control, gradual exploration and increased understanding without the risk of being out of one's depth. For example, using a piece of wood to symbolise a person.
Fantasy	Play which rearranges the world in the child's way, a way which is unlikely to occur. For example, playing at being a pilot, flying around the world.
Creative	Play which allows a new response, the transformation of information, awareness of new connections, with an element of surprise. For example, enjoying making something with a range of materials.
Role	Play exploring ways of being, although not normally of an intense personal, social, domestic or interpersonal nature. For example, child brushing with a broom, dialling with a telephone, driving a car.
Dramatic	Play which dramatises events in which the child is not a direct participator. For example, presentations of a TV show, an event on the street, a religious or festive event.
Imaginative	Play where conventional rules, which govern the physical world, do not apply. For example imagining you are, or are pretending to be, a tree or ship, or patting a dog which is not there.
Rough and Tumble	Close encounter play which is less to do with fighting and more to do with touching, tickling, gauging relative strength and discovering physical flexibility and the exhilaration of display. Playful fighting and chasing are examples.
Socio-dramatic	The enactment of real and potential experiences of an intense personal, social, domestic or interpersonal nature. For example, playing at house, going to the shops, being mothers and fathers.
Locomotor	Movement in any and every direction for its own sake. For example, chase, tag, hide and seek, tree climbing.
Social	Play during which the rules and criteria for social engagement and interaction can be revealed, explored and amended. For example, any social or interactive situation which contains an expectation on all parties that they will abide by the rules or protocols (i.e. games, conversations, making something together).
Communic-ation	Name calling, mime, Mickey taking, jokes, play acting, facial expressions (the play face), imitation.
Exploratory Play	Play to access factual information consisting of manipulative behaviours, such as handling, throwing, banging or mouthing objects. For example, engaging with an object or area and assessing its properties, possibilities and content.
Problem Solving or Object Play	Play which uses infinite and interesting sequences of hand-eye manipulations and movements. For example, examination and novel use of any object (e.g. cloth, paintbrush and cup).
Mastery Play	Control of the physical and affective ingredients of our environment, for example, digging holes, changing the course of streams, constructing shelters, building fires.
Deep Play	Play which allows the child to encounter risky or even potentially life-threatening experiences, to develop survival skills and conquer fear.

Table 2.3 Hughes' taxonomy of play

Just as we questioned the 'truth' of theory early in this chapter, and theoretical concepts were presented as ideas to be questioned, tested and adapted, so Hughes in his updated version of the above table also acknowledges that:

> *No taxonomy should ever claim to be the definitive listing of all play types...*
> *I write this... in the respectful knowledge and in the hope that others may*
> *observe play types or playful behaviours which are not included here.*

(Hughes, 2002, page 4)

Did you perhaps observe different play types in your notes for the above activity? Hughes' taxonomy of play is clearly open to interpretation and extension. It is a tool, or a starting point to stimulate discussion and analysis.

A different analysis of types: social play

While Hughes offers a very broad and useful categorisation of children's play activity into 16 types across a range of developmental domains and contexts, there are theorists and writers who very clearly limit their analyses to the impact of play on one aspect of development, such as social development.

Mildred Parten was a social psychologist who also classified play into *types* several decades before Hughes' taxonomy. Her play types (Parten, 1932) offer a perceived progress of development in children as they mature from solitary play through to much more sophisticated co-operative play. Her research indicated that as children develop, they become more advanced in their communication and social skills and so solitary play became less common.

THEORY FOCUS

Parten's play types

- *Unoccupied* – when the child is not involved in play.
- *Solitary* – the child plays on his or her own, without interaction with others.
- *Onlooker* – the child is not involved with the play, but looks on with interest.
- *Parallel* – the child plays alongside another child, perhaps echoing language and actions, but without social interaction directly with the other.
- *Associative* – the child is interested in social interaction with other children and this overrides the play activity.
- *Co-operative* – the child is interested both in the social interaction and the activity itself, and is able to manipulate the two domains.

There are many people (Broadhead *et al.*, 2010; Smith, 2011) who question Parten's concept of a simplistic progression through play type according to age. They highlight that children will choose to be either solitary or co-operative at different times according to context, environment, mood, and how well they know the other children.

Despite this concern, Parten's categories can still be useful as an initial consideration of young children's social play activity. Drawing on her play types, it is possible to see that younger children display more solitary play, exploring a range of objects in a treasure basket, for example.

You may equally see an 18-month-old child playing alongside a child of a similar age clearly illustrating parallel play in which, although they are not communicating directly with each other or sharing toys, they show they are very much aware of what the other is doing, echoing movements and discoveries.

It is possible in the later early years to see large numbers of children playing quite complex co-operative games, often with explicit rules (think of children playing with chalk roads and ride-on toys, for example).

ACTIVITY 4

Observe some children aged under three involved in playful activity. Try to use Parten's play types to analyse the stages of social interaction seen. Does this confirm her model, or lead you to agree with the critics that it depends on the context and environment?

Piaget's interest in play types and stages

Jean Piaget (Piaget and Inhelder,1969) considered play from a cognitive psychology perspective (being interested in the growth and development of intelligence). Piaget argued that play activity supported children's ability to take on new information and adjust their existing understandings as a result, leading to intellectual development. Piaget called the taking on of new information *assimilation*. He termed the subsequent adaptation of existing groups of ideas, or *schemas, accommodation.*

An important aspect of Piaget's theories is his argument that we are driven to seek a state of balance or equilibrium, in which our ideas match our experiences. He considered that children explore clusters of ideas (or *schema)* through practical action and play. An example of such a schema may be a child's repetitive interest in water, exploring concepts of form and volume. This may involve pouring it into and out of a range of containers. If the water behaves as expected the child is operating in a state of equilibrium, with their actual experience matching their cognitive understanding. However, if the water behaves unusually (perhaps because it is thickened in some way), the child's understanding is challenged and they must adapt what they already know. Through such play processes and adjustment of existing understanding, Piaget argued, children gradually acquire new knowledge

Piaget considered three broad types of play activity that followed the child's development stage:

1. *Sensorimotor* – meaning using senses and muscles or motor skills to explore. An infant up to approximately two years will explore and experiment with sight, smell, taste, touch and sound.

2. *Symbolic* – During this phase which occurs between two and six years approximately, the young child is able to translate experiences to symbols. By using symbols, a young child can recall images and understandings and re-play them in a meaningful way. In children's symbolic play, one thing can represent another. A block of wood might symbolise a telephone; a bucket might symbolise a saucepan, and so on.

3. *Games with rules* – Piaget argued that older children aged six and upwards, were developing their understanding of social concepts, co-operation and competition. Their play would reflect this understanding with greater emphasis on team behaviour with rules and boundaries.

Here Piaget is not only categorising what children do when they play, but is also offering an analysis of the stages of development and the impact of the play activity on the developing child.

Corinne Hutt's epistemic and ludic play

Corinne Hutt (Hutt, 1979) was a play theorist who also identified three broad *types* of play, but hers were not age related. She clearly drew on Piaget's work, but also stated that her perspective was a biological one. Hutt had studied mammals and monkeys at play and related their evolutionary behaviours to her observations of children. She considered a child's play behaviour would be altered and adjusted according to his current experiences. Children's play experiences prompt their adaptation which in turn ultimately leads to species adaptation and evolution. As a result of her studies, Hutt devised a *taxonomy of play* which distinguished between two main categories labelled *epistemic* play, and *ludic* play and included a third category of *games with rules*, a social or more elaborate play type that developed with age (Hutt, 1979).

THEORY FOCUS

Hutt's taxonomy of play types

Epistemic play is exploratory play, concerned with exploration of things and the acquisition of information and knowledge. Babies and young children are undertaking epistemic play behaviours when they are exploring the contents of a treasure basket, or a new toy. They may place items in their mouth to identify taste and texture, wave them around to establish weight and density, or bang them together to see what sounds they make. Epistemic play asks the question: *What is this?*

Ludic play is play which uses past experiences. It includes symbolic play, therapeutic play, fantasy and innovation. Role play is ludic play as children may act out past experiences

---

continued

THEORY FOCUS *continued*

such as tea time, cooking or car repair. They may fantasise as they dress up, or act in a therapeutic way, exploring difficult experiences. Therapeutic play may also be seen through the satisfaction of completing an action or game over and over again and confirming that things are as they should be. Children may therefore return to shape sorters or jigsaws that they can already do with ease, for the therapeutic, or ludic, reassurance it may give them.

Games with rules. Hutt also recognised the importance of games with rules in older children's play as they explore social relationships. She also included games of skill and games of chance in this play type which recognises a growing complexity in older children's activities.

Hutt argued that there was no age-related progression between the types of play, rather she understood that children would alternate between ludic and epistemic activity at any age. They would at one moment be exploring an object and, in the next, using the object symbolically for a make-believe exploration of some experience or feeling (Hutt, 1979).

Heuristic play: an epistemic activity?

Heuristic play is a term quite well known and often used in the field of Early Childhood, particularly in relation to very young children. Closely related to exploratory or epistemic play, it is often combined with the use of Treasure Basket resources for young children and babies (Goldschmied and Jackson, 1994). Heuristic play and treasure baskets, explored by Elinor Goldschmied and her colleagues in the 1980s and early 1990s have become interchangeable terms in common practice.

The term 'heuristic' is derived from a Greek word meaning *to find*, and is largely used to describe behaviours, including play, that involve an individual actively discovering something for themselves. Heuristic play is a term coined by Goldschmied (1994) for a type of play that is very closely related to both Hutt's epistemic play and Piaget's sensory motor play. Although often associated with treasure baskets and very young children, heuristic play can happen at any age, with older children playing outside with pipes, planks, ropes and guttering, or indoors exploring a jewellery box.

ACTIVITY 5

A treasure basket is merely a resource that prompts heuristic play. It is usually offered to children as a basket that contains a collection of everyday objects that vary in weight, size, texture, colour, taste, temperature and sound. Children are allowed to explore the basket of objects or 'treasures' at their own pace, using their senses to discover what an object is like, and what it does. Hughes (2010) describes the objects in a treasure basket as food for the brain.

Elinor Goldschmied is quoted as saying

> We can never truly know what it is like to bite into a ripe juicy peach until we have actually taken a bite for ourselves. Similarly, what do the concepts cool and smooth, prickly and rough actually mean unless we have caressed a pebble, picked up a pine cone, or fingered the bark of a gnarled tree.

(Cited in Hughes, 2010, page 3)

Why not find for yourself a wide, stable basket with no sharp edges, to fill with such textured objects to feed the brain?

Some suggested items are given below, but you can continue the list by considering whether the object is natural, of varied texture, safe, and stimulating to the senses.

My treasure basket contains:

* *Pine cone*
* *Wooden nail brush with soft natural bristles*
* *A bunch of metal measuring spoons (perhaps still linked together)*
* *A silk scarf*
* *A length of light chain*
* *Large wooden curtain rings*
* *Wooden spoons*
* *Metal pots to bang or put things in*
* *A fresh lemon*
* *Place mats smelling of the straw they are made of*

Now suggest some more items.

Play, involvement and flow

Eleanor Goldschmied recognised that children would become very involved in exploring the treasure basket and remain in a state of concentration for up to an hour. *One of the most striking features of a baby or child's behaviour, when playing heuristically is an intense concentration that is satisfying to the child and practitioner alike* (Hughes, 2010, page 3).

Such observable concentration in children at play has been noted by other theorists. Laevers (2000) combines the concepts of *well-being* with *involvement*, indicating that both are required to achieve a state of deep level learning. His is a constructivist perspective in which child and environment (including adults) interact and develop (or construct) knowledge together. A child who is in a state of well-being in a setting feels *at home* in the environment and therefore able to relax and get on with their exploratory play activity, leading in turn to greater involvement while playing. Laevers indicated that an involved person narrows their attention to a limited circle of concerns, there is a period of intense motivation, fascination with what is going on or being explored and *no distance between person and activity* (Laevers, 2000, page 24).

Another theorist, Csikszentmihalyi (1979), developed a concept of involvement or *flow* relating to play activity. A range of states that were indicative of *flow* were identified.

- Levels of concentration or involvement in which you are not thinking about something, but are immersed in doing it. You become unaware of alternatives, end products, or even the environment around you.

- There is a *filtering out* of other influences or stimuli. Memory becomes very short-term as the player is concerned only with the enjoyable, intrinsically rewarding activity of the moment.

- Time sense becomes warped, either seeming very compressed as the child is jolted out of their exploration or reverie, or expanded, as their involvement has led to fast complex thinking in this heightened state.

- While in *flow* you feel in control as no one else is reaching you to direct you to an external goal.

Both of these theorists considered that a state of deep involvement was achieved by play as the motivation was not stimulated by external concepts of gain or product.

The well-known early childhood author, Tina Bruce, also put these ideas together and coined the term *free-flow play*. Key features of free-flow play are that participants would *wallow in ideas, feelings and relationships* and *actively use first-hand experiences*. In free-flow play children would become immersed in the process and *operate in advance of what they could normally do* (Bruce, 2004, page 59).

SUMMARY

I am sure that you can by now see similarities between the above discussion on involvement and flow and those factors we drew on to define play in the last chapter. As we shift perspective from categorising observer looking to describe play behaviours to the psychology of involvement and flow, the complexities of play become more evident. We have journeyed from a complex consideration of what play can look like, to a consideration of the depth of concentration that it can provoke. We have considered play from the perspective of the observer, but we have not yet really considered what play can do for a child. Yet even in considering the importance of environment, developmental phase and emotional security, we are building our layers of understanding relating to this complex phenomenon. Take time to consider what these theories mean for your practice. In the next chapter we will explore some historical perspectives, theories and resources, and further develop our definition by considering how culture has affected children's play.

Brock, A, Dodds, S, Jarvis, P and Olusoga, Y (2009) *Perspectives on Play: Learning for Life.* Harlow: Pearson Education.

This is a very useful reference book. The first chapter offers three 'Perspectives on Play' and there are definitions of play throughout the book.

Hughes, A (2010) *Developing Play for the Under 3s: The Treasure Basket and Heuristic Play (2nd Edition).* London: David Fulton.

A very clear and interesting exploration of the ideas of heuristic play and treasure baskets including a section directly quoted from a conversation with Elinor Goldschmied, guidance on selection of objects and the adult role.

Hughes, B (2002) *A Playworker's Taxonomy of Play Types (2nd Edition).* PlayEducation.

A further exploration of the types of play, their potential purpose and indicators, supported by quotations from key thinkers about the theory behind these types.

3 Historical perspectives and principles

Through reading this chapter you will:

- develop an understanding of the changing perspectives, theories and concepts of play as they have emerged from the ancient times to the present day;

- consider the social environment, toys, resources and adult attitudes that have impacted on children's play experiences at different periods in time;

- reflect on some key policy responses to a growing awareness and understanding of the value of play in the twentieth and twenty-first centuries.

Throughout you will be encouraged to consider what this historical evidence means for today's early years practitioners – and how these understandings can further develop our individual approaches to supporting children's play in a range of contexts.

A Time line (at the end of this book) is offered to support your understanding of the journey through time to our current concept of play in the United Kingdom and Europe.

Introduction: play in historical context

It is not a new understanding that children play. There is historical evidence that, given freedom and space, children have always exhibited play behaviours. Children's play activity can be seen in ancient Egyptian paintings, Bronze Age toys and Victorian literature. Archaeology reveals that in primitive communities of the past children used objects as play resources much like the toys of today. In contrast to the historical constancy of the play behaviours of children, adult attitudes towards play have been far from consistent.

This chapter will take you through a range of historical perspectives on play from classical praise for its benefits to a confusion of modern perspectives and positions, some of which can be seen in recent government policy.

Despite changing perspectives and understandings, it is possible during this journey through time, to see the following tensions and themes:

- child freedom versus adult control;

- play as a vehicle for learning or play as recreation and release;

- play as cultural and socially desirable, or play as disruptive and distracting;
- play as preparation for adult life, or indicative of separate children's cultures.

The persistence of play

Recognisable toys have been found in China dating back to 5,000BC. There are Egyptian tomb paintings that depict children playing. The oldest toy found in Britain dates back to the Bronze Age (Owen, 2008). Vases dug from Greek and Roman ruins show how children played in ancient history some 400 years BC. A Greek wine vase of fifth century BC, 2,400 years ago, depicts a small boy pulling a wagon, or possibly a toy chariot. A painting over a thousand years old depicts one hundred children at play, riding hobby horses, juggling and dressing up as adults (Konner, 1991). Many of the toys the children played with centuries ago remain similar to those used until recent history. Small carts, whistles, balls, swings, spinning tops and hoops, dolls, miniature animals, and small versions of adult clothes and tools have been found as play resources from Roman to modern times (Frost, 2010). This would imply that children's play activity has changed little over the centuries, despite shifting adult perspectives.

Early interest in play for learning

As long ago as 360BC, the Greek philosopher Plato proposed that allowing children to play was essential to supporting the development of good future citizens. Plato considered play to be important to the establishment of a cultured, creative and artistic society (Plato, 360BC/1974). Frost (2010) identified that Plato uses the ancient Greek words for education/culture (*paideia*), play (*paidia*), and children (*paides*) which all have the same root, demonstrating their close link in Greek thinking. Play as the formation of future culture is a theme we shall see re-emerging in more recent history.

Plato recognised that children's enjoyment of learning was enhanced by play – and in fact that play was essential for learning to be embedded and sustained. Through play children could concentrate for longer and would learn social skills such as argument and debate or how to handle competition and defeat. The ancient Greek culture valued physical ability and active play, and play fighting was encouraged. Jenkinson (2001) attributes Plato as first recognising the *play leap*; a free movement of children who cannot keep their bodies still; purely wishing to move because they can.

While Plato gives little mention of play for the under-threes, he argued that the nursery child aged three to six years needed a great deal of free play. Supporting this play would be the Greek stories, myths and legends prompting fantasy and creative imagination (equivalent to our role-play). He seems to have recognised that children played and learnt in different ways according to age and experience. Plato offered a clear distinction between play and playfulness: he defined *play* as children's immersion in play activity, while he saw *playfulness* as an attitude of fun and creativity that could be applied to other activities.

Although the focus was on the education of the child as future citizen, Plato proposed education should work with the interests of the child. Through freedom in play, he thought, children may indicate unique individual dispositions and future career aptitudes which should be supported appropriately.

> *...anyone who would be good at anything must practice that thing from his youth upwards, both in sport and earnest... for example he who is to be a good builder should play at building... The most important part of education is the right training in the nursery...*
>
> (Plato, 360BC/1974, page 349)

Training in the nursery was reliant upon identifying and nurturing the child's dispositions, interests and aptitudes that emerged from their play activity.

THEORY FOCUS

Dispositions and aptitudes

A *disposition* is an interest, inclination or tendency to act in a certain way, or to be drawn to certain things or actions in preference to another. So a disposition for learning is a keenness to learn.

An *aptitude* is an emerging talent or tendency to do something well. Aptitude normally refers to a skill yet to be fully developed.

An example of a disposition is a young child's persistent curiosity towards engineering. Perhaps a child can be observed taking things apart to see how they work, or lining up blocks carefully and *levelling* the construction of walls and sides with their hands, head tilted to see the angle. Their successful ability to *engineer* solutions, making bridges that work, is perhaps an indication of *aptitude* for engineering, an emerging skill.

Many authors have suggested that we should nurture children's dispositions for learning (an intrinsic interest and curiosity for learning), rather than the traditional ability to remember the facts they have been exposed to. A focus on supporting learning dispositions is often linked to ideas of play and the child as leader of their own learning (Carr and Claxton, 2002).

ACTIVITY 1

A number of key points made by Plato have carried through time and continue to have resonance today. Read the following passage relating to current practice and see how many of Plato's ideas you can apply.

> Sally was first into the nursery and set out the room with resources drawing on her observations of children. She had noticed that Ruti liked playing with the blocks and was making long roads, so set out cars and small world toys, along with planks of wood, to see where her engineering would take her today. Kieran had recently

> ### ACTIVITY *1* continued
>
> had a baby brother and so Sally set out the home corner with dolls, nappies, a baby bath of water, towels and other resources relating to the experience of a new baby in the home. As she did so she wondered if both Kieran and Ruti were developing skills that they might need in later life. She was aware of how the children might change the doll's nappy in a certain way, or build a bridge, copying what they had seen more skilled others do. Within the resources there were opportunities for counting and measuring as she put out coins and rulers.
>
> Sally planned to tell a story about a dragon to stimulate imagination as some of the children had been 'fighting the monster' yesterday. The storybook tale had a moral point as the dragon turned out to be good, and this might stimulate debate in the children about whether 'monsters' are always bad, so considering what is meant by 'good' and 'bad'. She mused over the children's mock fights yesterday and wondered how far she should let these activities continue before they became a nuisance to others, or a fight for real! She considered that the children were learning how to manage difficult situations themselves through this play, and were gaining physical skills as a result of their rough and tumble outdoors. She decided she would let them continue, but would maybe suggest they think of some rules to give themselves boundaries.
>
> *How many did you spot?*
>
> - *The focus on the child's interests and experiences.*
> - *Consideration of the future citizen.*
> - *Use of story and fantasy.*
> - *Encouragement of physical activity.*
> - *Moral messages in the stories.*
> - *Managing the balance of mock fighting in play and responsibility for others.*
> - *The teaching of mathematics in a pleasurable way that would have some meaning to the children.*
>
> *Was Sally planning for play, or playful learning? Where is the boundary between the two? Perhaps there is no clear boundary?*

Finding the balance and setting constraints

Although he promoted play, Plato also considered that children needed to be encouraged to move towards self-discipline as they matured, so indicating a tension between play and responsibility. The Roman teacher Quintilian (35–97AD) expressed a similar tension when he wrote about accepting a love of play: *Nor should I be displeased by a love of play in my pupils, for this is a sign of alertness, only let there be moderation…* (Quintilian cited in Frost, 2010, page 12).

You can almost hear the exasperation as Quintilian appreciated the involvement and alertness that came from play, but also wanted moderation and direction to learning for an adult-directed agenda.

Perspective shift away from play

Unfortunately for children it appears that an interest in children and the value of play dropped away after the Romans left Britain and we enter a period in which there are few records, but themes of *work* and *duty* come to the fore in period literature. There is an argument (Ariès, 1962) that childhood as a concept, and therefore their related play activity, disappeared with the Romans and did not reappear until the late Middle Ages: *In Medieval society the idea of childhood did not exist... as soon as the child could live without the constant solicitude of his mother, his nanny or his cradle rocker, he belonged to the adult society* (Ariès, 1962, page 128).

If there was no childhood, then there was no play. A growing focus on productive *work* reduced the value given to frivolous and non-productive *play* which was time wasting and idling. Toys were more likely to be useful small versions of adult tools. As the power of the church grew, the doctrine *work is worship* increased in prominence and churchmen and elders (including teachers) often felt it was their duty to force compliance to the Christian work ethic upon children.

The historian Hanawalt (1993) describes a young twelfth-century child's day which required early rising, and much prayers and reverence to avoid a whipping by his elders. Hanawalt notes that the records indicate that there is evidence of children being severely punished on a regular basis. In part, this was to keep out the devil and model the child into the expected future adult form, preventing future sinful activity. Although we would not employ the punishments of the past, remnants of this perspective towards play may remain in Western culture today. Is this Christian work ethic of the past, where some of our ideas come from about keeping children productively occupied, rather than allowing them to waste time *just playing*?

ACTIVITY 2

Consider this scenario.
A carer drops off two young children at an after-school club. As the worker comes to greet them at the door the carer says, 'I don't want them just playing all evening, make sure they take part in the activities and make something to bring home!' Then she smiles at the children, says goodbye, and leaves.

There was clearly a bond between the carer and the children, but the carer had set the agenda based on her own principles arising from deep-rooted perspectives and values. The creation of something, a product such as a picture or object to take home had more value to the adult than the more elusive process of play which may in fact be more important to the child. The child may need to work through recent experiences and

ACTIVITY **2** *continued*

understandings, relationships and ideas in their play – without a mind to create a thing to take home.

Reflect here on whether you have experienced a similar attitude from parents and carers.

If you are a parent or carer consider if you have ever adopted a similar approach? If so, ask yourself why. If you were the worker what would your response be?

Are our habits and principles perhaps influenced by historic experiences and perspectives such that we need to take time to acknowledge them, think about why we have them, and then leave them behind in order to consider the child's agenda?

Begin to build your perspective in relation to expectations of product or process.

Play prevails

Despite the depressing picture of a play-free childhood offered by Hanawalt (1993), and Ariès (1962), play clearly prevailed. The famous painting *Children's Games* created by the Flemish painter Pieter Bruegel the Elder in 1560, shows children (portrayed very much like small adults) playing with a wide range of toys and games in the streets.

Although the meaning of this picture has been extensively debated, it does record the range of play activities of the late 1500s. Children are playing leap-frog, blindfold and group racing games. Some children are playing at role-play and dressing up, others are playing games of skill with balls and hoops. Some are physical in their play, others are playing seated on the ground. Whatever its purpose, this painting offers a social record of children's games at that time.

ACTIVITY **3**

Bruegel's painting Children's Games *is widely available on the internet and makes a great discussion piece, offering opportunities to talk about what children used to do, or what types of play can be seen, their social groupings, how play is risky and challenging, and so on. I found a version at:* **www.heuristics.org.uk/breughel.html**

It has so much resonance with children's play today that a modern interpretation of the image has been created for Play Wales, available through their website **www.playwales. org.uk**. *In this cartoon adaptation, children are pursuing many of the same activities as in Bruegel's time, but with the addition of a greater number of toys, and some modern inventions such as skateboards and electronic games.*

Why not also search for other images of children at play in artworks and old photographs? Take time to consider the similarities and differences of street play in historic pictures and from your experiences today. Do children today have a more restricted access to street play?

continued

ACTVITY 3 continued

Consider whether there are any adults in the images you look at. Was play directed by adults or largely adult free? Does this reflection on play add anything to your own perspective of play in today's society?

A more enlightened approach

By the time that Locke was writing in the 1700s the view that play was sinful was being challenged and a range of perspectives of children, childhood and play were beginning to emerge. A new *enlightenment* way of thinking was sweeping Europe, which drew on the classical writing of Plato and the ancient Greeks, but also emphasised the importance of science and systematic experiment. This period opened the doors to discussion and we see ideas presented and subsequently challenged or refined, building one upon another to establish modern thinking about life, education, culture and play.

The enlightenment journey began with Erasmus, a philosopher who had been to Italy and explored classical ideas. He criticised the way that children were often neglected, and instead promoted instruction for young children through enjoyable activity. Although Erasmus still believed that children were like wax and needed moulding, he also considered that nature had given them a desire to learn and gain knowledge. In 1497, he wrote that:

> *...a constant element of enjoyment must be mingled with our studies, so that we think of learning as a game rather than a form of drudgery, for no activity can be continued for long if it does not to some extent afford pleasure to the participant.*

> (Erasmus, 1497, cited in Cunningham, 2005, page 44)

Learning through play was back on the agenda. A century later, the philosopher Comenius (1592–1670) was also proclaiming that children should experience learning through pleasurable activity and the first-hand experiences we might today call play. He made a link between play and the environment. Much of the thinking of these early enlightenment philosophers can be seen in the later works of Rousseau, Pestalozzi, Froebel, Montessori and Piaget.

Locke and Rousseau

Both John Locke and Jean Jacques Rousseau argued for appropriate education of children, using what we might term play – yet they presented very different perspectives in their writing. Locke argued that children are born with blank minds to be filled with knowledge from experience. Rousseau, however, believed that children have an innate (or inborn) biological drive, instinct and understanding that leads natural choice and individual development.

Locke wrote of how children could be motivated to learn while at play:

> ...*learning might be made a Play and Recreation to children; and they might be brought to desire to be taught if it were propos'd to them as a thing of Honour, Credit, Delight and Recreation or as a Reward for doing something else; and if they were never chid or corrected for the neglect of it.*
>
> (Locke, 1689/1979, page 208)

ACTIVITY 4

Locke's writing contains the tension of play and restraint that we have already seen in classical writings. Children were to be encouraged to learn through playful experience, but an adult's role was also to form young children's minds and introduce good habits.

Are Locke's ideas so very far from those in settings today, which offer a play-based approach to readiness for school, but also encourage good sitting and kind hands, fixed periods for play and an expectation of positive behaviour and restraint?

Reflect for a few moments on your position. Do you think that adults have a role in introducing good habits and forming a young child's mind, as well as supporting their self-directed play? How should the two interests be balanced?

Contrast Locke's perspective of play, linked to balancing learning and moral restraint, with Rousseau's work which more readily highlights play as the right of the child. In the following passage learning appears almost incidental to the right to play:

> *Childhood is, or ought to be, the age of games and frolics... Work and play are all the same to him (the child Emile). His games are his occupations: he is not aware of any difference. He goes into everything he does with pleasing interest and freedom...*
>
> (Rousseau, in Boyd, 1956, page 67)

In the above passage, Rousseau positively advocates for play, rejecting the common perception that it was unimportant and time wasting. His was a romantic, nativist, perspective in which during the first five years of life children were to learn more from their own direct experiences, exploration of the environment and social contact than from any *taught* experience. Such a perspective might be seen today in a setting which emphasises free play over planned outcomes, and the adults adopt a *laissez faire* attitude to the children's activities (merely leaving them to play without intervention).

Later the extremes of this spectrum, of blank sheet or natural wisdom, were to be joined by a central perspective of the child as constructivist. Attributed to the philosopher Kant (1781/2004), this position asserts that children are born with some cognitive understanding and potential, but that this is developed through the child's informed interaction with their environment and other people. The child has an element of agency (ability to act as an individual thinker). It is this interaction that enables children to create their own meaning and understanding and new future perspectives. This latter position is one very much promoted in early childhood set-tings today, in which there is a balance of free play and adult direction towards learning arising from this.

THEORY FOCUS

Ideas of learning that relate to play

Empiricism (or blank sheet)	Constructivism	Nativism
Nurture	Combination of nature and nurture	Nature
Children's knowledge and behaviour stem from their experiences and environment and are *built up* from nothing through experiences. Children can therefore be *shaped* as they mature, and adults impart knowledge and mould the child.	A position which acknowledges that children are born with unique biological characteristics and potential, but that these are influenced by the child's interaction with the environment and people in it. The child has an *agency* or ability to act as an individual thinker from an early age.	Knowledge and concepts are partly innate and present in humans at birth. Children are pre-programmed to develop or mature in certain ways. Individual differences are biologically determined and inherited. Nature must be given time to work.
Adults lead the way. The child responds to the adult and environment.	A model which requires adult-child or child-child interaction as they learn together.	A *laissez faire* approach in which the child can lead his or her own way.
Play may be used as a vehicle for learning – to support children's sustained interest in an appropriate topic.	Children may explore their own interests through play and be supported in this exploration by an adult or more experienced peer.	Children have an innate drive to play and this will *naturally* lead to learning and development.

Table 3.1 Empiricism, constructivism and nativism

Now that we have these three *roots* of thinking about play, let us explore where each of the threads has taken us in relation to more recent understandings of play.

Nativism: from Rousseau to kindergarten and outdoor play

Rousseau had made a theoretical case for play in his book *Emile* but had not put his ideas into practice. It was Johann Pestalozzi (1746–1827) who took these up and established a successful school in 1805 with the intention of linking education to the power of nature rather than nurture. Pestalozzi emphasised play as spontaneity and self-activity. He argued that children should not be given ready-made answers but should arrive at answers themselves. To do this their own powers of seeing, judging and reasoning should be cultivated (Silber, 1965; Smith, 1997). He promoted the importance of observation in adults and argued against constraint: *...life for the young child should be happy and free, and education in self-control should be gradual and careful. Punishment and restraint should rarely be necessary* (Pestalozzi, 1801, cited in Nutbrown *et al.* 2008, page 29).

Froebel (1782–1852), the architect of the Kindergarten, trained at Pestalozzi's school, but went on to develop his own educational theory. He too believed that the nature of the child should be emphasised in both method and subject matter. He opened his first Kindergarten (which translates as *child garden*) in Germany in 1837. His approach was based upon an understanding of the child's innate *unfolding*, much as explained by Rousseau. Play was essential to his method. One aspect of his approach was the use of *gifts* (specific play items comprising balls, cones, cubes) and *occupations* (tasks such as paper-cutting, weaving, drawing, and so on). The gifts were play resources for discovery, the occupations activities for inventiveness and creativity. Froebel has been highly influential in promoting the play-based approaches to learning we have seen since his time, particularly in relation to the use of outdoor playgrounds. He has perhaps also influenced a romantic idealisation of play.

> *Play is the purest, most spiritual activity of man... It gives therefore joy, freedom, contentment, inner and outer rest, peace with the world. It holds the source of all that is good... play at this time is of deep significance... the germinal leaves of all later life.*
>
> (Froebel, 1887/2010, page 55)

Influenced by the culture of his time and the growing interest in man's place in nature, he presents a view of the playing child as free and at peace with the world, spiritually fulfilled and unfurling like a growing plant. However, his is a view which has been criticised for being too idealistic, not giving recognition to the darker side of play in which children contemplate danger and explore power struggles and even death (Greishaber and McArdle, 2010).

Evolutionary instinct and recapitulation

Play as instinctive action, perhaps in preparation for adult life is a persistent nativist theme. However, instinctive actions are not always romantic and with positive out-come. In the mid-eighteenth century, Herbert Spencer (1820–1903) promoted a theory of play as *surplus energy*. He argued that humans, being more highly evolved than other animals, were less dominated by the constant need for survival. As a result they possessed higher levels of energy than they used and this overflowed as play (Spencer, 2000). Spencer was writing in the time of industrial revolution and play was therefore, to him, like the steam from a pressure cylinder, a moment of release for the child. This view would align with perspectives of play as release from intense periods of study, a recreational release, school play-times, for example.

Spencer had been influenced by the industrial developments of his time. Darwin's *On the Origin of Species* was published in 1859 and influenced an interest in evolution. Groos (1896) drew on this influence and argued that play was essential for survival and arose from the necessity to practise instinctive behaviours that emerge before they are needed. He concluded that children and animals... *do not play because they are young but have their youth because they must play* (Groos, 1896/1985, page 67).

In other words, the long childhood of human beings exists so that children have time to practise the emergent instinctive skills needed in a more complex adulthood than other species.

Hall (1906) also promoted instinctive play as important for human evolution, a theme later picked up in the work of Bob Hughes in his book *Evolutionary Playwork and Reflective Analytic Practice* (Hughes, 2001). In his *recapitulation theory* Hall argued that just as a child's individual development from the womb goes through stages from fish-like creature to human so, he claimed, the child's later development follows the pattern of development of the human race. Through play, children go through the various stages of human evolution, re-enacting primitive behaviours such as tribal behaviour, wandering and den building (Hughes, 2001; Jenkinson, 2001).

ACTIVITY 5

Groos (1985) argued that the long childhood of humans exists to allow children to practise instinctive skills. Hughes (2001) in his final chapter offers this plea to parents and to practitioners:

> Where you can, ensure that your children have opportunities to engage in recapitulative play... To help them to keep the pressures of the here and now in proportion, try to make it possible for them to engage in 'primitive' or historical narratives. When it is 'safe' to do so facilitate play with fire, facilitate play in the dark, facilitate dressing up, ritual and story-telling.
>
> (Hughes, 2001, page 261)

Reflect on your practice and observations of the children you work with. Are they den-building and creating rituals?

Do they show an interest in the elements, earth, fire, air and water?

Do they like to play with dark cave-like spaces and shade and light?

Do you think children really do re-enact primitive behaviours in their play?

How might you offer opportunities for children to engage in recapitulative play?

Play and social optimism: giving children voice

We have now progressed to that point in history which prompted the creation of the state interest in social welfare and health. During this period, play was one of a range of tools to create better futures. Margaret McMillan (1860–1931) provided health clinics for poor children, and established an open-air nursery school in London to benefit the health of children. In Germany the Waldorf factory owner was concerned that the working classes were held back in education and well-being and opened a factory-based kindergarten in the name of *social progress* (Murphy, 1991).

The factory owner worked with Rudolf Steiner and they established the first Waldorf School in 1919 in Stuttgart. Steiner argued that teaching and learning took place in a community and meant taking one's place in the world, acting with consideration for and responsibility to others. He also argued for a holistic view of the child, in which identifying the spirit or *essence* of a child was more important than *spelling out the letters* (or separate parts) (Steiner, 1924). *To careful observers, a child's play reveals something of the innermost nature both of the present child and of the future self... In play the emergent self is revealed* (Jenkinson, a Steiner teacher, 2001, page 51).

To Steiner, the spirit of the future child would emerge in play, as also would the spirit of the future of society. If play were repressed, the child would become the mere *parts*, disjointed and constrained, and society would be less coherent too.

In 1939 at the start of World War II, the Dutch historian Huizinga (1976, page 687) had also written of play as a *culture creating force*, but one that *must be pure. It must not consist in the darkening or debasing of standards set by reason, faith or humanity.* Huizinga argued that true play is not led by political intention or propaganda but by freedom and inspiration. He argued that civilisation requires self-limitation and an understanding of one's own needs in relation to others, that is developed through play. Play *creates order and fairness* but also creates new cultures as rules are played out and become fixed in the child's social mind – and as a result a new, fairer society emerges. He illustrates this with examples of children at play establishing *forbidden spots*, fixed rules of play in games, and the often strong sense of justice in their activities.

ACTIVITY 6

Huizinga is among several authors who claim that play enables children to explore social rules and create order and fairness.

Again take time to observe the children you work with, perhaps older children playing in groups. Do you see any evidence of children creating social rules and establishing fairness? Are they perhaps saying there are safe areas in a game of tag, or making a game fair to give younger children a chance?

If children are to establish their own social rules and fairness, the adults' role must be reduced to allow them to reach their own conclusions.

Earlier in this chapter you were asked to consider whether it was the adult's role to inspire moral behaviour in children.

What do you think is important, the generation of new social rules by children through play, or the establishment of order and fairness by adults?

After World War II in Reggio Emilia, Italy, a new approach to play and learning was also developed from a resolve to provide a better future for children following the war years. The new approach that Reggio Emilia presents was also based on concepts of co-construction, community and citizenship. The philosophy was, and is, that if the children's development were appropriately supported their social cohesion would be stronger. In Reggio Emilia children are recognised as citizens who are powerful, competent learners and have a social and political *voice* through use of multiple forms of expression. They can inform others of their views and interests and play has a role in this (Abbott and Nutbrown, 2001). The Reggio Emilia method proposes that educators need to listen to the children as representatives of their communities, to hear their *hundred voices* and to support their development in an appropriate environment.

> *...we place enormous value on the role of the environment as a motivation and animating force in creating spaces for relations, options and emotional and cognitive situations that produce a sense of well-being and security... It has been said that the environment should act as a kind of aquarium, which reflects the ideas, ethics, attitudes and cultures of the people who live in it.*
>
> (Malaguzzi, 1996, page 40)

The environment for communication, play and creativity is here presented as important for children. In all of these approaches, there is an understanding that in play children are learning how to be citizens creating a better future, able to adjust their individual needs for a collective aim in order to maintain individual voice, create social rules, and deal with disappointments. These ideas of child as creator of the future were no doubt stimulated by the specific circumstances of the time, but still have resonance in current times. Is it the freedom of play that allows for the new culture to emerge, rather than constraint to a preconceived ideal towards which children are *educated*?

Empiricism and nurture: the influence of behaviourism

A growing interest in the mind and spirit, together with scientific methods of research, led to the rise of the discipline of psychology in the late-nineteenth century. The early psychologists recorded their own experiences to analyse conscious thought, separating thinking into basic elements, sensations, desires and so on, much as chemists analyse compounds into elements. In the early twentieth century, the behaviourists emerged from these early experiments, arguing that psychology was not about subjective introspection, but that there was a need to look objectively outside of ourselves to behaviours that can be observed by more than one person.

Behaviourism aligns with the empiricist or *nurture* perspective. It is a view in which the child is perceived as able to be conditioned by the adult who can, through persistent and consistent behaviour, set up conscious or perhaps subconscious patterns of behaviour in the children they work with. Pavlov (1849–1936) is perhaps the best known behaviourist for his experiments with dogs. By ringing a bell each time he fed the dogs he was, over time, able to make them salivate at the sound of the bell – whether food was present or not.

Skinner (1971) further developed behaviourism with his model of *operant conditioning*, which relied on reward and punishment systems. Positive reinforcement (a reward) is given for the required behaviour and *negative reinforcement* (in which the reward is withheld or a punishment is given) is offered if the behaviour is not as required. This model, if used with a child, places the power in the hands of the adult as reward giver. However, if a relationship exists between the children and the teacher, operant conditioning can use social systems of praise and disapproval rather than physical reward and punishment. Translated into current practice, concepts of *golden hour* (Friday play as a school reward) and *sticker charts* are behaviourist in nature and play time is often used as a reward. Behaviourism can also be used to establish the boundaries for play, perhaps creating the rules for a *frame* or space within which play can occur uninterruptedly.

Bandura extended the application of behaviourist understandings further to develop his *social learning theory*. He argued that imitation is important in children's development and that adults (and peers) can *model* behaviours that the child will copy. Reward, but in the form of praise or disapproval, plays a part in the social learning model. In play children may imitate the behaviour of their older siblings or peers, desiring their approval as friends. Adults may consistently model and praise the behaviours they wish to see, such as *please* and *thank you,* or they may model how a child might dress up, or drive a car, for example offering *templates* to the child.

There are many criticisms of the behaviourist approaches, mostly relating to issues of power, control and reward. If an adult is the reward holder and giver the child is largely disempowered. Greishaber and McArdle (2010) question what happens if the behaviourist power remains in the hands of dominant children able to create a mini *gang culture* in which some children are made to be compliant to the wishes of others? The emphasis of the behaviourists is on learning or *conditioning* and as such appears to have less relevance to play beyond approval and reward. It may also be that the influence of television programmes and peer influence are relevant stimulants for copycat behaviours of a social learning model.

Cognitive psychology and constructivism

Piaget's work (Piaget and Inhelder, 1969) was a direct response to the behaviourist claims. He valued play and saw limitations in the behaviourist understanding that children progressed from basic reflexes to conditioned understandings, responding only to external stimuli, as they layered knowledge onto the blank sheet of the mind. Piaget considered that cognitive development was not merely a passive building of layers of knowledge from external sources, but an active process in which the child was filtering information, working through adaptation and adjustment of existing understanding where needed. His thinking therefore aligns more with the philosophy of Kant.

THEORY FOCUS

Accommodation and assimilation

Key to Piaget's theories of the importance of play is the understanding of *assimilation* and *accommodation*.

Assimilation is the process of the child seeing or experiencing new knowledge and absorbing it to add to what they already know.

Accommodation happens when the new knowledge cannot be easily matched to what the child already knows. So the *old* knowledge must be adjusted in some way to *accommodate* the new understanding (Piaget and Inhelder, 1969).

UNIVERSITY OF WINCHESTER
LIBRARY

Piaget considered that active play generated thought. Through play actions, children are motivated to explore and understand the world, organise their thoughts and adapt. Play is essential for this continuing cycle of assimilation and accommodation. Later debates relating to Piaget's theories consider that play is concerned with bridging assimilation and accommodation in a safe environment, but also with offering opportunity to practise mastery of assimilated skills by repeating over and over the actions or understandings (Laevers, 1993; Hughes, 2002). Think here of the child who can bat a ball but wants to continue to practise with different balls to feel comfortable with the skill.

Piaget has also been extremely influential in the field of early childhood development in the twentieth century. His understandings are often used to argue for play-based approaches to learning in which children direct their own cognitive responses to the environment and opportunities before them (Athey, 2004).

Vygotsky's socio-cultural influence

The main criticism of Piaget's work is that he considered a child to be a *lone explorer* and did not take full account of the social context of the child. With a growing awareness of cultural differences in development came a growing interest in the social influences on learning.

Although Vygotsky lived from 1896 to 1934, his ideas did not really emerge as part of the play and development dialogue until the 1960s and 1970s, due to the need for translation from Russian. Vygotsky also placed a great emphasis on play as *a leading activity that determines the child's development* (Vygotsky, 1966, page 16). Unlike Piaget, his ideas not only agreed that activity and active learning generates thought, but also that other people (children and adults) have a role in the process. A social constructivist, his ideas recognised the importance of other people in creation of a socio-cultural environment and shared experiences. He saw a role for nearby adults in supporting children's play explorations. Vygotsky very much valued play as he considered that in play a child stretched themselves beyond the level they would normally be working at: *In play a child is always above his average age, above his daily behaviour; in play it is as though he were a head taller than himself* (Vygotsky, 1966, page 16).

Culture, society, global awareness and post-modernism

So from early political influences of the church, and simplistic perspectives of sin and evil, we can see that concepts of play become more and more complex as other influences impact on our Western European understandings. As we progress through the twentieth and twenty-first centuries, it is possible to see that increased travel and new research continue to bring new perspectives to understanding play. The adventure playground movement, for example, was established in the years immediately after World War II as a result of Lady Allen of Hurtwood's awareness of children playing on old bomb sites and her chance visit to a *junk playground* in Copenhagen.

Socio-political influences play their part too in the development of new play opportunities. In the 1960s the Pre-School Playgroup Association was established as a parental movement to provide group childcare and play activities for children of a growing number of working mothers, again influenced by women working during the war. The same political influences led later to the establishment of after-school clubs in the 1980s, largely for working parents.

Theory was being more quickly transformed into popular culture. The Plowden Report (DfES,1967) drew substantially on a popularised Piagetian theory and influenced a change of ethos of many primary schools to active and discovery learning. Broadhead and Burt (2012) note that during the 1970s and 1980s, play featured as one of the key approaches across early years education and care provision and that, with no National Curriculum in place, high levels of freedom allowed for a correspondingly high status for play.

Improved technology has continued to push the boundaries of research. One such example is where practice has been more recently influenced by research from emerging brain science, which highlights the importance of early play experiences (Smidt, 2005; Karmiloff-Smith, 1995).

The development of fields such as sociology and anthropology have brought awareness of understandings of children in their relative global, cultural or social contexts (Rogoff, 2003; Pellegrini, 2011) and challenge Western dominance in developmental theory (Walsh, 2005; MacNaughton, 2005). So it is that Konner points out that children in the United Kingdom may learn to run after a ball, while children in the !Kung tribe in Africa learn to run after grasshoppers (Konner, 1991). As a result the focus on universal stages of development such as promoted by Parten (1932) and Piaget (Piaget and Inhelder, 1969) have also been questioned.

With growing global awareness, and its poverty, children's needs and rights have become of greater interest. In 1991 the United Nations Convention on the Rights of the Child (UNCRC) was ratified by the UK Government. Article 31 of this convention clearly says that *state parties recognise the right of the child to rest and leisure, to engage in play and recreational activities appropriate to the age of the child and to participate freely in cultural life and the arts* (UNCRC, Article 31, Unicef 1989).

Children now have the right to play, and this has been supported in the UK by government funding. Note that play and culture are aligned once more.

Play now may be viewed from multiple perspectives at the same time, its complexity acknowledged. This is a post-modern view in which there are many influences and no single *truth* relating to the importance of play and the rate of development. There are many *truths* depending on the unique context of the child and the position of the observer (MacNaughton, 2005).

However, in the socio-political arena we seem to be turning full circle to a more restricted, structured perception of play. The free-play interest in schools (and pre-school) that was influenced in psychology and sociology in the 1970s came to a gradual end in England with the introduction of the National Curriculum in 1988, followed by the Curriculum Guidance for the Foundation Stage in 2000 and an increasing emphasis on childcare and education provision, rather than play, for children of pre-school age. With the Early Years Foundation Stage (DCSF, 2008a) play for the under-fives became compliant to the education system – and was very much about preparation for learning and school (although the documents still contained the language of play). This has been further reinforced in the wording of the new Early Years Foundation Stage (DfE, 2012) in which the early years experience is explicitly linked to preparation for school.

The shift in perspective from a focus on social play to education is clearly illustrated by the change of name of the Pre-School Playgroup Association to the Pre-school Learning Alliance in 1995 (Pre-School Learning Alliance, 2012). Meanwhile, government investment in play in early childhood during the early twenty-first century was in many ways also about creation of a promising future society as Sure Start and Children's Centres focused on regeneration and resilience to outcome targets. Every Child Matters (DCSF, 2003) supported children in *enjoying and achieving* and *making a positive contribution* through, for example, family play sessions.

With a new government elected in 2010, the former EYFS (DCSF, 2008a) has been reviewed and the new EYFS framework (DfE, 2011) seems superficially to be returning almost full circle to the empiricist philosophy of Locke, in which play is merely perceived as a motivating vehicle for learning. The Tickell Review of the EYFS (DfE, 2011) recommends that *playing and exploring, active learning, and creating and thinking critically are highlighted in the EYFS as three characteristics of effective teaching and learning.*

Moreover, the Foundation Stage Profile milestones (DfE, 2012) offer a minimal vision of play as a series of actions through which children will *play with materials, role play, or play co-operatively.* I hope that there will be a much richer interpretation of the value of play in the implementation of this curriculum, one that recognises our intellectual heritage and, as in the Welsh Foundation Phase (2008a), supports the holistic benefits of a play based approach.

What history does tell us is that there are many ways of viewing the child and their play activity, and we should adopt a broad perspective, different from thinking of play as a *child's work*, a vehicle for learning, or merely as recreation and release. Play is both created by, and creating of, culture; it is informed by society and science; it creates health and future resilience and offers opportunity to practise responses to the unknown. It is perhaps about spirituality and an instinctive connection to the past. It has been tested for generations. Essentially it is a right that children have, to explore and practise a range of skills, concepts and relationships that have meaning for them, not merely something to be shaped by those adults to meet blunt education targets.

ACTIVITY 7

Take time here to consider the many perspectives and understandings of play raised in this chapter. Reflect on your own position and highlight which of the following have resonance with you and your practice.

- *Play as recreation*
- *Play as time wasting non-work*
- *Play as a release of energy*
- *Play as a tool for physical development*
- *Play as a social activity enabling future conflict resolution*
- *Play as a vehicle for learning*
- *Play as 'innate', an instinctive biological drive*
- *Play as practice of survival skills*
- *Play as hope for the future*
- *Play as spiritual oneness with nature*
- *Play as a re-living of human evolution (recapitulation)*
- *Play as a behaviourally conditioned response to others*
- *Play as exploration for development of cognitive understandings*
- *Play as a cultural activity copying and expanding the activities of others*
- *Play as universal and timeless*
- *Play as a right*

SUMMARY

This chapter has sought to explore a very wide range of historical perspectives in relation to play and perceptions of its purpose. It has ranged from an early understanding of play as essential to the creation of culture, through concepts of play as sinful and work as good, to a final understanding that play is both shaped by and shaping of society and culture. The chapter reveals how understandings of play have been influenced by the experiences and philosophies of different times, illustrating thinking that builds on or challenges ideas that went before. You can continue to update and inform your practice by looking for more and varied historical perspectives; play in other cultures; and current research to maintain a healthy criticality and up-to-date understanding of play.

FURTHER READING

Bruner, JS, Jolly, A and Sylva, K (Eds) (1985). *PLAY: Its Role in Development and Evolution.* Harmondsworth: Penguin.

This may be an old book but it is a really useful collection of essays about play gathered in one place. Here you can find Huizinga, Bruner, Piaget and literary comments about play.

Froebel, F (1887/2010) *The Education of Man.* Charleston, S Carolina: Forgotten Books/Classic Reprint.

This book can be accessed online and is surprisingly more readable than I expected. So no excuses – go to the original works of this very influential thinker.

Frost, J (2010) *A History of Children's Play and Play Environments.* London: Routledge.

Although American in approach, this is a thoughtful book that offers something of the history of play, and a consideration of current issues of environment and place.

Nutbrown, C, Clough, P and Selbie, P (2008) *Early Childhood Education: History, Philosophy and Experience.* London: Sage.

A really good, accessible summary of the key pioneers and thinkers relevant to Early Childhood Education: it also contains creatively imagined conversations between key theorists such as Pestalozzi, Piaget and Froebel giving greater insight into interpretations of their theories.

WEBSITES

http://wales.gov.uk/topics/educationandskills/earlyyearshome/foundation_phase/?lang=en
Wales has adopted a 'Foundation Phase' for the Early Years which very much draws on a play based approach to learning and development.

https://www.pre-school.org.uk/about-us/our-history
This website offers the history of the Pre-School Learning Alliance.

www.infed.org/index.htm
The encyclopaedia of informal education offers the opportunity to look up and read about many of the pioneers of play based approaches. Here you will find articles on Maria Montessori, Pestalozzi, Owen and many more.

www.ltscotland.org.uk/earlyyears/cpd/pastevents/playandactivelearning.asp The different countries of the United Kingdom have as a result of their historic perspectives, adopted slightly different approaches today. Look at this site to consider the past events that have impacted on play and active learning in Scotland.

www.playengland.org.uk/about-us/about-play-england.aspx
PlayEngland website that promotes children's right to play and gives access to a range of freely downloadable publications and research on play.

www.heuristics.org.uk/breughel.html
Bruegel's painting *Children's Games* is widely available on the internet and I found it at this site. This makes a great discussion piece and there are related activities on this site.

www.playwales.org.uk
The Welsh charity supporting children's play contains useful resources and publications.

4   Observing play

Through reading this chapter you will:

- consider the importance of observation and the methods you use to capture children's play behaviours;

- be introduced to some theory relating to perspectives on observations of children;

- explore ethics and intervention issues – how you might observe children at play without disturbing their flow;

- reflect on the issues of a practitioner 'researcher' role;

- be informed of some ways to analyse what you have seen.

Introduction: the importance of observation

Why do we watch children at play? Perhaps we do so for the enjoyment of seeing their excitement, remembering our own childhood play? Perhaps for the purpose of identifying what play is? Perhaps because we are told we should observe and assess children's development? Most of us are already expert observers. People are generally naturally curious, and will watch things or other people to see what they are like, how they act, or what will happen next. It is through such observation that we understand the way in which people behave around us, the culture that we operate within, the templates of our society.

If we believe that play actually leads learning and is a part of, but also creates culture, then we should take care to observe children's play in a way that seeks to identify the child's intentions and perspectives (i.e. in what the child is doing and not the adult-shaped outputs). In order to understand children's play intentions, practitioners need to actively engage with observation and reflection, trying to see what is happening from the child's perspective. They should try to capture the detail and seek to find out from the child – as well as take time to reflect on what they consider children are really doing when they are *at play*.

In this chapter we will consider how we might observe children, what the issues are as a practitioner 'researcher', and how we might then analyse what we have seen to be better informed about a child's play activity.

Considering current practice

Observing children is one of the most obvious and most effective ways of examining play behaviours, meanings and impact. Most of us are already skilled observers of our world. Using an innate curiosity we will watch events or other people to see what they are like, how they act, or what will happen next. However, we will watch such activities with our own 'lens', or perspective, on the world. We are effectively assimilating more information into our own existing cultural schemes. Although skilled in observation, our personal lens means we may make choices and judgements about what we see. The angle of our lens depends on our experiences, job roles, culture, personal values and interests. We may also take a narrow focus or a wide-angled perspective according to our interest in a single child or children within a group or complex environment.

When I ask my students to undertake an objective narrative observation of a child, the written pieces that are returned will often show specific biases in the individuals undertaking the observations. Some students will focus more on social relationships, others on speech and language, some will spot schemes of thinking (Piaget and Inhelder, 1969), and others will focus on emotional difficulty. Many of the observations will try to *measure* the child against the normative framework of the Early Years Foundation Stage (EYFS) development matters indicators (DCSF, 2008a), and subsequent updated versions (DfE, 2012).

Because of these varied perspectives and individual biases, it is useful to share observations and see other perspectives of the same child or event by working in teams rather than alone. This shared understanding will offer a more detailed and complex picture of the child's play actions.

As a practitioner you should take time to identify your own dominant observation lenses. Consider also whether you do share your observations with colleagues. Finally, and obviously, consider whether the primary source of information about their play activities – the child who is playing – can tell you of their intentions and help to inform what you see.

ACTIVITY 1

How often do you just sit and watch children with no prior expected outcome?

Take a few moments to think about (reflect upon) a recent observation you made in relation to a young child or children's play activities. The questions below are intended to prompt you to step back and consider your own position as an observer.

- *Why did you watch the child or children?*
- *What did you see?*
- *Did you have any prior purpose or intention?*
- *Do you think you saw what you expected to see?*

ACTIVITY *1* *continued*

- *Did you ask the child what they were doing?*
- *Did you write your observation down (missing vital information while writing)?*
- *Did you limit what you could capture from the observation by the size of your paper for writing notes? (Sticky notes clearly restrict recording space, as also do fixed columns in a table.)*
- *Could you hear the children's speech (or were you guessing what was being said)?*
- *Did you share your observation with a colleague, or with the child?*

Could you identify a personal bias or interest whilst observing? Could you identify a favourite method and approach?

Awareness of personal perspective

What we learn from observation of children depends on what stance we take when looking, what our expected outcomes are, and what 'baggage' we bring to the event we are observing. A parent or grandparent watching their grandchild in a new setting may well look intensively for emotional well-being to see if the child is settling in. An early years professional in a nursery class may observe to assess developmental progress and identify information for planning. An experienced practitioner in the baby room will look for the propped baby's increasing back and stomach muscle control that will enable him or her to sit up unsupported.

No observation is ever done in a vacuum (Smith, 2011). Observers will be influenced by conceptions of what play is and what perspective and position they adopt in the observation. It is impossible to observe everything. Selections will inevitably be made as our own interests will dictate what we note. However, if we are truly trying to explore children's play as revealed to us in their behaviours, we should allow an immersion in their experience to shape our understanding – rather than being led by preconceived adult ideas and expectations.

Qvortrup (2000) and Hendricks (2010) point out that we are effectively interpreting children's behaviour as outsiders. In observing we create a situation in which children's lives and actions are being interpreted by another, older, generation whose interests may be at odds with those of the children themselves. Adults are *immigrants* entering a child's culture (albeit informed by the specific understanding of their own childhood cultures). Furthermore, when analysing observations of children, we are not only trying to make sense of what we see in front of us, but may also be drawing on something we have left behind; for example, our own play experiences, belonging in a different era, with different social influences. Hughes (2001) actively encourages reflection on observation using our own childhood experiences.

In order to enter the children's own experiences, environment and culture, we should as far as possible discard our own expectations. This will allow understandings to emerge objectively from what we see. This is not easy as Drummond (2003, page 67) recognises.

- *The mind unconsciously distorts what it hears and sees according to its own prejudices.*

- *The mind cannot grasp things that are totally unknown to it.*

- *The mind is inclined to see that which it has already noticed.*

- *The mind is unable to see things that it has not been trained to accept.*

She explains how practitioners or teachers are inclined to project onto the children the ideas that they formed in childhood, drawing on their own experiences. In this way they see children not as they are, but as they think they should be.

An expectation of observation outcome?

Many early years practitioners, as a result of inherited practice, adopt a technician approach (Moss and Petrie, 2002) to observation of children that can in turn lead to a deficit approach to *spotting development*. In England for example, under the former Statutory Framework for the Early Years Foundation Stage (DCSF, 2008a) practitioners were required to undertake developmental observations:

> *Practitioners should:*
> - *make systematic observations and assessments of each child's achievements, interests and learning styles;*
> - *use these observations and assessments to identify learning priorities and plan relevant and motivating learning experiences for each child;*
> - *match their observations to the expectations of the early learning goals.*
> (EYFS Statutory Framework, DCSF, 2008a, page 16)

Under the old *Practice Guidance for the Early Years Foundation Stage* practitioners were encouraged to undertake ongoing observations for assessment, identifying children's progress against a number of developmental goals such as *can repeat words or phrases from familiar stories* (DCSF, 2008b, page 52).

Although the language of the EYFS (2008a) was positive about play, this model offered a development chart which reinforced the deficit model or gap-identification and gap-filling exercise in which practitioners were looking out for children who have either met or not met the predicted next expected stage.

The new Statutory Framework (DfE, 2012) takes a slightly softer approach which focuses on:

> *observing children to understand their level of achievement, interests and learning styles, to then shape learning experiences for each child reflecting those observations. In their interactions with children, practitioners should respond to their own day-to-day observations about children's progress, and observations that parents and carers share.*

The focus of this document and the accompanying non-statutory guidance Development Matters in the Early Years Foundation Stage (EYFS) (DfE/British Association for Early Childhood Education, 2012b) is on observation as formative assessment and entails observing children to see what they can do, using the indicators on the development matters charts as *examples... to help identify where the child may be in their own developmental pathway* (page 3) and to plan ways to support the child in their own journey. This approach more readily aligns with play.

ACTIVITY 2

Consider the two passages below. One is an account of a current practitioner's approach to observation in a nursery setting; the other is Margaret Carr's critical awareness of her former practice.

In a pre-school room children are playing with bowls of small objects of similar colour and with ten items in each bowl at the start of the activity. A nursery practitioner sits down with a pad of sticky notes waiting to capture a child's demonstration of number awareness appropriate for the age group she is working with. Drawing on the EYFS Practice Guidance (2008a, page 65) she will look for children to 'show awareness of number and quantity'.

The practitioner has an idea of six points from the areas of learning that the current adult initiated but playful activity will offer to her. When she has seen the expected actions for each child she will jot them down onto a separate sticky note and then stick these onto the child's daily notes chart. Where a child does not use the resources in the way expected their actions are either ignored, or it is noted that they had not achieved the expected outcome.

The approach of the above practitioner captures children's activities as if they were individual actions only relating to the materials on the table. She does not take into account social interactions, cultural or environmental prompts. Children are each perceived as individuals or lone explorers and a range of social, emotional or cognitive behaviours is thus reduced to a single sentence; indicating that child X can sometimes match number and quantity effectively *(EYFS Practice Guidance, DCSF, 2008a, page 67). The focus was on meeting adult targets.*

Margaret Carr also recognised this limited observation for assessment technique in her own emerging practice as is shown in the following paragraph:

When I was a beginning kindergarten teacher, twenty years ago, I believed that observation for assessment was about checking to see whether the nearly school aged children had acquired what I considered to be the requisite skills for school: the list included early writing (writing their name), self-help skills, early mathematics (counting), turn taking, scissor-cutting. I therefore looked out for the gaps in a school-readiness repertoire, keeping a checklist, and used some direct teaching strategies to do something about them in the months before school. I did not find

---

continued

ACTIVITY **2** *continued*

the process interesting or helpful to me, but I certainly saw it as linked to my reputation as a competent early childhood teacher...

(Carr, 2001, page 1)

Carr subsequently noted that she found it difficult to align this practice with her preferred play-based approach in which she became more interested in children's dispositions for learning than acquisition of knowledge.

Do these approaches sound familiar in relation to your own experiences?

What are the benefits and disadvantages of the assessment for development and skills approach?

What may be the limitations of this approach to identifying the breadth of interest and learning of children at play?

Did you spot the insecurity in Margaret Carr's comment that she saw such observation for assessment as related to her competence as a teacher?

Seeking direct and dispassionate observations

It is inevitable that the whole spectrum of children's behaviours cannot be recorded by one person during a period of observation and that many of the very interesting play-based actions that children do will not be captured and will therefore go unnoticed. Practitioners merely take a number of short records of the day's activities, unless they film them in some way and spend hours analysing them later.

However, such models as those in Activity 2 not only limit the observer's perspective in relation to the child's interests. They also reduce the importance of play, prompting the practitioner to see only those aspects of play: a) as development, and; b) that are important as part of the adult recording system. As a positive example of objective observation, Drummond (2003) and Arnold and the Pen Green Team (2010) draw on the narrative records of Susan Isaacs (1930). They highlight how these close observations of daily life were *more than isolated anecdotes* in a year of play, and they were the starting point for Isaac's exploration of the process of children's cognitive and social development through play activity.

Susan Isaacs argued that qualitative observation records of children's play behaviours should be:

> *...direct and dispassionate observations, recorded as fully as possible under the conditions; and as free as possible from evaluations and interpretations. Ideally no interpretation should appear in the records. Vague evaluatory or summarising phrases such as, 'the children were very interested or polite or quarrelsome' are better avoided. Only full verbatim records of what was said and full objective records of what was done should be given.*

(Isaacs, 1930, page 1)

Verbatim records try to capture everything that is said or done in sequence. Isaacs' careful observations of children are still used today, acknowledged in importance by current researchers: *These first hand observations can be treated as raw data, even today, nearly 80 years later* (Arnold et al., 2010, page 14).

So what do these observed snapshots of early childhood play in the 1930s read like? In Isaacs' book they are usually fairly small passages of six to ten lines, but written in complete narrative with no comment relating to assessment. The activities she captures in this way may be seen as play, or as discovery, depending on your position. She was interested in cognitive development and was in correspondence with Piaget – and this interest undoubtedly comes through in her notes. Many of the activities that she records (such as children trying to light a gas fire or playing with dead animals) would not be considered appropriate today for safety reasons, but such topics do acknowledge children's interest in the unusual and macabre, and children's drive to playfully explore the world as they encounter it. Here is an observation written by Isaacs that is less challenging to contemporary health and safety concerns:

> *The children had a set of large wooden blocks, perforated right through in many places, with wooden sticks to fit, for constructing various things. Most of them made carts, engines for motor cars etc. Phineas' (4.1) interest however seemed to be in observing the particular hole on the far side of a block out of which a rod would come when pushed in on the near side. Some of the holes ran diagonally so that it was not always quite obvious where the rod would come out. He took a long steel rod and spent some time pushing it through, saying beforehand where he thought it would come out, verifying his idea, and showing great pleasure when he was correct.*
>
> (Isaacs, 1930, page 143)

From this record we can see that Phineas' play activity was exploratory, and he was working something out. Some people may say he had a *schema* of *going through* as he is interested in the rods going through the blocks and coming out the other side in different places. In this example, Phineas was the lone explorer; we have no idea of his language or social activity. We know that other children were also playing with the blocks, but not whether he interacted with them. He was saying where the rod might come through, but we do not know if he was talking directly to an adult or other child. There is an indication of emotional reassurance and cognitive equilibrium in his acknowledgement that the rod has come out where it was expected. Phineas was in control of the pace of his own activity and learning and therefore this could be seen to be *play*.

If we believe that play gives ownership of actions to the child, leads learning and creates culture, we should take care to observe children's play with the same patience and depth as Isaacs shows. We should seek to reflect objectively on what we have seen and to identify the child's perspective and their intentions in their play.

Papatheodorou, Luff and Gill (2011) raise the question of the depth of detail that might be required in such observations, given that the context may also be important. They ask whether an observer should also include statements about the weather or the colours in the classroom. They conclude that such decisions must relate to the intention and choices made by the child. If the bright sunlight or coloured door affects the child's approach or response to an activity then perhaps they should be mentioned in the observation record.

ACTIVITY 3

Read the passage below:

> It was a blustery day with strong gusts of wind that seemed to nearly blow the children over. Ezra and Sian were playing outside by the horizontal tree trunk that was lying on the ground in the open, grassed play area. The top of the trunk was just 60cm from the ground and it had been left so that the children can climb up and walk across the top of it, usually with assistance.
>
> Both children were showing signs of excitement and seemed to enjoy the feeling of being buffeted by the wind. They ran round the tree trunk, then ducked down on the sheltered side realising that it stopped the wind. They then went through several sequences of the same behaviour, standing up to feel the wind and then squatting down so that they were protected from it. They laughed out loud as the wind caught their hair and the hoods of their coats, blowing them backwards. They appeared energised and jumped on the spot several times. Then Ezra picked up a leaf and let it go in a strong gust, laughing as it flew upwards and then settled by the school building. He squealed with laughter and jumped on the spot, Sian copied him, and they then went to seek more leaves. They carried the leaves to the tree trunk, placed them in a heap on the sheltered side, and then kicked them out into the wind, watching them disperse across the playground in erratic waves. (End of observation)

Is the mention of the weather and environment here relevant to the understanding of the play activity?

Was there sufficient detail in the record above?

What do you think the children were exploring and learning through their play?

How would you normally record such actions?

Has anything been left out of the above record? What would you add to it? (Usually the date, time and ages of the children are recorded.)

A reciprocal relationship

There is no doubt that my capturing of the above experience was informed by my own childhood experiences of playing in woods near to my house. I can recall just those moments of playing with the elements of wind and water because they were there, and did different things according to the conditions and the materials we had to hand. My early play experiences have greatly influenced the way in which I see and support children's play today, and are reflected in my choice of words.

Furthermore, if we consider, as I do in this book, that people and environments affect each other, then our observations should also take care to focus not merely on the child as lone explorer, but also on the ways in which the dynamic processes of children, environments and other people interact at different times. Ezra's excitement was prompted by the wind, but further supported by Sian's response. Together they were collaborating in exploring the elements and impact of strong wind and shelter.

Seeking a breadth in positive appreciation

It seems to be human nature to adopt a convergent approach to observations. We sometimes close down situations looking for things that are *wrong* rather than branching out with a wide lens to positively appreciate the bigger picture. This convergent perspective can be constraining. Sian later tried to climb the trunk and stand on it in the wind. This was risky behaviour. She did so because Ezra was encouraging her, and she felt safe with a practitioner nearby who would pick her up if she fell. While looking for risks and skill shortfalls may be a human protective mechanism which normally works to keep us safe, it also has potential to restrict our approach to understanding children's worlds and constrain their play adventures. It is almost as though the danger to the child is something the practitioners can *fix*, making their role active and is therefore more likely to be spotted by them.

More careful reflective observation of the situation would indicate that the children did not take risks they could not manage. They first knelt on the log and judged the pressure of the wind, only trying to stand when they felt confident that they understood how it might push them over. Reassured by the distant presence of an adult who would pick them up if they fell, the children were capable of exploring and managing their own risk, gaining useful knowledge about how to balance in gusty winds. These are all important early childhood experiences worth observing with a wide lens so that we too can judge the context of the risks they take. In this way we can facilitate the appropriate support, rather than adopting a deficit approach of an assumed childhood incompetence (Gill, 2007).

There is also a difficulty in finding the language to richly capture the positive play experiences of children. I find that there is also a tendency in practice, if children are enjoying themselves, to just note *they are happy*, or even to fit that enjoyment into one of the former early learning steps or goals, for example that they *enjoy the company of others* (DCSF, 2008a, page 32). Does such language really capture the joyful interaction of children rejoining their nursery after a holiday break, when all want to talk at once, and the energy of revived friendships is displayed in physical action?

If a child is showing emotional distress, or perceived developmental delay, the practitioners may observe intensely and break down what they have seen into small parts to analyse and address those *problem* areas and thereby reach their own sense of equilibrium (a sense of knowing that they have done what they can to support the child). We seem to have far more words to note down difficulties, shortfalls and the need for additional support – or *moving on* – than we do for achievement, exploration, exhilaration and creativity. I am not here arguing that we should neglect the child who is in distress or experiencing developmental delay, but I wonder how much more we could see and acknowledge if we paid the same detailed attention to the analysis of children's enjoyment and small achievements in their play. Such a positive approach requires a perspective that sees children as competent and able.

THEORY FOCUS

Positive appreciation

Adopting a positive appreciation stance when undertaking observations of children seeks to identify the positives in what we see rather than having a deficit perspective – which looks for the shortfalls and things to fix. A positive appreciation observation draws on the theories of *appreciative inquiry* (Cooperrider and Whitney, 2005) which argues that instead of continually asking:

- *What is the problem?*
- *What has not quite worked?*
- *What needs to be fixed?*

We should ask the opposite, positive questions:

- *What is going well?*
- *What is good about what is happening?*
- *How can we do more of this?*

Applied to observations of children, this requires us to positively look for the good things that are happening (the children's achievements through play) and to spend an equal (if not greater) time on these. We should perhaps consider how we can offer more opportunities for *what works*.

A process-orientated approach

Increasingly there is an argument for a process-orientated approach to a child's play activities. This requires revisiting the child's world and attempting to identify, through careful observation and reflection, what is really going on, with whom, and in what context (Dahlberg *et al.*, 1999; Rogoff, 2003). Taguchi (2010) warns against the use of development charts and *habitual developmental thinking* that limits our perspective, preventing us from visiting the child's world. Hughes (2001) argues for a *reflective analytic practice* in which playworkers reflectively immerse themselves in playwork at such depth that new and important insights regarding the mechanisms and motivations behind it begin to emerge. He recognises the value of personal perspective and memory and he notes that such new practice has *the effect of opening up long-forgotten sensory and affective play memories* (Hughes, 2001, page 183). These memories are useful in analysing the play actions of children today.

By using such approaches to observation, practitioners seek to capture something more of the essence of the child, and children's dispositions and interests in play.

Foregrounding and backgrounding what we see

Rogoff (2003) adopts a socio-cultural approach to observation of a child in context in relation to others and their culture. She points out that with the influence of Piaget and Inhelder (1969) and the scientific approaches, we often view a child at play as lone explorer, dissociating them from their cultural and environmental situation. We choose to '*foreground*' and '*background*' certain aspects of the things we see as if one is more important, while the other is a secondary influence. She highlights how we might therefore carry out two observations of two children next to each other – each child separately foregrounded and noted – but without the relationships between the two being fully explained and developed.

She, like the authors above, also argues that we need to be more sophisticated in our approach, making choices in our records that reflect how the context and other people affect the behaviours (i.e. seen not as a single influence but as a reciprocal relationship). She argues there is a need for a system that acknowledges how things function in ways that influence each other at the same time. In the earlier example (Activity 3), Ezra was influenced by the wind, the shelter, his friend Sian and possibly past experiences. She too was influenced by him, and by the presence of the play staff. If the focus had been only on Ezra without the other details we would probably only note that he could duck down, jump and run round the tree. It is the richer picture, the inclusion of the wind, the direction of the wind, the presence of other people, which give the greater detail and understanding.

In this way we capture the interpersonal, environmental and cultural information necessary to interpret what the child is doing. The choices and distinctions between what is in the foreground and what is in the background still lie with us, but we are aware of these choices. I considered that the wind, the tree trunk and Sian are influences on Ezra's behaviour. There are still cultural aspects I have not recorded. For example, I do not know whether Ezra has been encouraged to release other objects into the wind before, or whether his setting encourages or restricts such exploratory behaviours. I have not noted whether Ezra looked to adults for approval or disapproval. It may be that releasing leaves into the wind is his anarchic play response to a previous restriction on such activity!

Ethics and adulteration

Whenever you watch a child in a professional context as researcher or practitioner, it is important that you consider the ethics of the situation. When undertaking an observation, you are closely watching someone else, or many people, and then keeping records (even if only in your memory) of the detail of what you have seen. Sometimes that detail is personal. You may also be intending to share that detail with colleagues. You are effectively a researcher of children's behaviour and as such you have a responsibility.

A standard ethical awareness is a consideration to:

- be fair;

- do the right thing; and

- do no harm.

The British Educational Research Association (BERA) guidance indicates that we should adopt an ethic of respect for the person, the knowledge and the democratic values of the community in which you are researching (BERA, 2011, page 4).

Consent should be sought from the child. However, we then move into the position of potential *adulteration* of the play experience as the child will be more aware of your presence. If you were told *I am going to watch what you do for 30 minutes to see what your normal practice is like*, I expect that your *normal practice* would suddenly be different through awareness of the onlooker. Be reassured that children do get used to regular observations, and over time will usually forget the presence of the camera or notebook. You will then be able to gather information that is more reflective of their spontaneous play behaviour.

Participant or non-participant observer?

Another ethical consideration is the awareness of your impact on the situation you are observing. Perry Else (2009) raises a concern of *adulteration* in which a child's play is effectively interrupted by the presence of an adult. One of the first decisions that should be made in relation to observing children is whether one is:

- a participant observer – seeking to enter the child's play world or;

- a non-participant observer – detached from the event and watching as if through a window as an excluded outsider.

Both positions are valid, and each presents particular issues for consideration.

Participant observers seek to immerse themselves in children's play activities to enter childhood play cultures. They will be a part of the interactions, be close to and aware of the environmental impacts, hear the speech of the child, and experience the emerging ideas. The participant observer will find it harder to write notes on the spot and will probably have to write down recollections of the activity after the event. They are also a part of the action, in danger of shaping the play, *adulterating it* (Else, 2009) depending on their own restraint or engagement. Questioning or leading the play activity will shape the experiences. Imagine if a participant observer had been in the Ezra and Sian situation (in Activity 3) and asked which way the wind was blowing; or pointed out that other things would also give shelter from the wind; or perhaps offered other objects to let go in the wind. These may be helpful ideas, but would also shape the play that occurred – offering different roads to explore than those of the children's unsupported choice. So a participant observer may overtly or inadvertently shape the play to their own dominant interests, even if they too are engaged in the play with the children.

Non-participant observers on the other hand are objectively detached, stepping outside of their role as facilitative practitioner. They observe as if looking through a window. They are not immersed in the play and may not pick up all of the language and social nuances of the actions they see from a distance. They may be trying to ensure that their impact on the play responses is minimal (though, as we have seen, even a non-participant observer may constrain children's play behaviours, creating the awareness that they are being watched). Non-participant observation is the most common approach to observations of children – despite the disadvantage that the practitioner will be slightly detached from the experience and therefore may be unaware of its true, and felt, intention.

THEORY FOCUS

Some methods of observation

I have so far argued for detailed, short narrative observations taking a wide 'lens' to capture children's play behaviours in context. However, there is a range of observation methods you may choose for different purposes. Here are a few of the common approaches:

- *Narrative* – A record in writing of the play behaviours or development actions seen. The practitioner effectively *tells the story* in as much detail as he or she considers appropriate. So narratives can be extremely short *snapshot* comments or longer detailed records over an observation period of an hour or more.

- *Time sample* – This method allows the practitioner to *capture* what a child or several children are doing at different identified times of the day. They involve very short observations at fixed times. For example, at 8.00 a.m. the time sample may capture arrival and settling in; at 9.00 a.m. engagement with resources and peers; at 12.00 noon lunchtime behaviours; at 2.00 p.m. whether the child's energy levels are waning, or whether they are still engaged in that same play activity as at 9.00 a.m. the same morning.

- *Environmental tracking* – This can be a very useful approach in observing play, particularly in outdoor areas. Environmental tracking follows a child's progression around the environment and is usually drawn as a diagram with arrows indicating the child's movement. So it may show Ezra coming into the play space and initially exploring everything in it and the boundaries to get his bearings. It may then show how he has *favourite* spaces he keeps coming back to such as the tree log, or the balancing ropes. Other people may be included in the environmental tracking, for example if a

---

continued

THEORY FOCUS continued

classroom assistant is normally found in one area and the child keeps returning to her for reassurance, she effectively becomes a part of the *environment* for the child and this should be recorded.

- *Sociogram* – A sociogram records who the child interacts with and is often a blunt tool, only recording contact as one incident, regardless of the length of that communication. So it may be recorded that Ezra had social contact with Sian three times in an hour, but also two contacts with Ben, three with Ella and two with Miss McEwen. A sociogram will often indicate friendship groups, children who are broad-ranging communicators, or those who are withdrawn and make little contact. It may indicate surprising, unnoticed relationships, such as the importance of the caretaker, or parent helper.

There are many more methods that may be used; some of which are indicated in the suggested further reading below.

Why not try a range of approaches to find the *best fit* for what you are interested in?

Reflective practice

I have throughout this chapter mentioned the word *reflection*. My understanding of reflection in the context of observation of children at play is one of taking the time to step back and consider carefully not only what the child can do, but also what the child is intending to do, what they are influenced by, and what other things we can draw on to build a deeper understanding of what the child is doing. Argyris and Schön (1978) argue for a *double loop* reflection that presses the reflector to consider not only what is going well, but the values and principles, the *whys* of the activity. Why did Ezra throw the leaves to the wind? Why did I see only that aspect of the observation, when someone else may have seen very different detail? Rogoff (2003) prompts the observer to consider the socio-cultural influences in her reflections on observations of children in other cultures, she also prompts us to reflect on what we *foreground* and *background* in our observation choices. In relation to people and cultural activity Hughes (2001) cites *reflective analytic practice* as a process of immersion in the children's experiences, while also drawing on theory and the contemplative and regressive skills of considering *what if this had happened to me, what does this mean?* Reflective practice in observation of play is therefore about the ability not merely to act or react, but to consider thoughtfully what it is that we have seen or done and what we bring to the shaping of that understanding. It is thinking about our own actions and analyses. It should also be about the views of others, seeking the comment from the child at play, and the colleague with a different perspective.

SUMMARY

This chapter has sought to explore the nature of observation of the play activities of children. It has recognised the potential limitation of observation for normative development in relation to play. I have argued for observer self-awareness and reflective analysis, seeking to capture through detailed narrative what a child is doing at play to reach a deeper understanding. Reflective observers recognise that the opportunity for and analysis of what the child is doing is shaped by the environment, the cultural and institutional features, and by their own history and experience. Practitioners make choices in their observations, but those choices should always be in consideration of the child's rights, the impact of the intrusion (even by non-participant observation) and the quest for honesty of knowledge and understanding.

Whatever method we use, it is clear that there needs to be more observation of play to ensure that we have captured a full picture – in order to understand the child's world, a world we have largely left behind. We should also remember that it is only really the child participating and shaping the play who truly knows what it is about. Bob Hughes reminds us how we may immerse ourselves in the child's experiences, concentrating on recall of our own play and, through reflection, be in an approximate situation to the child. It is in this way that we are not in the cockpit with the child, but certainly flying in parallel! (Hughes, 2001, page 184).

FURTHER READING

Harcourt, D, Perry, B and Waller, T (Eds) (2011) *Researching Young Children's Perspectives: Debating the Ethics and Dilemmas of Educational Research with Children.* London: Routledge.

A really useful series of chapters that consider the challenges and complexities of rights-based, participatory research with children. Ethics, methodological frameworks and methods are discussed, including consideration of observation of the very young.

Hughes (2001) *Evolutionary Playwork and Reflective Analytic Practice.* London: Routledge.

A playworker's perspective on observation and this technique of immersion in a child's experiences through using our own. It offers a series of examples of play experiences and reflective analytic analyses of these.

Palaiologou, I (2008) *Childhood Observation.* Exeter: Learning Matters.

A clear examination of a range of methods of observation of young children. Includes a section on ethics.

Papatheodorou, T, Luff, P, and Gill, J (2011) *Child Observation for Learning and Research.* Harlow: Pearson Education.

A very useful and accessible book, written for students, which clearly outlines a range of methods for observation and explores in greater depth the issues of bias, objectivity and ethics.

Part 2

The benefits of play

5 The value of play in child development

Through reading this chapter, you will find out more about the relationship of play and development. This includes:

- early social development;
- physical development;
- cognitive development and learning.

You will also find out more about how, through play, children work out ideas and thoughts and learn how to express these to others.

Introduction

This section of the book will consider the benefits of play to the developing child. Many of the philosophers, theorists and writers we have considered so far have already linked the freely chosen, intrinsic activity of play to developmental and learning benefits. Their claims have crossed a wide range of areas from the importance of play for social development and resolution of conflict, through to cognitive or intellectual development and training for adult life. One difficulty that we face when considering the benefits may be in deciding what is 'play' and what is non-play activity. Perhaps such a distinction does not matter as the two processes of play and development are so entwined. Hughes (2010) considers that *a person should not presume to understand children's development without having a complete understanding of children's play* (Hughes, 2010, page xv).

With our growing awareness of play, we should be aware of the holistic and reciprocal relationship of the two processes, even if we do not have the *complete understanding* that Hughes recommends.

THEORY FOCUS

Holistic and reciprocal

We often hear the term *holistic* in relation to child development, but are we clear what it means? Langston and Abbott (2010, page 93) merely describe holistic development as

---

continued

the way that children *develop physically, intellectually, linguistically, emotionally and socially.* Having divided development into these recognisable areas for ease of understanding, they are clear that we should look at these areas together, without emphasising one above any other. Lindon (2005) explained that a holistic approach stresses the importance of thinking about how the parts act together to benefit the child's development, thus physical well-being cannot be separated from intellectual areas or other aspects of development.

Reciprocal is a term we will use again when considering social play in the next chapter. There are different parts or separate aspects of development that work together in a harmonious give-and-take relationship that benefits each. So in child development terms, a reciprocal relationship would be one in which social development (understanding of encouragement by others, for example) influences physical skill (the action of clapping or 'dancing' in a young child) which is then rewarded by a social response which further encourages physical action and so on.

Vygotsky has famously also indicated a clear link between play and development, arguing that all of the developmental tendencies can be found in a condensed form in play (Vygotsky, 1966, page 16). He considered that play was not a supporting activity that helped learning and development, but that it was the source of development, a leading activity that determines how the child grows and develops – *as in the focus of a magnifying glass, play contains all developmental tendencies in a condensed form; in play it is as though the child were trying to jump above the level of his normal behaviour* (Vygotsky, 1966, page 16).

Some perspectives on child development

Child development is the study of changes in children over time in relation to maturation and learning, but even this can be considered from differing viewpoints or perspectives.

Some perspectives we may take when considering play and development are:

- *A biological/maturational approach*
  This considers how all children grow according to similar patterns which unfold over time. Such an approach is often divided into stages with milestones. All children may be expected to follow similar patterns (although there will be individual differences within these according to experiences). Think here of health workers' growth charts, and those child development charts which try to indicate what a child can do at various ages.

- *Psychological/behavioural approaches*
  These approaches focus on the mind and its growth and adaptation. There are a range of psychological approaches such as behaviourism, cognitive psychology and psycho-analysis. The mind grows from a primitive operating of reflexes and responses to a

complex structure able to represent thought and feeling in reality, symbol and imagination. In child development terms exploration and external stimuli are important in shaping psychological development in different ways.

- *Socio-cultural approaches*
  These are concerned with the way that the child responds to the other people and their ideas in the period of learning and development. These approaches recognise that children live with people and will be influenced by them. Social contexts of other people and culture prompt particular development. So Konner (1991), for example, noticed differences between the development of the !Kung in Africa and the Western child as a result of differences in parenting and community influences.

- *An ecological approach*
  Bronfenbrenner (2005) considers the dynamic relationship between the developing individual and their place in the complex 'ecology' of relationships, places, time, and resources and so on. It recognises that the developing child influences the people and contexts as much as they are influenced by them in a two way process. As such it draws on the other perspectives and combines them to recognise complexity in the child development process. Development in this perspective is no linear maturation, but a process in which the child is both influenced and influencing of other contexts and factors.

In this chapter we will look more closely at interpretations of play in relation to children's development, considering what play is *for*, and how children might jump above their level of 'normal' behaviour as Vygotsky has suggested. In order to give some structure to the discussion we will consider the three following areas in turn:

1. Early social and emotional developmental play;

2. Physical play;

3. Cognitive development through play;

Please remember that in practice these three parts should not remain separate but be seen within a dynamic system of development in which each plays a part and influences the other.

There are two key questions we could ask in relation to play and child development.

1. How does play help to stimulate development across different areas of growth?
2. How does play arise differently through the phases of development?

Think about these two questions.

a) In relation to point 1 above, how do you think play could stimulate development? What might this mean?

continued

ACTIVITY *1* continued

Think of how children are motivated to continue to try the same thing in play until they have developed the skills they need for that game. The enjoyment stimulates repeated attempts which gradually lead to development and mastery of the activity. So an infant around four months may continually find pleasure in grasping and letting go, holding and dropping objects. An older child may continually try to catch a ball she threw in the air, enjoying the challenge, until she can finally control her muscles and hand-to-eye co-ordination sufficiently to regularly catch the ball successfully. For both children the playful element ceases as they become fully competent at the activity. The game finally loses attraction and so the child moves on to something else.

Can you think of some other examples?

b) In relation to point 2 above, take time to consider children of different ages at play. Do you see different types of play at different ages?

We have already considered how a young infant who can sit, will probably be solitary in her play, exploring treasure baskets alone, using senses and fine motor skills in the process. Older children, say four to five years, may play elaborate social role-play games in which both social and fine motor skills are much more developed. They are able to undo zips and buttons, get dressed and run around, far beyond the grasping and sitting of the younger age.

A dynamic systems approach

Smith and Thelen (2003) recognise that children are complex systems made up of individual elements also operating within a complex environment. Rather than there being one dominant factor in the brain that co-ordinates all of the others, there is a coming together of factors that stimulate action in a specific response to the context or situation. To illustrate this random *coming together* of the factors, Smith and Thelen offer a scenario of the infant who is just crawling.

They recognise that crawling itself is a behaviour that babies use to move around once they have sufficient muscle strength and co-ordination to lean on their hands and knees. They are not yet strong enough to balance and walk upright. The nature of their crawling will depend on the environmental conditions, their muscle strength and motivation to move. Babies crawl differently according to their circumstances (Karmil-off-Smith 1995). Some will bottom shuffle, some will crawl on hands and knees and still others will flop forwards and wiggle like fish to get around. These responses may be stimulated by the conditions of the environment (carpeted floors give grip for traction, wood floors allow for sliding), or patterns of muscle control in the individual. There is no *programme for crawling assembled in the genes or wired in the nervous system* (Smith and Thelen, 2003, page 344), but rather it is a solution to a problem that is going to be replaced by a more efficient solution (walking) in due course. It is therefore something of a *free-style* response to a number of stimuli.

Smith and Thelen (2003, page 344) describe such responses as a *self-organised solution to a problem* (in this case the 'problem' is the child's desire to move across the room). It is a temporary response that *will do* for now as it later becomes *'destabilised by the patterns of standing and walking'*. Once the child can stand and walk the efficiency of those actions mean that they no longer need the crawling action and so those skills become redundant.

The dynamic systems approach draws on the ideas of *emergence*, new responses or ways of acting arising through processes intrinsic to the system or individual. In other words the response is not *patterned* or conditioned externally. Crawling merely emerges as a consequence of several aspects of development coming together and impacting upon each other. The act of crawling may not be mere locomotion, but playful and enjoyable, as signified by the child's *play face*, their smile and persistence with the activity. Play often offers flexible opportunity for responses to the environment creating optimum opportunity for emergence of new ways of acting.

Early social development: a secure base for play

Do very young babies play? It has been argued for some time that *precursors of the things we call play have their origin in early social relationships* (Lewis, 1979, page 24). Lewis was highlighting here that play emerges in very young babies as a dialogue between parent or main carer and child. It has a role in supporting social development, but is reliant upon a strong social response from someone else.

In order to participate and explore both the social world and wider environment when they are mobile, young children must first draw on an innate reflexive system that makes the human face attractive to them and prompts communication and response behaviour. Early reciprocal communications build a particular relationship to give infants a *secure base* (Bowlby, 1988) or attachment to another person. This security then acts as an emotional *anchor* which allows for later wider exploration as the child feels their needs are *held in mind* (Bion, 1962) by another person who will look after them.

Before the young infant can move their body with any skill at all, they can 'tune in' to the human face, and respond to sounds and visual and sensory contact. Bowlby noted how a mother and baby of just three weeks will face one another and demonstrate phases of lively social interaction he called social 'play'. He describes the phases of interaction:

> *Each phase of interaction begins with initiation and mutual greeting, builds up to an animated interchange comprising facial expressions and vocalisations, during which the infant orients towards his mother with excited movements of arms and legs; then his activities gradually subside and end with the baby looking away for a spell before the next phase of interaction begins. Throughout these cycles the baby is likely to be as spontaneously active as his mother. Where their roles differ is in the timing of their responses. Whereas an infant's initiation and withdrawal from interaction*

> *tend to follow his own autonomous rhythm, a sensitive mother regulates her*
> *behaviour so that it meshes with his... she lets him call the tune and, by a*
> *skilful interweaving of her own responses with his, creates a dialogue.*
>
> (Bowlby, 1988, page 8)

Bowlby was highlighting how adults will respond to the *cues* thrown out instinctively by the young child. There is a clear link to playful behaviour, with the child's excited movements of arms and legs. There is enjoyment in the relationship as each partner adapts to the other. Long before speech occurs, there are alternating patterns of communication which appear synchronised, or working together, in a rhythmical response to each other (Trevarthen, 2005).

The attached pair may also be synchronised in response to external environments. Bowlby (1988) offers a research example in which mothers and children were introduced to a scene in which there are a large number of brightly coloured toys designed to attract their gaze. Careful observations of their behaviour showed that very often both partners were looking at the same object at the same time, and that invariably the child again led the play response, with the parent following the cues.

We may no longer consider that Bowlby was correct in his assumption of the importance of the 'mother' as opposed to father or other key carer, but what we do still recognise is this need for a close bond, or bonds with other humans which then provide a *secure base* from which the child can progress to increasing levels of exploration and play as they become more mobile (Ainsworth, 1969). Watch young children who are at the crawling stage in a safe space that allows for roaming. As the child explores he will circle away from and back to the person with whom he has this key bond, regularly seeking eye contact, or showing objects he has found in his explorations. This bond is normally considered in a social and emotional development context, but clearly physical play will also be restricted if the early conditions are wrong.

Ainsworth (1969) identified that those children most securely attached were most likely to be confident in their subsequent separation and exploration activities. However, children who did not have this close bond (being therefore insecurely attached) were more likely to show great anxiety when they separated from their parent/carer in due course. Positive early experiences of reciprocal social relationships between a primary carer and child are therefore essential to later separation, exploration and play activity.

These research findings also indicate that we should not consider a baby or child to be merely a passive recipient of adult care or planned experiences. The baby seems *pre-programmed* to *play* and actively stimulate a non-verbal *conversation* that is enjoyable. Parents too are stimulated to offer playful social behaviour to a young child, echoing sounds, tickling toes and tummies, blowing raspberries, throwing them in the air and so on. These adults actively invite their babies' participation in play for social interaction. In communicating in this way, they are, without necessarily being aware of it, creating both the safe space (Ainsworth, 1969) to enable later adventurous exploration, and the basis for essential physical development.

The EYFS (DCSF, 2008, pages 7–8) clearly articulates a perspective that play supports development and learning. We are told in the practice guidance for the foundation stage that play underpins all development and learning for young children, and furthermore that it is through play that [children] develop intellectually, creatively, physically, socially and emotionally (DCSF, 2008a, page 7).

However, rather than asking how play can support development, Sutton-Smith asks the question the other way around and with less of an expected agenda, merely reflecting, what are the outcomes of play? (Sutton-Smith, 1979, page 214)

The position of the EYFS is that play supports development and learning, whereas for Sutton-Smith enhanced development and learning is a consequence of play, an outcome.

Is there a difference in these perspectives?

Does play support development, or does development emerge from play and playful activity? Do children have to play to develop to their full potential?

Play and physical development

The early social play activity of parent and child zooming in and out, rocking up and down, and 'throwing' children playfully into the air may have important impacts for physical development as well as social and emotional security. There is a close link between intellectual development and physical play as the brain needs to control the nerve system and muscles before physical activity can happen. Practised physical activity will increase the ability to control the muscles through experience. It is possible that the adults playing with the child with exaggerated movements such as *bouncing* baby into the air are offering experiences for signals to the brain relating to balance and consequent muscle control that is not yet fully established in other conditions (Pellegrini, 2011). The DCSF stated that *young children need to move, and learn and remember things by taking in experiences through the senses as they move* (DCSF, 2009, page 9).

It has been widely recognised that play amongst the under-eights involves a significant amount of physical activity (Hughes, 2001; Brown, 2003; Smith, Cowie and Blades, 2003). The physical aspect of play is often overlooked in favour of the cognitive, social and symbolic aspects of play. Pellegrini (2011) identifies *locomotor play* as *exaggerated and non-functional behaviours and behavioural sequences* involving the large motor muscles. In other words babies and young children will swing their limbs around, kick, and later jump and run, because they can, and so that they can do so better in future. They are exploring what their limbs can do, 'playing' to stimulate and control their developing muscular growth.

Esther Thelen (1980) has undertaken a longitudinal study of babies' and very young children's physical actions which she considered did not have a goal or purpose (therefore being perceived as play actions). Examples of such movements include body rocking and foot kicking (think of babies kicking happily at bath time). These movements she termed *stereotypic behaviours*. Pellegrini (2011) found that young children spent a long time on such behaviours, particularly at around six months of age when *infants spend as much as 40% of a one hour observational period engaged in [such] stereotypic behaviour (*Pellegrini, 2011, page 174*)*. Infants of around six months therefore spend almost half of their time playfully moving.

ACTIVITY 3

Smith, Cowie and Blades argued that there were three developmental phases in physical activity play.

1. Rhythmical stereotypes – bodily movements that babies make such as kicking legs, waving arms.
2. Exercise play – during pre-school years which involves running around, jumping, climbing – whole body movements which may be done alone or with others.
3. Rough and tumble play – which crosses the ages and progresses from vigorous physical play of parents with toddlers to play fighting in the middle school years.

(Smith et al., 2003, page 220)

Consider 1 and 2 above:
Look at the children you work with. Identify the playful kicking and arm swinging of infants and very young children. Why not list the range of physical playful stereotype movements you see?

Take time to also look at the exercise play of older children. What kinds of things are they doing in their physical play? Note again the range of physical play activities you see.

How much time in an hour do you think the children you watch are playing physically?

A point for reflection: If we know that children are involuntarily stimulated to such physical play for developmental reasons, is it unreasonable to expect long periods of sitting still in young children at nursery or play setting?

Pellegrini argued that locomotor play (play using gross muscles for movement) increases from the first year to a peak at around four or five years, declining in the primary school where children area expected to sit still for longer periods and running around is discouraged. However, he also noted that this perception of a peak may be incorrect as there is a lack of research into physical play behaviours outside of the school setting. Certainly from my work experiences in an adventure playground I would perceive the peak as around 7–8 years of age, but that is purely speculation from informal observations and does need more research. Perhaps early restriction in physical play is in part responsible for increasing obesity in the young population of the UK?

Revisiting the surplus energy theory

In Chapter 3 we considered a historical *surplus energy* theory of play. Smith and Hagan (1980) also argue a case of surplus energy. They considered that young mammals usually have access to sufficient food and that physical play is about preventing obesity by using *surplus energy* to develop muscle rather than fat. They highlight how during rapid growth periods children may need to consume higher levels of protein and running around balances the excess. Pellegrini reminds us to consider how the younger child carries more fat in contrast to the lean and active seven to eight year old. Physical play may therefore condition energy regulation behaviour in children, forming a foundation for future health.

What is physical play for?

Physical play leads to the ability to do things requiring muscle strength, and muscle control or dexterity. Such play also enables the child to develop the ability to continue to use the muscles for a long period of time, so consolidating and refining those skills. A child of seven or eight can not only jump, but may, with a skipping rope, jump for many minutes or even hours. Physical play is also about control of muscles ensuring economy and efficiency of movement. The more skilful and controlled the action is the more effective, and less wasteful of the body's energy. Perhaps think here of the ability to run round a tight corner. The unformed toddler muscles may take a wide loop round the corner, being not sufficiently in control of muscles to balance on a tight turn. The mature seven year old in contrast will use balance and muscle control to run a tight corner without falling over. Children's play will echo their levels of development and allow for opportunity to practise emerging skills.

Think of how a toddler that is just mastering running (the toddler jog) will run around for sheer joy in the ability to do so. Is this play? I recall watching a toddler at a festival doing the toddler jog up and down the metal road that cars had used to enter the site but that was now entirely quiet. The look on his face clearly illustrated that he was at play. He seemed to be simply enjoying the freedom to use his muscles to 'run' in a linear fashion, also making a good noise with his feet as he did so. He ran on this road whenever he could, along to one end and then back again to the watchful adult. He ran for hours, building up his running related muscle power, and control. He was also building stamina. The toddler may run in straight lines, just because he now can, while the seven year old will play chase games to enhance co-ordination, change of direction and balance.

Smith and Thelen (2003) argue that the developmental systems of children are interconnected and the physical movement of a child is linked to other aspects of development. When a child can crawl and explore, the benefit is not just a physical one, it also develops the child's ability to remember and *map* the space that they are in, which is a cognitive skill. Other authors have highlighted the importance of physical play aligned to emotional release at the same time. Kalliala describes this as the *dizzy side of play* as she highlights that children all over the world seem to like swivelling and the feeling of dizziness that comes with it (Kalliala, 2006). She also notices that children like falling onto a pile of mattresses, or playing *rough play* with another child. They like riding on the backs of adults crawling on the floor, and playing wild rough and tumble play with their parents on the bed. These physical play activities are about physical ability, but also about social negotiations, and challenge or competition. She describes dizzy play as the kind that *wells up inside us* and highlights that Callois calls this kind of playing *ilinix, using the Greek word for whirling water* (Kalliala, 2006, page 94, citing Callois, 1961).

ACTIVITY 4

Figure 5.1 A child plays with waves

Look at the photograph above. Locomotor physical play is about young children doing physical things because they can. They enjoy the element of practising and mastering the skills of jumping, running, hopping etc.

ACTIVITY *4 continued*

Bjorklund and Gardiner (2011) highlight the influence of culture and environment on children's play and development. They note that in Western cultures pre-school children are often given toys such as blocks or connecting bricks to promote constructive and fine motor play indoors. In Brazil young boys primarily play outside with miniature bows and arrows encouraging gross motor play. These opportunities have a subsequent effect on development.

The child in the photograph above is stimulated to physical action by the sea and sand. Consider what environmental factors stimulate the physical play of the children you work with. Are there things that invite physical play and development in your setting?

Do not forget that physical play can also involve fine motor skills. By the end of the first year most children will be able to pick up small items using the forefinger and thumb together. To perfect this skill requires that they have the opportunity to pick up smallish items, which must be available as play things. However, the child is still in a development period in which everything will be tested in the mouth, so the chosen items must also be safe for the child's age.

What items do you offer to stimulate fine motor play in the children you work with?

Play and motivation

Play is intrinsically motivated, and encourages persistence in activities as we have indicated above. Such persistence may consolidate previously learnt activity, or may be about reduction of anxiety through therapeutic confirmation of control of one's own body. Some authors (Berlyne, 1969; Csikszentmihalyi, 1979, 2002) have argued for an optimal level of satisfaction or arousal in play, in which the activity is neither too challenging to be uncertain or too easy to be boring, but somewhere in between that keeps the player *aroused* and in *flow*.

Bruner cites the *Yerkes-Dodson law that states that the more complex a skill to be learned, the lower the optimum motivational level required for fastest learning. Play then, may provide the means for reducing excessive drive and frustration* (Bruner, 1976, page 15).

In the above passage, Bruner is writing of play having the ability to reduce or neutralise the pressure of goal-directed action and the push to successful completion – which ironically makes it more likely that the child will persist in that activity. It seems that in play children are also able to maintain the flow level by choosing to opt in or out, or change its sense of reality and fantasy, so there is no pressure to complete the task chosen. As a result it is more likely to be completed!

In physical play this may be seen when a child is trying to run over an uneven but soft surface. The child slips and falls down in front of his friends but immediately shouts 'I meant to fall, this is how we fall'. He then falls down a few more times to consolidate this false tale before again trying to run across the whole width without falling down. He adjusted his goal by making the falling down fantasy, and so maintained his level of competence within his flow zone. The challenge still remained for him, but he was able to remove the pressure of failure. Sutton-Smith (1979) indicated that such challenges were in a particular zone of understanding in which *children prefer to play with those areas of competence which are not fully mastered and yet not completely unknown* (page 309).

Play and cognitive development

Piaget (Piaget and Inhelder,1969) also held the concept of internal motivation through play – a motivation which led to persistence in exploration for cognitive development. Piaget considered the child very much as an individual connecting to his or her environment. For Piaget, intelligence came from action. Play provided the conscious space for exploration of concepts.

THEORY FOCUS

A quick summary of Piaget's key ideas

For Piaget, the actions of play were broadly classified into four levels.

Sensori-motor
This is the initial stage, when the child is using senses to understand things and concentrating on developing his or her motor control. Control of limbs is a cognitive act as the child's brain is developing connections and understanding of hand-to-eye co-ordination, spatial awareness and self-determination. They are taking on information through their senses and experiences. At this stage, children need lots of things to explore that have different sizes, shapes and textures.

Pre-operational
From two to seven years, children's interest in exploring really comes to the fore. Thought processes are developing during the pre-operational stage. This stage includes the *symbolic* phase, when children increasingly recognise and use symbols to represent the world. Ideas still largely relate directly to objects rather than to abstract thought and objects may be given person-like qualities (animism). Piaget argued that children would not understand the concept of *conservation*. By this he meant that they could not distinguish volume accurately – given a shallow bowl and a tall glass containing the same amount of water, children in pre-operational stage would believe the latter had the greater amount. At this stage, exploration of the world is important to the development of concepts and children will work out their ideas through concrete activities or doing things – playing with water and cups to identify properties of liquids and ideas of volume and flow for example.

THEORY FOCUS *continued*

Concrete operational

This stage is from seven to 11 years. A period in which the older child is able to understand and obey logical rules (Piaget's *operations*) and begin to generate abstract thought, initially moving the object they are thinking about, and subsequently progressing from the 'concrete' act of doing. A child of seven or eight will understand *conservation*, so they need more complex resources and things to explore. Games increasingly have rules, social ability is increased and explorations become more 'scientific' as interest in classification, speed, number and space, for example, come to the fore.

Formal operational

A child aged 11 and above can visualise and work out concepts (Piaget's *operations*) in their heads. They are able to undertake abstract thought.

Play and cognitive development through the stages involves both Piaget's concepts of *assimilation* and *accommodation* and *schema*.
Assimilation = the taking in of new information.
Accommodation = the adjustment required to adapt existing understandings or schemes of knowledge to include the new information.
Schema or *schemes* = are clusters of ideas, or the organisation of actions that are generalised or reduced for understanding such that they can be repeated in similar situations or circumstances (Piaget and Inhelder, 1969, page 4).

Many authors have questioned Piaget's theories, and as I read them again to write this I note that the ages given seem arbitrary and not entirely accurate. I know of quite young children who understand *conservation*, for example, because they have had experience of pouring the same quantity into different vessels. However, Piaget's theories are a useful starting point. Athey identifies that for Piaget, children develop through stages from struggle, through practice, to play. *Playfulness signifies knowledge so well assimilated it can be played with* (Athey, 2004, page 75). Both Athey (2004) and Arnold (2003, and Arnold *et al.*, 2010) draw on Piaget's work to explore the importance of play or active learning for cognitive development as children explore complex ideas by doing things. She argues that playfulness (the humorous positive emotional affect) emerges as an indicator of something very well understood and assimilated. An example of this is the game of ring-a-ring-a-roses. This cannot be played in the toddler's early stages of upright balance as the child is usually furious when they have fallen down. Such a game involves having fun with pretending to fall down, and in order to get to that stage it would imply that the player has great confidence in their ability to stand up again, so that falling down becomes a joke.

Athey indicates that play does have a role in cognitive development, but not so much with play as exploration, but play as mastery, at the point of Piaget's accommodation of understanding, the adjustment of existing ideas. Schematic play may involve deep concentration. Athey simplified Piaget's concept of schemas describing them as *patterns of repeatable actions that lead to early categories and then to logical classifications* (Athey, 2004, page 49). Children are, through schemas, exploring in a physical way more abstract concepts. Athey probably considered these actions to be exploration, however I prefer to link them to play as the child is choosing how far to take the exploratory activity, and is very often showing deep involvement, flow and enjoyment.

Athey's categories of schema

Athey (2004, page 130) gives the following categories of schema:

- *Dynamic vertical schema* – An interest in up and down, falling and falling down. A child may drop things on purpose, drop a stone in water to see the splash 'coming up'; building towers with blocks.

- *Back and forth, or side to side* – Athey does not mean zigzag here but a horizontal linear schema. The toddler on the metal road may well have been exhibiting such back and forth or side to side linear schema behaviour.

- *Circular direction and rotation* – A child will show interest in things going round, trains 'going round' an oval track, looking at wheels going round (even whilst riding a toy), things that rotate such as windmills, records on a record player, a food mixer and so on.

- *Going over, under or on top* – Children are interested in the position of things and will mention that a house has 'a chimney on top', or that something is 'under the bridge'. Athey gives an example of junk construction or collage in which a child sticks a cake paper on top of a cardboard lid and then puts a yoghurt carton on top of that stating clearly their position 'on top of'. She also explains that this schema is about positionality and some children may be interested in the concept of 'next to'.

- *Boundaries and enclosure* – This may involve making enclosures such as laying string in a circle, or putting toy fences up to contain toy animals. It may reveal itself as children wrapping themselves up in fabric, tying things round their waists. It may show itself as an interest in the edges of an area or approved limits.

- *Containing and enveloping* – Children are very interested in putting things inside other things – think of stacking cubes that can either pile up, or be stacked inside each other. Children like play with things in small boxes. They may discuss concepts of *empty* or *full*. They will go in and out of spaces, build tents, and wrap things (including themselves) up.

- *Going through a boundary* – Susan Isaacs' (1930) observation of a child playing with metal rods going through a block is an example of *going through*. The child was interested in something coming out of the other side. So children may be interested in holes (an idea incorporated into many story books), they may be interested in light coming in shards through the branches of a tree, or a hole in the wall. Pushing pencils or fingers through clay is another example of *going through* as a schematic behaviour.

There may be many more categories of schema and you will see different lists of schema categories in different books. That does not really matter. What is important here is to

---

THEORY FOCUS continued

understand that rich play opportunities and flexible resources enable children to work out concepts through practical actions. If we are aware of the cognitive significance of what children are doing it achieves a different importance for us. It is our adult need to label that creates the list of categories, not the child's need to work things out!

Combinatorial flexibility

Combinatorial flexibility (Piaget and Inhelder, 1969; Bruner, 1976; Hughes, 2001) is the final idea I will raise in this chapter. It is the idea that humans *combine* a number of thoughts and ideas to reach a solution. So a child may in play be consolidating some skill or knowledge as well as introducing some novelty and alteration to encourage and extend their own *combinatorial flexibility*. It is about the child's mind being able to process information at speed and come up with new connections and combinations.

> *What the term combinatorial flexibility describes to me, is a process of looking at a problem and then scanning one's memory bank for the tiny pieces of information that have been learnt, to see if any of those pieces, or any combination of those pieces of information, might contribute to a solution of the problem.*

(Hughes, 2001, page 138)

The child at play will often act out the solutions – and so the solutions are arrived at through a process of trial, error and elimination. Alternatively children may seek to challenge themselves by increasing the combinations, introducing new challenges to further develop their skill or understanding. So a child may have an idea to build a bridge, but one plank will not cross the span he wants. He will consider what he already knows about bridges, and about how things balance. He may recall that bridges are arches, or that planks can stack one on another. He will bring all of these together to reach a potential solution to his problem of bridge building!

The level of combination will increase with greater knowledge and therefore with age, but even quite young children are combining thoughts to reach a toy, or to plan a physical action, such as jumping off something without risk to themselves. This is combinatorial flexibility. This also happens all day long in appropriately flexible play environments and again forms the basis of understandings we will use as adults.

SUMMARY

In this chapter we have progressed from a consideration of the beginnings of play in infant:parent interactions, through an understanding of the contribution of play to physical development and finally to the exploration of ideas by doing. I have purposely

continued

SUMMARY *continued*

avoided the maturational approaches of indicating the ages at which children may be expected to do things because I believe that this does alter according to opportunity. In the further reading section is a prompt to look at a video clip online of a 20-month-old child playing with an iPad for the first time. The combinatorial flexibility is clearly at work as she explores this new item, drawing on what she already knows and skilfully using fine motor skills, brushing the screen with her index finger to change pages and select games. I wonder what Piaget would have made of such an observation? It clearly challenges some of his stages.

Hopefully this chapter has stimulated you to think about the child's context and the importance of the resources and opportunities you have available for children. In this chapter we have largely concentrated on the child as an individual player and explorer, operating within a safe space. The next chapter will draw your attention to the relationship of play and social development.

FURTHER READING

Arnold, C (2003) *Observing Harry: Child Development and Learning 2–5.* London: Sage Publications.

A very accessible book which explores the development of Harry through use of observation and theory. Arnold recognises Harry's possible schemas in play, for example as he ties things up with string.

Athey, C (2004) *Extending Thought in Young Children.* London: Paul Chapman Publishing.

This is not an easy read, but a book to keep returning to, to understand the application and importance of schemas practised by young children and how to share this understanding with parents.

Hughes, FP (2010) *Children, Play and Development.* (4th edition). London: Sage.

A very clear consideration of the relational nature of play and development or play in the process of development. Introduces key terms at the end of each chapter and considers the value of play for development beyond the first five years of a child's life.

WEBSITES

www.youtube.com/watch?v=kT3dBKIzHNY&feature=relmfu

The French Test of the iPad which shows a 20-month-old child skilfully negotiating a piece of electronic equipment seen for the first time.

6   Play and social development

Through reading this chapter, you will:

- explore play from a social and ecological perspective;

- consider the importance of others and the tensions of social connection and space framing activity;

- reflect on the relevance of Vygotsky's zone of proximal development and issues of *flow* in relation to self and others at play;

- explore concepts of enculturation and social rhythms in play;

- reflect on issues of rough and tumble play, emotional containment and enculturation.

Introduction

Play has for many years been linked to children's social development and the process of learning to live with others in a social community or society. Recall here our discussions in Chapter 3 and Plato's emphasis on play as important to the creation of a cultured society. Plato argued that through play children explored social ideas, and learnt about relationships, failure and resilience. You may also recall that the Reggio Emilia approach in Italy was concerned with creating a more effective future society through play. This approach both engineered social spaces within its learning environment to allow for communication, debate and discussion. It also offered opportunities for children to be influenced in their play by cultural artefacts and images. In Reggio Emilia, children are encouraged to work with each other in small groups, and to *copy* adult roles as teachers play a part in role-play activities *acting shopkeepers*, for example (Abbott and Nutbrown, 2001). The link between play and social development is such that some authors have gone as far as to argue that the strongest argument for play is in terms of its role in supporting social development (Smith, Cowie and Blades, 2003).

The UK Department for Children, Schools and Families also considered that:

> It is through play that babies and young children learn, grow and have fun. It helps them understand the world and to develop socially and emotionally. Singing songs, reading together, playing games with letters and numbers, and having fun with friends gives them a head start.

> (DCSF, 2008b, page 1)

This statement mixes social and cognitive skills but implies that play is important for social and emotional development – having fun in social groups also helps learning.

Play can offer opportunities for the development of social relationships (Parten, 1932) or insight into the social patterns (the cultures) of the society in which children grow (Rogoff, 2003). The social and cultural contexts of play can in turn influence children's choices of who and what to play with, their understanding of roles to copy and even the ways they behave with each other. The development of language is also a social development though it involves cognitive skills.

In this chapter we will look at both:

- how children develop in relation to other people (their ways of being); and

- how children are influenced in their play by social context and learning (the influences on them as 'becomings' (Else and Sturrock, 2007).

ACTIVITY 1

Jayden, Susan and Jack are playing in the home corner. It is laid out like a kitchen today, with food from different countries, aprons, chef hats, and cooking utensils. There is a supermarket shopping basket in the corner, filled with plates, cups and saucers.

'I am going to cook today, we must cook the best meal ever,' says Jayden in a very loud and excited voice. 'You see what I can cook'.

'OK chef,' Jack says with a particular accent as if copying something he has seen on TV.

'You must have an apron or the food will be dirty,' Susan adds to the conversation, 'I will cook too; I know how to cook'.

'No, no, no...I am chef,' Jayden says very forcefully.

'Yes, he is, and I am going to help him,' Jack says aligning with his best friend.

'But it is my kitchen,' as Susan's fast fantasy thinking gives her the upper hand for a second.

'OK you can be the manager. You have to wear a jacket,' says Jayden, as he again controls the game.

'...and managers can cook too!' Susan keeps to her theme.

The game goes on all morning, with Jayden often the most dominant voice heard in the group. At one point Jayden and Susan argue over who is going to stand by the cooker. Susan is now wearing her jacket and stays firm to her ideas. As manager, she can cook, and she tells chef what to cook. Jayden is happy to pretend to be chef. Jack seems quite happy to transport objects from the basket to the table and so their play revolves around each other, at times playing in parallel, at times fully co-operatively and at times in conflict. During the course of the morning they skilfully negotiate a series of social conflicts and compromises in their play.

ACTIVITY *1 continued*

Can you spot the children as 'beings' or 'becomings' in this example of social play?

a) The intention of the play resources and the way in which the children approached the activity could be considered to be supporting children as 'becomings' – children being led to consider what they need to know or do for adult life. The children were exploring potential adult roles in their play. They seemed to have seen a video or TV programme about a restaurant. Jayden and Susan definitely have clear ideas of the relevant adult roles. Jack too is mimicking a voice and phrase he has heard. They are in tune with their perceptions of a commercial kitchen. The classroom home corner had been purposely laid out to help children explore this range of adult job roles.

b) However, this example is also about children as 'beings', competent and skilful now, enjoying playing with others and exploring power and social relationships with relative ease. Jayden uses dominance, particularly in volume of voice. Susan is smart, as she can assert herself by adjusting the fantasy, choosing to say that the kitchen is hers. Jayden is smart too, as he plays the next challenge when he tells her she can be the manager. Susan retorts with the fact that managers can cook. If you watch pre-school children at play you will see these regular shifts in fantasy and power. The three children are already good negotiators, working out their roles and importance in the game.

Why don't you watch some three to five year olds at play in the home corner or other role-play situation? See how skilfully they can negotiate with each other, often using fantasy to change the direction of the play. Of course there will be some conflicts too, but watch and see if the children can sort them out before adult intervention.

What is social development?

Social development encompasses learning about the society (or social context) in which the child is growing and also learning how to relate to other people. It encompasses emotional development, communication and social cognitive skills. A child begins to develop socially as soon as she is born and use her early reflexes to begin interactions with others. A baby can make his needs known and encourages responses from others. Infants will also listen to those around them, and respond to the noises and rhythms of the life into which they are born. The nature of the child's later understandings and responses is very much influenced by the social context into which he or she is born. Bronfenbrenner's bio-ecological model is useful to consider the complexity of the social system and influences at play in relation to the developing social child. Usually drawn as a series of concentric circles with the child at the centre it is clear in this model that not only is the child affected by the adjacent 'system' but he or she is also able to affect it. So a child is influenced by family, but also changes family structure merely by existing and responding.

The ecology of childhood

Bronfenbrenner (2005) recognises the importance of social and environmental context and influences in child development. Although initially concerned with cognitive development, he expanded his theory to consider social and emotional development implications too. Bronfenbrenner was influenced by the psychologist Kurt Lewin's (1936) work on force field analysis. This recognised tensions between *field forces* or events influencing a person's present awareness. Bronfenbrenner's model (1992) recognises the socio-cultural tensions within *systems* of opposing influences on society, family and the child. He described this as a scientific recognition of the belief systems in the world of the developing person. The model demonstrates the importance of the interaction of the developing child within a series of influences or forces of importance to its development. The child both influences and is influenced by the *systems* within which he or she develops.

Usually drawn as a series of concentric circles, Bronfenbrenner's theory comprises:

Microsystem – A pattern of activities, roles and interpersonal relations experienced by the developing person in a given face to face setting (Bronfenbrenner, 2005, page 148). A microsystem would be the relationship between child and family, or child and setting or other social context with which the child is very familiar. Bronfenbrenner added the social development understanding that the microsystem included influential others who had particular characteristics, temperaments, personalities and belief systems which would also influence the child's own developing beliefs and social characteristics.

Mesosytem – Comprises the linkages and processes taking place between two or more settings containing the developing person (Bronfenbrenner, 2005, page 149). This system would therefore hold a series of microsystems perhaps offering conflicting characteristics. I find it helpful to picture it as the jelly that holds a number of nuclear eggs like frogspawn. So it is that there are a number of microsystems known to a developing person or child. There is movement and tension as the different influences come to the fore at different times. Think of how a child can respond differently in their actions when playing with siblings or with grandparents. The different influences offer different social prompts and responses.

Exosystem – Comprises the linkage and processes taking place between two or more settings, at least one of which does not ordinarily contain the developing person (Bronfenbrenner, 2005, page 149). So here the link is made between things not directly experienced by the developing child but which will also have an influence on him or her through culture and belief systems. This sphere may indicate the influence on family culture of the parents' work, or any social groups they have.

Macrosystem – The overarching pattern of micro, meso and exo-systems of a given culture... or other broader social context (Bronfenbrenner, 2005, page 149). In the macrosystem would be resources and government policy, culture and opportunity structures in society, life course options, media and patterns of social interaction. This system is the ideological system that shapes the broad social context and culture in which the other systems exist, and the child develops. So it may be that the macrosystem places an emphasis on merit and achievement and the child is presented with a pressure to achieve. Alternatively, we could focus on the influence of commercial media, and recognise the influence of this on our developing child who recognises the M for McDonalds and plays with Barbie dolls.

Chronosystem – Time. Bronfenbrenner added this later to his model to indicate how things change over time. It is time that makes something important at that moment, but shapes it differently in future. This system also recognises that previous life experiences will have an impact on subsequent development.

Bronfenbrenner's use of the terms 'bio' and 'ecological' for this model clearly indicates that the system is presenting a complex relationship and series of tensions that together create a balance.

Playing with the tension

Just as play occurs in Piaget's space between assimilation and accommodation (between the taking in of new information and becoming familiar with it, and the struggle of adjustment to existing understandings), so play occurs at the points of tension between Bronfenbrenner's *systems*. Children will explore the tensions between the cultural systems they have experienced, taking them on, exploring through play, and reconciling the tensions over time.

What does this all mean in practice for a developing child? The child will not only initially be influenced by their relationship with their mother, father or other primary carer, but will also be influenced by the interactions of different microsystems. For example, home to school, and the macro and exosystems which feed down to the family in terms of cultures, political and moral understandings (and ways of being or understanding their world). Children establish roles in play – such as superheroes, princesses, wrestlers, dinosaurs, doctors and vets. There appear to be constant power struggles in the creativity of such play (for example, the mummy tells the baby what to do; the super heroes' powers are always extending to be stronger than their play partners').

So it is that our children in Activity 1 are influenced by media, the economic culture that enables restaurants to exist, by conformity to dress codes perhaps (in the manager's jacket), perhaps their parents' work, and certainly the child as manager recognises that she, as a female with a job can also cook in a kitchen as her mother or father does when home from work. In a different time different influences would be at play (as seen in the historical Chapter 3). In a different macrosystem there may not be the influences of the media or commercial play resources available to our children. Think again of the !Kung and their clumps of mud as people reported by Konner (1991) in contrast to the commercialisation of play in the UK and USA.

THEORY FOCUS

Enculturation

Enculturation is the process where people existing in an established culture teach an individual the accepted norms and values of that culture or society – in which the individual also lives. So a developing child learns the contextual boundaries and behaviour from other members of the culture (adults or children). They learn what is acceptable and not acceptable, the lifestyle and templates of that society, and perhaps the roles expected of the individual (Kottak, 2011).

To continue our example from Activity 1, in the UK children are *enculturated* into the use of cooking and eating implements particular to this society. Think here of children *tea making*, for example, with the use of tea pot and cups and saucers. Children are shown how to use them by others. They are also a symbol of English culture. Other communities in the world do not drink tea made in teapots, and may not use implements to eat with. Children are also enculturated into understanding boundaries of behaviour for example, being shown the boundaries and the ways to behave as staff model good behaviour.

The importance of role play and fantasy

Role-play has many important social functions for young children, and one of these is related to exploration of cultural and socio-cultural influences. Another is the acting out of the tensions between the range of complex systems which are transmitting social and cultural messages to the child, thereby influencing their choice of play activities and toys. A child may, for example, act out the tensions she has seen between parent as mother and parent as worker, or her own experiences of being at home and going to a friend's family. Much role-play seems to focus on actions of transition, for example using phrases such as 'I am going shopping now,' or 'I am going to the doctor's'.

> *...the place where cultural experience is located is in the potential space between the individual and the environment (originally the object). The same can be said of playing. Cultural experience begins with creative living first manifested in play...*

> (Winnicott, 2005, page 135)

Again play is offered as that process of transition between what is known and what is not yet fully assimilated. Play happens between people, but also in the *space* between the individual and the socio-cultural environment in which they develop. The fantasy space of play allows for a safe exploration of social concepts and rules. Vygotsky (1933) cites an example of two sisters playing at being sisters.

> *One day two sisters, aged five and seven, said to each other: 'Let's play sisters.' ... the child in playing tries to be a sister. In life the child behaves without thinking that she is her sister's sister. She never behaves with respect to the other just because she is her sister... In the game of sisters playing at 'sisters,' however, they are both concerned with displaying their sisterhood.*

> (Vygotsky, 1933, page 7)

So, in this game, the girls can explore what it means to be a sister, what 'rules' there are in society about how sisters should behave, they could explore how they perceive *other* sisters to be. Just as children work out cognitive or intellectual understandings through actions relating to how things behave or act, so fantasy and role-play allows children to *work through* relationships and the rules of *being* in relation to other people.

We should remember within these models that the child is not the passive recipient of the external culture, but an active partner in the exploration and accommodation of cultural understanding. The children work through things they have seen and their new perspectives will emerge as a result, in turn impacting on the future systems and culture within which they operate.

THEORY FOCUS

Vygotsky's zone of proximal development

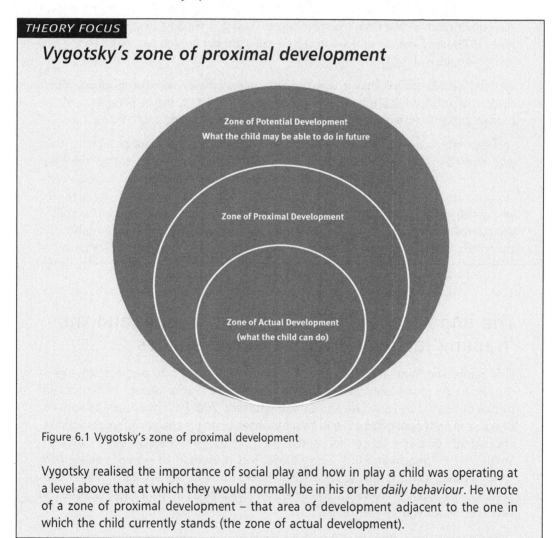

Figure 6.1 Vygotsky's zone of proximal development

Vygotsky realised the importance of social play and how in play a child was operating at a level above that at which they would normally be in his or her *daily behaviour*. He wrote of a zone of proximal development – that area of development adjacent to the one in which the child currently stands (the zone of actual development).

---

continued

THEORY FOCUS *continued*

> *Play is the source of development and creates the zone of proximal development. Action in the imaginative sphere, in an imaginary situation, the creation of voluntary intentions and the formation of real-life plans and volitional motives – all appear in play and make it the highest level of preschool development.*
>
> (Vygotsky, 1933, page 20)

In the diagram above the inner circle represents the zone of actual development – what the child can do now.

The outer circle represents the zone of potential development – what the child may be able to do in future, but which would be too stretching for the child at present.

The zone of proximal development is that area of potential growth that is just beyond and within reach of the child's current capabilities. It is within Csikszentmihalyi's *flow zone* (1979) being not too difficult to put the child off, but not too easy to be boring and non-developmental.

Vygotsky (1933) argued that it was the influence of more experienced *others* (other children or other adults) that could lead the playful child to the achievements of the zone of proximal development by showing them and scaffolding experiences.

So a child who can just stand and walk forward with relative ease watches an older child who can move backwards dragging a pull-along caterpillar toy on a string. The older child watches the caterpillar intently. The younger child watches the older child. A few moments later the older child had dropped the string and moved on in his play. The younger child picked up the string and tentatively tried to move backwards whilst pulling the caterpillar. He had been ready for a further challenge, and observing another had shown him what to try next. He was operating in his zone of 'proximal development'.

The importance of relationships in play and the 'framing' activity creating social spaces

Play frames and frame negotiations are further topics relating to play that emerge in the conclusion to the Johnson and Johnson Conference (Sutton-Smith, 1979), and are further developed by Perry Else and Gordon Sturrock (2007). From as early as one year of age, a child is engaged with a protracted series of negotiations with other children and parents or carers to develop and sustain his or her own *play frames* (Sutton-Smith, 1979; Trevarthen, 2001; Else, 2009). This is a world of power-management which involves learning how to set up play frames (offering signals and systems about pretending and not-pretending). Even children as young as in the image opposite can negotiate space within their den.

Children must negotiate before they can even play, and perhaps negotiate during play as it changes direction. By adulthood negotiations become part of the work environment, teamwork, debate, and sports activity (Sutton-Smith, 1979, page 305). However, now we get to the difficult bit … although we can see that children negotiate and

Figure 6.2 Three children in a 'den'

establish such play frames (the situational contexts for play) before role-play can occur, for example, we also know that play is about contrast, anarchy and disruption. Children's role-play is as much about moving in and out of negotiation as it is about the dramatic content or *storytelling* that takes place. The negotiations themselves become play and offer a *get out* for the child who is rejected by the other potential players. Young children will negotiate by *taking space* physically moving in and shifting sideways until they are where they want to be. Older children will use language much more for their negotiations.

We have already considered in the previous chapter how a parent and child create a *play frame* in their early conversations, based on infant reflexes. Sutton-Smith (2011) draws on the work of Lewis (1979) and Stern (1977) in arguing that a main carer (he said the mother) provides the safe expressive frame within which her stimulation and the infant's response assume the characteristics of play in a social environment when she creates that *proxemic bubble* by close eye contact. This is a safe ludic space in which the child can gently begin or end the communications. As the child grows and creates their own *play frames* things get a little more complicated; they invite their *friends* into their play frames, and eject them just as easily!

Sutton-Smith (1979) writes of dramatic exchanges within play frames, and of there being director, performer and spectator in play. He summarises a range of play competencies relating to communication and role-play:

- *The exchange routine*, in which the partners are equal in gently responding to each other. This is the routine we considered with parent and very young infant. We could also consider that Jayden and Susan's negotiating dialogue was also an *exchange routine*.

- *The central person routine* in which there is a main performer and counter-actors. Here we may think of Jayden being the chef, loudly trying to create a central role for himself. He was also forming a *director* role at the beginning, clearly shaping the play frame around his needs. Although Jack was a participant he was also very much a *spectator* and therefore the audience for the central person.

- *Unison routines*, in which the players work very much together as if in harmony, but not necessarily all doing the same thing. In Activity 1 the children spent much of the morning in harmony once they had negotiated their roles and importance. Sutton-Smith saw this aspect as very important. *If much of society rests on turn-taking and performing, so even more rests on our ability to act in concert with each other* (Sutton-Smith, 1979, page 302). The ability to operate in unison in play perhaps leads to team working in future?

Finally there are *contest routines*, in which there are *sides* and implicit *rules* – for example of baby pulling mother's hair and then mother escaping, or of stopping the young child running, then letting them go. As children get older these social exchanges may become rough-and-tumble play, a more explicit contest type of play.

ACTIVITY 2

Esmee has two brothers, Ethan and Jake. They are playing in the garden. Ethan, the oldest of the children, starts organising a game of throwing a bean bag around. They are playing near to a tree and the bean bag gets caught on a branch just out of reach. A competition starts between the children as they try to get the bean bag down. Esmee gets a stick to poke it down and Ethan is trying to climb the tree. They are both laughing, displaying the play face whilst trying to perform this complex action. Then Esmee knocks the bean bag to the ground and all three children lunge for it at the same time. Laughingly they push each other around, grabbing the bean bag off each other when they can. Somehow Ethan and Jake end up sitting on Esmee, tickling her to release the bean bag from under her back. There is a burst of energy in this play, and much laughter. Jake grabs the bean bag and runs a few metres only to be brought to the ground by Ethan. The children are not intentionally hurting each other though there may be a few bruises from this play. They are engaging in a physical form of social play.

Would you allow for this form of play?

This is rough-and-tumble play. This play is also about exploring boundaries, power and strength. Here it takes the form of a physical contest, but it is not about aggression. The unwritten rules are of play and not intention to hurt. This form of play can be seen in quite young children who may pretend to karate kick other children and fall to the ground. Often there is no contact at all, it just looks aggressive. There is a balance of approach and submission in the play. Rough and tumble play includes running, climbing, chasing and play fighting (Pellegrini and Smith, 1998; Tannock, 2011). These authors recognise that the play face is an important characteristic of rough-and-tumble play as it signifies to the other person that it is not aggression, and therefore the players do not

ACTIVITY 2 continued

have the intention to hurt. Pellegrini (2011) considers it to be an important form of social physical play. Tannock suggests that rough-and-tumble play evolves as the children mature, progressing from non-contact play to the kind of contact we show in this scenario. She concluded that there should be more observation and awareness of the developmental impact of rough-and tumble play. She also considered that there should be more opportunity for children to play in this way.

What is your view on rough-and-tumble play? Should it be allowed within your setting?

Social rhythms and language in play

Sutton-Smith (1979) identified that play is *biphasic* and involves antecedents, entry points, a phase of increasing excitement or involvement and then tension release, catharsis and euphoria. In other words there is a rhythm to play. The child is encouraged to play, tentatively enters the play frame, is increasingly involved and excited, but gradually reaches the peak of interest (the flow) before breaking the frame to move on. This can be seen in the rough-and-tumble scenario above.

Trevarthen (2005) also identified that there is a rhythm to play, but for him it is to the sounds of play to a very young child. Language is an aspect of social development and Trevarthen identified patterns of timing across parent-child interactions and use of rhyming games. There is a musicality in the sounds exchanged, and common rhythms. However, these rhythms may be different across cultures as ways of talking to babies are culturally learned behaviours. Mothers and carers *create frameworks of interaction in jointly constructed worlds* (Bruner 1987, cited in David *et al.* 2003, page 68).

Language development is a social skill which involves elements of play in a series of widening play frames. Language is learnt on several different levels at the same time (Karmiloff-Smith, 1995). Children must get to grips with the sounds of language, its rhythms and words, as well as how to use the language, putting the elements together. Children's first spoken words have arisen from a period of intense listening, experimenting or *playing* with sounds and imitating familiar people. Early play and ritualistic games in an adult-child relationship or in parallel with other children offer strong rhythmical patterns to follow. Later, children need opportunities to rehearse language – they may secretly narrate their own behaviours to practise language before joining communication with others. Often early language is not words, but sounds that mimic words (for example, *uh-oh* if something is going to topple).

Again, play allows for the removal of barriers and tensions in the exploration of words. There is no *wrong* in play and children may explore and share word sounds, looking for rhythm, and seeking to mimic those they have heard around them. I recall my children in pre-school years wandering around chanting together words and word sounds, practising the muscle control needed for more sophisticated combinations of words and phrases.

Moyles (1994, 2005) suggests that play, particularly *role-play*, provides a very appropriate context for language development across both the intellectual and emotional areas. A review of literature on play and language found an *undeniable association* and concluded that play was an *effective medium of stimulating language development and innovation in language use* (Coulter and Taylor, 2001, page 16).

Play helps the child to explore understanding and production of language. Symbolic play and naming of objects also relates to language development and later socio-dramatic play allows children to copy the language of others, further embedding their understanding through practice and comprehension in relation to context.

SUMMARY

In this chapter we have considered briefly some of the main themes of social development and play. Social play is concerned with learning about the culture within which we live, and learning how to operate alongside and in collaboration with others. It is concerned with negotiating play space, and power relationships in action. It is also about learning from those around us, whether that learning concerns cultural patterns, or merely the next idea to try. Social play is about fantasising what we may become, and negotiating to establish who we are.

We have here also briefly considered communication and the importance of signals and sharing. Children and adults offer play cues, and seek play responses (Else and Sturrock, 2007), and this extends to the use of the play face to signify non-aggression in rough-and-tumble play. Konner (1991) recognised this use of play cues in rough-and-tumble play and praised the way that fairness, rules, sanctions and oral contracts arise during the natural course of social play' (Konner, 1991, page 297).

The social benefits of play may therefore not merely be imparting behaviours to integrate the players into relevant cultural systems, but may also be generating innovative alternatives to change the cultural systems of the future, which in turn will influence the next generation of players.

FURTHER READING

Bronfenbrenner, U (2005) *Making Human Beings Human: Bioecological Perspectives on Human Development*. London: Sage.

For those who want to look at Bronfenbrenner's work in the original. I would always suggest going back to the author's own writing as the models do get adjusted a little in translation to regular textbooks. You may need to read this more than once.

Hughes, FP (2010) *Children, Play and Development*. (4th edition). London: Sage.
A very useful book that links child development and play very clearly with insight and more opportunity to expand on some of the ideas I have mentioned in this chapter.

Johnston, J and Nahmad-Williams (2009) *Early Childhood Studies*. Harlow: Pearson.
A very clear introduction to child development that offers a clear chapter on language development and another relating to social development.

Konner, M (1991) *Childhood: A Multicultural View.* London: Little, Brown and Company.

A little old now, but this book is full of insights into the cultural impacts on human development.

Vygotsky, L (1933) Play and its Role in The Mental Development of the Child in *Voprosy Psikhologii,* 1966, No.6; translated by Catherine Mulholland available through Psychology and Marxism Internet Archive (marxists.org) 2002 **www.marxists.org/archive/vygotsky/works/1933/ play.htm** accessed 30/01/2012.

Again, a chance to read Vygotsky's mention of proximal development in an original translation of his work relating to play.

7 Play, creativity and risk

Through reading this chapter, you will:

- find out more about concepts of creativity and possibility thinking in early childhood and beyond;

- explore both the emotional impacts of play (the desire for exhilaration) and the risky aspects that result;

- consider the meaning and implications of deep play;

- discover more about concepts of risk and risk benefit analysis, creativity and possibility thinking, and make links with relevant observed play behaviours.

The chapter will also have exercises to help readers to consider their perspective on risk, emotion and creativity.

Introduction

At first glance this chapter may appear to be considering three concepts that are not entirely related. You may be wondering about the leap from creativity to risk. We have already considered how play is sometimes about turning things upside down, seeing the world from a different perspective, challenging the 'normal' way of doing things. A child will therefore try to go up the slippery part of a slide, or down a slide head first. Children will push at the boundaries of *what is possible* and create new ways of doing things, new understandings for themselves. These new ways of doing things might be seen as creativity or creative thinking. However, such ideas will not always align with the adult's perspectives and rules, nor indeed be operating safely. There is therefore a risk element to the promotion of children's creativity through play. This risk element needs acknowledging and managing in a way that does not stifle further creativity in young children, but rather supports the creative spirit that emerges through play.

So in this chapter we will initially explore the concept of creativity and the importance of supporting children's creative play in a range of contexts, considering the difference between creation and construction. The chapter will then move on to a consideration of the emotional aspects of creativity, and the management of potential risk or benefit.

What is creativity?

Creativity means many things to many people. One of the problems of discussing creativity is that it does not have a neat definition. In society as a whole technically skilled artists are described as *creative*; creativity is used in business to stimulate *thinking outside the box* to generate new ideas; and creative activities in early years settings are often about gluing, sticking and constructing artefacts to take home. The terms 'creative' and 'art' are often juxtaposed, as in the phrase *the creative arts* and some practitioners may consider creative activities therefore to be painting, drama, dance or music.

ACTIVITY 1

Take a few moments here to reflect on creativity in your setting.

Would you say that your setting stimulates creativity? How?

What kinds of things do the children do that you would consider as creative?

Do you plan for creativity? What kinds of activities do you offer?

Are there creative artefacts, paintings, wall hangings and so on in your setting?

Do you have a consistent view of creativity within your team?

Could you define creativity?

These are useful prompts for reflection on your setting's practice and you may find it helpful to revisit your answers to these as you finish reading this chapter.

It is interesting to note that there appear to be conflicting views of creativity emerging in government documents. The Practice Guidance to the Early Years Foundation Stage (DCSF, 2008a) promoted creativity as an area of learning which offered to practitioners a broad definition of creativity.

- *Creativity is about taking risks and making connections and is strongly linked to play.*
- *Creativity emerges as children become absorbed in action and explorations of their own ideas, expressing them through movement, making and transforming things using media and materials such as crayons, paints, scissors, words, sounds, movement, props and make-believe.*
- *Creativity involves children in initiating their own learning and making choices and decisions.*

(DCSF/EYFS Practice Guidance, 2008a, page 106)

In the new Development Matters (DfE 2012b, page 7) we are also told that *play is a key opportunity for children to think creatively and flexibly, solve problems and link ideas.*

Compare the above quotations with the one below which is taken from the newly issued 'Final Areas of Learning and Early Learning Goals' (DfE, 2012a) in which creativity has been replaced with *expressive arts and design*:

> *Expressive arts and design involves supporting children to explore and play with a wide range of media and materials, as well as providing opportunities and encouragement for sharing their thoughts, ideas and feelings through a variety of activities in art, music, movement, dance, role-play, and design and technology.*

(DfE, 2012a, page 5)

Here the idea of creativity returns to a position of the alignment of creativity to art, and the breadth of opportunity for creative activity in a setting is reduced to the use of a wide range of media and materials. Interestingly it also encompasses emotional expression. Thomson and Sefton-Green (2011) acknowledge that whilst there are emerging common understandings about the meaning of creativity in the broadest sense, it may also be squeezed into association with particular subjects such as *the arts* and be limited to a particular understanding, such as manipulating materials.

ACTIVITY 2

Some three year olds are sitting around the nursery table. It is close to Christmas and on the table are six green cards, six cut-out shapes resembling a horse's head, 12 sets of antlers cut out of card, six red noses made of small fluffy balls, a marker pen and some glitter. 'Come on,' said the practitioner, 'we are going to make reindeer cards to take home'. She was full of enthusiasm. The children were each given a green card and a glue stick. It was pointed out to them where they should glue, and then stick down onto the glue the card reindeer head. 'Well done,' was the response when the head was in the right place. 'No, not that way up, let me do it for you', when the head was upside down. The children then drew on the eyes and stuck on the two antlers per reindeer. They glued on the red nose. Finally the children were allowed to put the glitter wherever they liked on the card. Some children did big sweeping marks with the glue, others did dots or swirls. The glitter and the drawn eyes were the only differences between the six cards. The children seemed to enjoy the activity and each proudly went home with their reindeer card.

Would you consider the above to be a creative activity?

Was it of value to the children? In what way?

Was it play?

Is there a difference between construction (the putting together of parts to make something according to a pattern or template) and creativity (which is more aligned to possibility thinking – and children making their own choices and decisions).

To my mind this activity was about manipulating materials for construction. There was a product for the child to take home (which in turn can give esteem from praise). The children seemed to enjoy the activity.

ACTIVITY 2 continued

However, I would not consider this to be creative, but construction. The children had no choice where to put the different elements, which were all pre-cut and offered no real challenge. They were merely putting them together. There was no opportunity to alter the design or freely choose what they did with the pieces so, although enjoyable, I would not term this a play activity.

The Early Years Foundation Stage approach clearly aligned creativity and play across a range of activities. Anna Craft (2001) identified creativity as an everyday activity, aligned with *possibility thinking* and involving a shift from asking *what is this and what does it do?* to *what can I do with this?* (Craft, Cremin, Burnard, and Chappell, 2007, page 267). This aligns with Corinne Hutt's (1979) epistemic and ludic play acknowledged in Chapter 2.

Here is another approach, an educator's perspective: *When educators talk about creative learning they generally mean teaching that allows students to use their imaginations, have ideas, generate multiple solutions to problems, communicate in a variety of media and generally think outside the box* (Thomson and Sefton-Green, 2011, page 2). Here the definition is about generating ideas, possibilities and solutions, as well as communicating these ideas in interesting ways.

Jenkinson offers a similar perspective when making the point that creativity is linked to the concept of *what might be*. The creator moves from the position of concrete explorer of *what is* to considerations of:

- What was...?
- What could have been?
- What can one try for...?
- What might happen...?

And use of an imagination that moves right away from the concrete to *the purest realms of fantasy using that miracle of human experience, the imagination* (Jenkinson, 2001, page 58).

She expands creativity to the clear sky thinking, of an imaginal space that can lead the child anywhere. In order to make this clear she gives the example that *few men and no women have set foot on the moon, yet thousands and millions of children have been there, in a variety of self-assembled play spacecraft, or in invisible flights of swift and soaring imagination* (Jenkinson, 2001, page 59).

Finally let us look at a definition that does offer a kind of playful, carefree energy, but is also slightly chaotic:

Creativity to me means mess, freedom, jumbled thoughts, words and deeds each fighting to claim their own space in my mind, and deciding, given even small amounts of free time, whether I shall write, paint, draw, take off to the beach with a camera, run outside, turn my house upside down to create a new environment...in a more formal sense it is the original thought, the spark, the ignition, the original design concept of the blueprint.

(Thorne, 2007, page 17)

Thorne here expresses an understanding of creativity as rather random, chaotic, the chance coming together of ideas and the motivation to take action.

This section may feel rather like a list of different definitions of creativity, and in a sense it is. The intention of this list is to help you to think about the range of under-standings about creativity, and to consider which you would choose. Do you perceive creativity as artistic expression and the skilled manipulation of materials and other resources (including the human body in dance) to reveal messages about emotions and ideas. Is it controlled artistry? Or are you adopting a broad definition in which creativity is about generating new possibilities every day? I am definitely with Kay Thorne and the last slightly chaotic approach. Creativity for me does involve juxtapo-sition of unusual elements, a fight between the energy of creating something new, and the need to control this freedom to produce the things needed. Creativity is about access to a wide range of resources, enabling you or the children to suddenly mix together the unusual to be somewhere new. This last definition of Thorne's perhaps also aligns to the idea of play as being a process operating *on the edge of chaos* (Battram and Russell, 2002).

THEORY FOCUS

The edge of chaos

Battram and Russell (2002) compare the management of play to the experience of a wave. Before the wave breaks, there is calm and order but stasis, and lack of energy. After the wave breaks, there is turbulence and chaos, unpredictable energy. At the curl of the breaking wave there is a delicate balance between order and chaos.

If we apply this to an early childhood setting then the pre-wave state may represent a very calm and ordered setting, with expected daily activity. It is a little dull and not inventive, prescribed and with expected outcome.

On the other hand if we look at the chaotic setting represented by the broken wave it is poorly organised and haphazard. There are perhaps safety issues, and care is not taken with the materials and resources available.

At the crest of the wave is where the balance is between order and chaos. It is where there is most energy. Resources and environment are ordered to allow for spontaneity and creativity in children's activity and unpredictability. The crest of the wave offers a framework for creativity.

This metaphor of surfing successfully on the edge of chaos indicates how a creative, energetic play setting would work. It does indicate the role of the adult at the point of balance, and that it takes some skill to surf!

Play and creation: possibility thinking in action

If offered open-ended and freely chosen play, the young child can select from her own resources, and behaviours, and control them, manipulating them in new ways. This allows the child to generate new thoughts and options. Play opens up more possibilities than are usually seen in a more structured approach; so it is in play that interesting things happen.

Imagine children being read a fairy story that has a moral tale. Usually the practitioner reads the story then sits with the children at circle time and the children are asked questions to check they have understood the tale. This indicated to the practitioner varying levels of understanding by the children, particularly in relation to the emotions. She asked questions about the character's feelings in the story. The children answered the questions, but remained a little unsure about the feelings.

The next time the practitioner told a similar story she made sure that she had resources available for children to dress up and dramatically re-tell the story to each other. This was a great success as children were exploring the story by *doing*. They were also taking the story further, exploring what it was like to be the farmer's boy or the princess locked away. This gave them greater understanding of the feelings of fear and happiness, as well as of friendship and adventure.

Such benefits have been researched and the use of *thematic-fantasy play* has been found to be more effective than adult-led discussion in developing story comprehension by children under eight years of age (Pellegrini and Galda, 1982). Furthermore, the use of *thematic-fantasy play* also had a positive effect on the ability of children to retell stories in future. The creativity of active exploration of the tale by acting it out (with embellishments) led to greater ability to both explore options and understand more.

The greater the encouragement to play; the greater the child's developmental ability to take control of his or her play and so the greater potential for creativity in future. I am not writing of artistic creativity alone, but the creative ability to adjust, amend, overturn and create new possibilities and ways forward not yet imagined. Most artists will say that the more they paint the more ideas spring into their minds. If they do not paint for a while, or are constrained by the boundaries of a commission, the painting becomes harder! Here we may revisit Csikszentmihalyi's *flow* and the optimum zone for creativity that has not too much, nor too little pressure for the artist in flow (Csikszentmihalyi, 2002).

The Singers in their work showed at considerable length the levels of cognitive flexibility that imaginative children possess – their capacity for delay, for redirection, for alternative routes. Such flexibility they argue, exceeds that of other animals, because it moves beyond a use of play as practice for the future, to the realms of human imagination in which things can be used as other things, ideas can be embedded in symbols, and children can imagine they can fly. As Sutton-Smith claimed (1979, page 315), *to play with something is to open it up for consideration and choice. Play opens up thought.* For the Singers this thought is opened up to the *limitless range of the human imagination* (Singer and Singer, 2001, page 22). The story-telling practitioner allowed children to *play with the ideas of the story* and so they were able to pursue their thinking in a relaxed way, which in turn led to both consolidation of the under-standings, and further creative thinking stimulated by the ideas or materials used.

Creative object play

You may recall that object play was another category of play that Hughes (2001) identified in his taxonomy. This too was a creative response in the broader sense of possibility thinking of *what can I do with this object?* There is a close link between exploratory play and object play. The former being about finding out about an object's properties and possibilities and the latter about novel use of it, or manipula-tion of it in unusual and interesting sequences, often with increasing challenge. Nunnally and Lemond (1973) indicate that a child's specific exploration of an object leads to play which consolidates ideas and fosters creativity again. Think here of how young children will explore a bucket or pot, and then try out some basic but different uses, perhaps as a hat, or a pretend bowl. Older children will explore what a ball can do: how high it can bounce; what ways they can catch it; what happens if it bounces on different surfaces; can they throw it and swivel round before catching it again? The sequences of creativity get more and more complicated the older the child becomes. The player is seeking alternative possibilities and also seeking mastery over these possibilities.

Emotional aspects of play: possibility thinking about self

Another aspect of creativity is the potential for play to allow exploration of alternative aspects of self. A baby will be struggling with concepts of sense of self in relation to others. Their understandings of themselves are very concrete at first, based on what is experienced, immediate behaviours and experiences. They then progress through a phase which has a little more flexibility, but with clear rules and fairly rigid concepts so they gradually acquire more abstract understandings of self and others. Role-play has an important part to play in children's exploration of self. Children can be creative in seeking alternative possibilities, perhaps initially such as *I am a builder like the char-acter on TV*, or even, as in Vygotsky's example two sisters undertaking meta thinking on what it is like to be a sister. Children can play creatively: *who can I be like today?* They can dress up as adults, shopkeepers, dentists. Young children can select from their own behaviours and manipulate them in new ways in a safe space. So testing their self-concept and how they may be perceived by others. A child can come to nursery in his superman costume and be superman for the day. This is creativity with ideas of self. Depending on the context such playful behaviour can lead to increased self-esteem.

Therefore creative play has potential for adaptation, experimentation, new potentials including potential self. Through play many other alternatives are possible. Creativity in play increases the repertoire of behaviours, understandings, actions that children may subsequently use in life. Whether the skills or perceptions of self are maintained or pruned depends to some extent on the cultural encouragement of others.

Let us now look at a more problematic play, one that may not receive the cultural encouragement of others, but which is important.

The problem with play: dizzy and deep

Children may take this emotional exploration through play a step further by exploring a form of play that Hughes (2001) calls *deep play* or Kalliala (2006) names *dizzy play*. Deep play is play that allows the child to encounter risky or even potentially life-threatening experiences, to develop survival skills and conquer fear. Kalliala, in writing of the culture of play in a changing world, recognises a destructive, challenging *dizzy play*, which *holds itself across time* and is at one moment a physical spinning round to feel good about dizziness, and in another using foul language purposely. It is the moment of rough and tumble and mock fighting, jumping on the bed, and doing just enough to *turn the world upside down* (Kalliala, 2006, page 102).

The creativity in this kind of play is the seeking of alternative ways to test oneself physically and emotionally. It is by undertaking risky behaviour that children learn what they are capable of. Play can be an appropriate way of channelling children's energies into controllable situations, where they experience *danger*, explore *appropriate* behaviour and gradually learn the nature of behaviour with others. For example, Coulter and Taylor, (2001 citing Stone, 1971) contend that *much childhood play takes the form of deliberately perpetuating loss of poise with the unintended, but highly important, consequence of preparing the child for the maintenance of self control in later life* (page 11). We could think again of Athey's (2004) recognition that children play on the edge of their comfort zone, needing to be safe in standing before they play ring-a-ring-a-roses, which requires falling down. Such play will have emotional effects, whether positive or not, and children may misjudge the challenge. Therefore play is the place to take risks and make mistakes, to learn and amend behaviours before the pretence is really experienced. The creativity here is in seeking future possibilities, including death and danger, and testing them in the current.

The act of destruction: creativity and impulse

If creativity is possibility thinking and the creation of something new, how do we perceive the act of negation that indicates control by one of the players in a social space? We now know that even the young baby will close its eyes and end the social dialogue of play. Slightly older babies will turn their heads away. Pre-school children may try to control others in, or run away from, the play space they have created if it offers negative emotional effect to them. They may join another nearby as they *flit* from one frame into another. The emotional experience and reaction to it may offer opportunity for resilience; *finding ways to function in a world in which bad things happen* (Gill, 2007). Such play behaviour involves willpower, the junction of self-will and power, enabling children to explore and cope with life experiences, making decisions for action, now and later.

Research tells us that the uncertainty and challenge of much of children's play is both a large part of its appeal to them but also that it enhances development of their brains, making them more adaptable and resilient as they grow (Sutcliffe and Voce in Ball, Gill and Spiegal, 2008, page 5).

It has become more acceptable that taking risks is an integral part of play. Risk cannot be entirely eliminated for any child, and there is a question as to whether it should be? How will children learn to manage risk if it is removed entirely from their experiences.

Exploring risk and play

ACTIVITY 3

What do these words mean to you?

Safe

Hazard

Risk

Chance

Reflect on what you have written. Are these all negative in your eyes?

Tim Gill recognises the need for risk in play for older children: *We need to move from a philosophy of protection to a philosophy of resilience. Instead of doing risk assessments where the goal is always risk reduction we should be doing risk benefit assessments: to recognise the upside of risk* (Gill, 2010, National College of School Leadership Viewpoint). He cites the Health and Safety Executive (HSE) which also recognises that *sensible risk management is not about creating a totally risk-free society* (HSE, 2008, cited by Gill, 2007). If we had a risk-free society children would not be encouraged to walk on the top of walls, to jump down steps, or even to run on uneven surfaces. There is a tension between fear of potential harm and enabling children to take those chances that offer deep play experiences. Gill considers we may be protecting children too much such that they cannot manage their own risks.

> *Unless children are allowed to take a degree of responsibility and to gain some experience in how to do this, adults in many contexts will feel under ever more pressure to intervene. At worst this could fuel a vicious circle where children's alleged vulnerability provides the rationale for excessive interference, leading to a loss of experiential learning opportunities that in turn leaves children more vulnerable.*
>
> (Gill, 2007, page 84)

Protection from risk resulting in a vicious circle of vulnerability and over-protection is something that many disabled children report they have experienced: an over-protection preventing their opportunities for creativity, risk and physical challenge – all essentials of play. In order to put this into perspective think of how risky it is for a young child to take their first steps between two people with outstretched arms. There is a high chance they will fall down. There is a likelihood of a few bumps and bruises in the process of learning to walk. We would be safer on all fours, but we don't stop children learning to walk for fear of the risk!

Deep play and risk benefit analysis

Children need an element of self-direction and opportunity for challenge or *risk*. Gill (2007) highlights that there are *good risks* and *bad risks* and we should learn to distinguish between the two. The good risks are those that challenge children and prompt actions to support growth and development. Good hazards and risks include different levels, steps, slopes, things that move and things to climb on. Having animals in a setting offers hazard and risk, as do loose outdoor materials (sand, gravel, water play) that allow children to explore and create. These may be good resources too.

Bad risks and hazards are those that the children may find it difficult to assess for themselves or that have hidden dangers. So sharp points, nails sticking out, uneven and wobbly steps are bad hazards with a high risk of accident and no play purpose. A knife may be a bad risk or hazard if unsupervised, but become a good hazard with lower risk if supervised to a high level in an activity appropriate for the ages of the children.

An element of creativity is the way that children seek out chances to test themselves and develop their abilities as they get to grips with the world around them. In order to achieve a full experience there will inevitably be some risks and hazards to engage with and manage. It is surely better that they learn how to do this than to later experience hazards having only ever been safe from them before, such that they have no experience of how to handle them?

> *...given children's appetite for risk-taking one of the factors that should be considered is the likelihood that children will seek out risks elsewhere in environments that are not controlled or designed for them, if play provision is not challenging enough. Another factor is the learning that can take place when children are exposed to and have to learn to deal with environmental hazards. Play provision is uniquely placed to offer children the chance to learn about risk in an environment designed for that purpose and thus to help children equip themselves to deal with similar hazards in the wider world.*
>
> (Ball, Gill and Spiegal, 2008, page 17)

A risk benefit analysis considers whether there are any benefits of hazards in terms of challenges and learning in relation to safe management of risk by children.

THEORY FOCUS

The meaning of words

Safe: A concept of a position in which there is no risk of harm at all. However, children of all ages need challenge in their play: *you can't make everything safe and a balance is needed between risks and fun. Children recognise that knowing about risks and how to manage them is an essential part of growing up* (DCSF, 2007).

Hazard: A hazard is anything that may cause harm, such as chemicals, a broken step, a frayed rope holding a swing, broken glass in the nursery and so on.

Risk: Risk is the chance that someone could be harmed by a hazard. It should be scored high or low depending on the likelihood of that harm and how serious the harm could be.

Chance: The possibility, probability or likelihood of something happening. However, it also means luck, fate and fortune. The word chance both implies unpredictability, and sounds inviting, positive. We may use it in a positive way: There is a chance that x will happen... or in a more controlled way, there is a high chance of Jim falling off that slide! A chance may or may not happen.

You were asked earlier to think about these words. How do these definitions match up to your own? Does your own response indicate anything in particular about the way that you perceive risks and hazards? Are you *risk averse*, seeking an entirely safe space, or *risk careless*, perhaps allowing too many hazards (operating in the chaos?). Perhaps you have revealed a balanced position.

SUMMARY

We have considered opportunities for creativity and how creativity may reveal itself as possibility thinking across a range of contexts; from creative play with materials and fantasy to creative, risky, play relating to physical and emotional self. This concern for risky play led to a consideration of health and safety management in the childcare setting and the need to promote opportunity for manageable risk, highlighting the risk benefits, of a situation or experience.

FURTHER READING

Thorne, K (2007) *Essential Creativity in the Classroom: Inspiring Kids.* London: Routledge.

Although the title may imply it is a book of activities this is in fact a great little book that offers a range of insights into creativity, what it is, and what you need to do to both realise your own creativity and to help stimulate children's creativity.

Wyse, D and Dowson, P (2009) *The Really Useful Creativity Book.* London: Routledge.

Aimed at primary school age range, this book has useful concepts and activities that can be adapted for the nursery setting. Includes information on Heathcote's 'Mantle of the Expert' in which children take on the roles of experts, exploration of the environment and a chapter on 'everyday creativity'.

8 Contexts for play

Through reading this chapter, you will:

- consider the many and varied places in which children play;
- reflect on your use of indoor and outdoor play and the environmental connections;
- be prompted to consider the value and limitations of a range of contexts, including time boundaries to play;
- learn about concepts of *affordance*, *loose parts*, and the *imaginal theatre* (that is self-constructed).

Through reading this chapter you will become more aware of the many and varied opportunities for play that lie beyond the nursery, and that these may in turn shape your ideas for qualitative improvement within your play spaces.

Introduction

Having considered in previous chapters how play benefits children physically, socially and emotionally, this chapter will change perspective to consider the environment for play. It focuses on where it happens: indoors or outdoors; a theatrical space, or challenging space; the importance of nature; or a calm interior.

Play in an early years setting with its concerns for safety and routine must be to some extent *play within boundaries* (there are boundary fences if not doors with high handles and limited flexibility for movement). We will consider how these bounded spaces may be managed to maximise play opportunity. In order to consider the alternative experiences we will look at what research tells us about children's views of play spaces.

ACTIVITY 1

And that park grew up with me, that small world widened as I learned its secret boundaries, as I discovered new refuges in the wood and jungles; hidden homes and lairs for the multitudes of imagination, for cowboys and Indians and the tall terrible half-people who rode on nightmares...

(Dylan Thomas, Reminiscences of Childhood, BBC Radio, 1943)

continued

---

*ACTIVITY **1** continued*

The above passage is a transcript from a radio interview with the Welsh poet Dylan Thomas. Here he reminisces about the park he used to play in as a child and offers us an indication of some of the important aspects of the environment on children. He mentions boundaries, in this case secret *boundaries, and also the opportunity for multitudes of imagination; there are opportunities for dens in* hidden homes and lairs. *There seems to be an excitement and risk indicated.*

- *Recall again your own childhood play spaces (this can be outdoors or indoors).*
- *If you have children consider where they like to play now.*
- *Try to identify what it is about those spaces that made or make them favourites for playful behaviours.*
- *Make a list of the characteristics of the places you recall or identify*
- *Use this list to audit your setting space. How does it measure up?*

Many settings are now aware of the need for outdoor spaces designed with different areas and hiding places. However, there are still many places that have large grass expanses without slopes to run down or shrubs to hide behind. Indoors the emphasis may be more on teaching with room layout limited to the six areas of learning and offering little in the way of child initiated and fantasy play adventures.

What do we know about children's play environment needs?

The Opies (1984) undertook a major piece of research into children's play in the 1960s and identified a wide range of street games and activities. Many had complex rules, and offered risk and challenge within these. Many were very similar although spread across widely different parts of the country. Children in Northumberland played similar games to children in London, but with different names. One of the major conclusions from this piece of work was that consideration should be given to the environments we create for children's play.

> *Children's games are ones which the players adapt to their surroundings in the time available. In fact, most street games are as happily played in the dark as in the light. To a child 'sport is sweetest when there are no spectators'. The places they like best are the secret places 'where no one else goes'... to a child there is more joy in a rubbish tip than in a flowering rockery, in a fallen tree than in a piece of statuary, in a muddy track than in a gravel path...Yet the cult among his elders is to trim, to pave, to smooth out, to clean up, to prettify, to convert to economic advantage...*
>
> (Opie and Opie, page 15)

In this passage the Opies highlight that children will play anywhere, adapting to the surroundings and the time available. They raise the issue of needing spaces away from adults, spaces *where there are no spectators*, where no one else goes. They also highlight a child's interest in the messy parts of life; interests in a fallen tree, a muddy track, and even 'rubbish'. Children love to dig in the garden, and climb on fallen trees (largely because they more easily offer the opportunity for climbing). We are also more aware of children's love of 'rubbish' for the flexibility it affords them in their play. The classic example is the large cardboard box that can become a house, a spaceship, a lorry or many other things in a child's fantasy play. At the Eden project's Den Building activity other kinds of 'rubbish' such as rubber inner tubes, pipes, bits of fabric, poles and ties, become play things with which children can make and decorate their dens. Settings regularly use small pieces of 'rubbish' for junk modelling and craft activities. The scrapstore PlayPod project allows children at school break time to play with recycled 'scrap': pipes, fabric, blocks, foam, large wooden reels and other factory off cuts or society cast offs.

Children are natural fiddlers

Children are natural 'fiddlers'. They do not need to be told to interact with any new object, apparatus or environment. They do so spontaneously, and in so doing discover important properties of objects and how things work. Adopting a naïve approach, but perhaps informed by past experiences, they will identify novel uses for existing objects, even those designed for adult tool purposes (Bjorklund and Gardiner, 2011). Hands-on, experiential opportunity is important, and objects will invite *discovery* such that a child will experience its properties through exploration. Children (and adults) seem programmed to pick up something that looks interesting, or to press something that looks as if it should be pressed. Gibson's theory of *affordances* explains a little further how this mechanism works.

THEORY FOCUS

Gibson's affordances

The affordances of the environment are what it offers [a person], what it provides or furnishes either for good or ill. The verb to afford is found in the dictionary but the noun 'affordances' is not... I mean by it something that refers to both the environment and the [person] in a way that no existing term does.

(Gibson, 1996, page 133)

The term 'affordances' is one made up by Gibson to reflect the fact that objects, or aspects of the environment invite us to use them in certain ways. It implies the complementarity of the person and the environment, influencing each other for a reaction. Something in the environment triggers a response that leads to behaviour. In well-designed objects the response may remain obviously consistent even where there are two people looking at it (a chair for sitting on, for example, or a button to push). In other cases two people may have two very different responses according to their own experiences.

---

continued

Here are some examples of affordance.

- A chair looks so obviously for sitting on that it invites 'sit on me'.
- A piece of fruit that is known to the onlooker says 'eat me'.
- A glass of water placed in front of you on a table says 'drink me'.
- A slot in a post box says 'post something in here'.
- A handle, whether on a door, or a box says 'grasp me'.

Portchmouth (1969) recalls his response to the affordances of a bucket, spade and sand.

> *I don't remember how it started. There was me, and sand, and somehow there was a wooden spade: and then there were castles! I don't even remember asking how to do it; the need was big enough and the way was there.*
>
> (Portchmouth, 1969, page 1)

Portchmouth was invited by the sand, bucket and spade to create the sand castles!

There may be many affordances in an object – which include its 'proper' use and some potential variants of this use. So a table has the affordance of sitting at it, but may also have the affordance of being overturned or being something to crawl under. Gibson states that the affordances are always there in the objects and the participant can choose whether to take them up or not.

In children's play terms we should be very aware of the affordances of objects and select our resources carefully. The more potential affordances an object has the better its play value will be. The cardboard box that says 'put things in me', 'climb in me', 'sit in me', 'push me around', or even 'squash me', has a great number of affordances. A piece of rope will invite children to tie it, make boundaries with it, measure it, skip with it, make it wiggle or make a shape with it. Some commercial toys have limited affordances, having been designed for specific actions, there may be buttons that say 'push me', and something pops up...but that is the limit of the flexibility in what they do. The button pops up, and the baby pushes it down. Fixed into a white plastic frame it can do nothing else and so has limited affordance.

Gibson argued that the affordance of something does not change as the need of the person near it changes, but is always there in the object, waiting to be perceived. The object offers what it does because of what it is. However, there is also an element of experience required in the perception of the affordance. It is perhaps the experience of seeing sand castles made in a bucket on a beach, for example, that makes the bucket have an affordance of a sand castle mould for Portchmouth.

Children may also perceive affordances slightly differently to adults who have expected ideas of what an object is for. Again a classic example of this was the slot designed for video tapes. The slot was designed to say 'post in me' – but only video tapes. Young children perceived the affordance of this slot to be 'post in me' without knowing the expected limit to purpose, and busily posted all the small toys they could find into the slot.

Cultural influence on interpretation of affordances

Although Gibson argued that affordances are always there in an object to be perceived, it may be that the perception is culturally determined. It is only when the bucket is seen making a sand castle that it is perceived as a mould. Bjorklund and Gardiner (2011) also identified that although hands-on, experiential activity is important in discovery of the properties of an item, it is observation of others that often promotes an item's use as a tool. Gibson argues that a round object of a certain weight invites throwing, for example, but Bjorklund and Gardiner would claim only if a child had seen something similar being thrown. Children's ability to learn through observation plays a critical role in learning to use these tools or objects with a particular primary affordance. So children in majority world countries may from an early age use tools like toys, but for their proper purpose (Rogoff, 2003; Konner, 1991).

Bob Hughes (2002) had identified two closely related play types: *exploratory play*, which involved exploring an object in order to see what it could do; and *object play*, which involved playing with one object in a number of new and interesting ways. Bjorklund and Gardiner (2011) are concerned that there is no clear delineation between these play types, but that children will swiftly move from identifying the properties and key affordances of an object to object play, with interesting sequences of use. So the rope is explored to be a rope, of certain weight, but then the variations in its affordances are tested as it is used for physical play in jumping or skipping, cognitive play as it becomes a boundary, or therapeutic play as it is gently swung around with a knot at one end, the weight making it feel good to the person swinging it.

The affordances are there to be perceived and used. The exploratory play may identify them, and the object play will repeat them.

THEORY FOCUS

Nicholson's loose parts

Whilst Gibson argued objects have affordances, the architect Nicholson (1971) recognised that a range of things with affordances in an environment prompted greater creativity and possibility thinking: *In any environment, both the degree of inventiveness and creativity, and the possibility of discovery, are directly proportional to the number and kind of variables in it* (Nicholson, 1971, page 30).

By this he meant that the more different things lying around, that could be moved, changed, and used in different ways, the more that the users of these spaces could be inventive and creative in responding to the objects. Flexible opportunities exist for individual development within the environmental space. Think here of a play area that has crates, planks and guttering (with water too perhaps). Children will probably begin to build, they may balance, and they will roll things down slopes, and will learn by exploration without being led. The types of *loose parts* provided may be directed in part by a

continued

THEORY FOCUS *continued*

practitioner's understanding of some children's needs (perhaps for extension of interests, perhaps bearing in mind such as grasp or pincer grip development so requiring some larger, easier to grasp objects) but the parts themselves should be arranged to invite use and be subsequently rearranged by the children according to their needs or interests. The environment as a whole, not merely the object, has flexible affordance to the children using it.

Moveable items crossing boundaries

It is important that children are able to move objects around in the play space. Bilton (2010) highlights how restrictive it can be to a child to be told that they cannot follow through their explorations, giving the example of a 'cake' that a child made of sand not being allowed in the home corner for fear of getting sand on the indoor toys. You may recall that we considered Piaget (Piaget and Inhelder,1969) and Athey (2004) in their realisation that children have *schemas* or clusters of thought that need exploring through action at the pre-accommodation stage. They will need to follow their particular interests or concerns in non adult-directed activity (which I call play). Therefore it is important that if children have a *transporting* schema they are able to *transport* or carry objects from one place to another. That rope with plenty of affordances may then be used to *enclose* a number of other items taken out of the indoor context to an area that allows for this laying out.

Bilton (2010) cites Matthews' (1994) discussion of visual representation and how a child followed an interest in fire, mixing drawing materials and toys such as blocks, straws and a sleeping bag as he explored his interest. It was an ongoing project that needed a flexible environment and supportive staff who would not clear it away at the end of each session but would leave it for him to rediscover and take to another level – when he returned. Sutton-Smith argued that it is important to allow children the freedom to *attempt the varying permutations of the possibilities before them* (Sutton-Smith, 1979, page 315). In so doing children can explore Craft's (2001) possibility thinking, and the shift from *what is this?* to *what can I do with it?*

THEORY FOCUS

Compound flexibility

Frazer Brown also recognises this connection between the child's thinking and the flexibility of the environment. Building on Piaget and Inhelder (1969) and Hughes' (2001) discussion of *combinatorial flexibility*, he proposes the notion of *compound flexibility*. This was an *interrelationship* between the flexibility and adaptability of the child and a flexible/adaptable environment.

THEORY FOCUS *continued*

The ideal developmental cycle for a human being (especially a child) involves the gradual growth of an interaction between a flexible environment and an increasingly flexible human being. In other words, given ideal conditions, the growing child makes use of whatever flexibility there is in the environment, and so becomes more flexible, and able to make even better use of elements of flexibility in the environment – and so on. This process may be characterized as 'compound flexibility'.

(Brown, 2003, page 53)

These authors are arguing for environments for play as fundamental to flexible learning and development. This approach entails using resources which are made available for children to adjust and adapt as they wish. Outdoors this may be crates, guttering, planks, seating and other large construction type materials.

The theory of loose parts could also be applied to indoor play, think of block play, or the use of Lego® or other construction play resources. It may mean putting different resources for different *areas of learning* together. Surely having Lego, sand and small world play together is a *loose parts* approach? Even the home corner could be an area of *loose parts*; offering structures and things that children can have the freedom to put together in different ways.

ACTIVITY **2**

Why not do another quick audit of your setting and see how many flexible loose parts resources you have available for children's play.

Do you have expectations of use of objects or materials that may constrain children's creative play?

How do you feel if children move things from one area to another?

Are they able to shape their own environments?

Where might your boundaries to such flexibility be. Why?

Is there a balance to be found between flexibility and a structured environment?

Exploring some contexts for play

Children will play anywhere there is time, space and resource. That means that there are endless environmental contexts for play. Children play in the countryside, in the streets, in the nursery and in the home, indoors and out of doors. They will play in school playtimes, in after-school clubs, and sometimes in their own neighbourhoods after school. Babies play in the nursery, largely with people, or with their own bodies, on the changing mat, and at meal times. Time is key to this process and perhaps the first boundary we should consider.

Children need time to play. In just ten minutes they are not going to be able to create their environments, explore affordances and progress to the deeper forms of play. They may only begin the cycle of play. It may be that a child does quickly get into *flow* but then must be jolted out of it again for *snack time* or some other routine. Montessori settings allow for set periods of time, taking most of the morning session for children to pursue their *occupations*. Resources are displayed in order of difficulty, encouraging the child to pick up the challenge (Lilliard, 1982). One of Montessori's contribution to modern understanding of play was the importance of a managed environment within which the child is not directed but facilitated. Time boundaries do shape how children play, and thought should be given to time as a *context* for play.

Let us now move on to explore what some of the options for play and playful behaviour might be in different environmental contexts.

Play indoors in an early years setting: learning or playing or both?

The capacity for the indoor setting to offer play depends on how you perceive your role and the way in which children learn. Indoor play potential can as a result be either restricted or very much encouraged. The EYFS (DfE 2012a, page 3) indicates *Children learn and develop well in enabling environments in which their experiences respond to their individual needs...* and that children must have opportunities to play indoors and outdoors. It also requires that providers ensure a balance of child-initiated and adult-led, play-based activities.

There should, therefore, be plenty of opportunity for a range of indoor play experiences. However, the form the indoor play takes often depends on the confidence of the practitioner to allow for a more child-led approach. If one is less confident with both child development and the learning outcomes, then more time will be spent on planning to the guidance. Experienced practitioners with well assimilated understanding of child development and good recall of the *development matters* indicators will often work from the child's play, merely *capturing* those aspects required.

Indoor play in an early childhood setting consequently varies from setting to setting: with some very structured areas for learning intending to lead playful instruction according to the curriculum outcomes; to a flexible space with resources and planning that follows a child's interests in play, from which the learning will occur.

It is interesting that there is much currently written on the outdoor space, and yet there seems to be a need to revisit approaches to indoor spaces for play. In their longitudinal study of an early years setting Broadhead and Burt (2012) focused initially on the outdoors but noted the restriction of the indoor space as the latter was more structured and less fascinating for both the children playing and adults observing. Although some children liked the structure of the prescriptive spaces indoors, the researchers identified that the children usually started to tentatively play in a defined space such as the home corner, gradually warming up to allow the play to progress across the whole indoor space having 'raided' other resources to take there.

The flexible 'whatever you want it to be' space

Having carefully observed the children's play actions in their indoor room, and in order to create a more playful space, Broadhead and Burt (2012) and the staff team created a *'whatever you want it to be'* space. This space is described as *the environment and its possibilities as perceived and engaged with from the child's perspective* (page 142). Effectively a den space created indoors with a canopy of fabric, this was a space where anything was possible, and children can engage alone or with others in *exploring and exploiting that environment to match the images, plans and memories that emerge from their own minds, experiences and skills* (page 142). The researchers found that although the den might be empty in the morning, children would gather items from all over the nursery to take to the den in some very complex play activities, both social and cognitive. By the end of the day, the den would be full of items explored and transformed. This in turn led the researchers to highlight how limiting the learning outcomes were against the richness of achievements and developments seen in free play within the *'whatever you want it to be'* place. They had effectively designed an *indoor theatre or arena for play*, a play space for creative action.

ACTIVITY 3

a) *Try to put yourself in a child's shoes and look around the setting you know. Take time to observe not just one child, but how the children use the space. You may wish to use a series of tracking observations.*

Is it attractive to a child or laid out for the convenience of adult planning?

Which areas do the children use most?

Drop down to a child's level. Try to see the visual impact of the room. What do babies see, for example? Is the ceiling bare? Is everything above a metre high on the walls?

b) *Try giving a camera to older children to take around their indoor setting and take pictures of things they like and things they don't like. You may find some surprising results. In some settings this has revealed a dislike of high blank walls and the ways in which the toys are presented. In others the photographs show children's pride in their creations on the walls or even those heaped on the floor which look to an outsider just like a pile of 'things'.*

c) *Look for the affordance of the space you have created. What does it invite you to do? Are there areas it invites you to move towards, and some that are less inviting? Has it encouragement to 'fiddle' with objects and materials, or does it look as if permission is needed to do so? Is there a theatrical space of the imagination?*

Generating an appropriate context for play indoors or out of doors requires an awareness of what it is like from a child's perspective. Long corridors have an affordance of walking along swiftly, but may also be given affordances of exploration if lined with pictures or textures. What does your research tell you about your setting?

Can babies have creative space?

In my visits to nurseries I have seen some very poor areas for babies. They are hygienically clean, have grey lino floors, and bright toys scattered about at intervals. The children are cared for according to an appropriate routine. However the children are not *at home* in the setting. It does not invite play, or offers only limited opportunity for creative juxtaposition of ideas.

In contrast I have seen attractive spaces for babies that have floors of different textures (lino, carpet, rugs and wood) that allow for exploration of texture and different crawling motions. The settings make use of light boxes, projectors and the safe strings of light that babies can sit among and explore. Toys are not all of the bright plastic kind but a mixture including natural materials, metals, and fabrics of varying textures. The settings are not afraid to get saucepans and lids out as a resource. There are cushions to prop children with and books to read. The sounds are soft, except for the children's banging. Some toys encourage reaching, some exploration, some stacking and containing. The changing mat is also designed as a place for adult-child play interaction: pictures on the wall, hangings above and clean toys to hold whilst being changed are all good practices to encourage enjoyment and play at this time. Effectively there are plenty of baby play *affordances* in the space, invitations to grasp, to explore texture, sound, relationships and so on.

The baby room spaces can offer opportunity for the child to initiate their own play activity – whether reaching for the next toy or playing with texture such as cooked spaghetti on a large floor tray. Nicholson's theory of loose parts still has validity here through the objects inviting heuristic exploration. There are things to bang and items such as fabric, cushions, or light toys that can be pulled and moved by the child so encouraging efficacy. Young mobile children will try to carry things around and make their own *places* within the nursery. I often see very young children making *sleep spaces*, carefully building a *nest* then lying on it contentedly for example. Early creative flexibility aligns with the self-centred infant focus, initially interested only in their own needs, but becoming more abstract as they grow and develop.

ACTIVITY 4

Creating a 'whatever you want it to be' space

> The environment and its possibilities as perceived and engaged with from the child's perspective. The child enters a space where anything is possible – whether a large or small space – and where they can engage alone or with others in exploring and exploiting that environment to match the images, plans and memories that emerge from their own minds' experiences and skills.
>
> (Broadhead and Burt, 2012, page 22)

Else and Sturrock (2007) wrote of the ludic (or play) space as an imaginal theatre of their own construction (page 21).

ACTIVITY 4 *continued*

Is there potential to create an indoor 'whatever you want it to be' space within your setting, pre-school, toddler or even baby room?

Perhaps you already have a den space, but it is restricted to being a quiet area for reading?

Could its intention be changed, or do you perhaps need two such spaces?

Do enclosed den spaces work as flexible spaces or arenas for exploiting resources and materials?

Is there perhaps another way of creating a play frame within the room?

Explore the possibilities for your setting. Why not continue to draw on the observations of Activity 3?

If, as we have considered, children *frame* their play activity before they can enter into the drama or *flow* of play, then an antecedent to that must be the environment that stimulates the play *framing* in the first place. The environment or context is vital to support the play activity. Gibson (1996) writes of the *affordances* offered by a landscape, or item, Else and Sturrock (2007) write of the ludic space, or *imaginal theatre*. So in play there is an ever-changing relationship between the play context and the play text. Initially it is perhaps only by adopting a fairly rigid frame that young children can even get their act onto the stage. They rely on the support of others, and of social templates to boost the emotional impact of entering the frame. As children get older, the boundaries of the play space and the frame within it get larger. Play usually moves into larger playing spaces and there are new *spaces between* – not only the space between adult and child, or child and child, but the spaces between setting and home, streets walked along and journeys made. Although there is recognition that children's independence and areas to roam are more restricted than the time of the Opies, 40 to 50 years ago (Gill, 2007; Coulter and Taylor, 2001) children I meet still seem very aware of their home neighbourhoods, and know of the local play spaces and areas of interest.

Play outdoors

There is a range of outdoor opportunities for play for young children: the outdoor provision at the setting; local parks and street play areas; wild places; these interstitial places on the way home, and the built locality.

Malaguzzi asserts that early childhood practitioners often fail to appreciate the role of the environment as the *third teacher* (the first two are the parent and the pedagogue or practitioner). He identifies outdoor, experiential play and contact with nature as significant contributors to children's learning and development (cited in Davis, 2008). However, the outdoor play spaces must be more than flat grass and fencing. It is important that an outdoor play area offers a range of affordances to stimulate children's play. Wild spaces, and the obstacles on the way home offer obvious affordances of looking, balancing, jumping off, stepping over. However, Coulter and Taylor (2001) identified that traditional playground equipment in a flat grassed area was *underused by children because it lacks complexity and is regarded as uninteresting* (Coulter and Taylor, 2001, page viii). It is not enough to just go outdoors – again you should be aware of the prompts to play that the environment can offer.

Shackell *et al.* (2008) highlight some key pointers for successful outdoor play spaces:

- they offer movement and physical activity;
- they stimulate the five senses;
- they are good spaces for social interactions;
- they allow children to manipulate natural and fabricated materials;
- they offer children challenge.

I would add one more: that they offer opportunities for children to connect with nature and the elements in some way or form.

Wild spaces

Vadala *et al.* (2007) researched the impact of early childhood experiences by asking 51 adults about their childhood experiences. Wild play was almost universally reported by conservationists as a formative experience showing the importance of the early connection as foundation for life. Adults questioned also identified that building forts, dens and bush houses is almost universal in middle childhood across the world, and that these forts and dens were used for games, social role-play and solitude. It is also interesting that they found that children who play in natural environments with irregularly sloped surfaces showed greater co-ordination than those who played in traditional level playground settings (Fjortoft, 2004, cited by Vadala *et al.* 2007). Within this report the authors identified a range of outdoor play types including:

- exploratory play;
- social play;
- fantasy play;
- creative play;
- gaming play;
- searching and trapping play;
- play based on outdoor chores (cutting and trimming, or picking and harvesting);
- alternative homes and dens.

They concluded that a part of the attraction of natural spaces is that they are dynamic spaces, growing and changing as the child does, and so offering new challenges.

Vadala *et al*. made a distinction between *playing with nature* and *playing with friends in a natural environment.* They express concern that there are decreasing numbers of people engaging with nature rather than in nature and therefore develop less strongly held environmental interests and concerns. In an answer to this, Davis (2008) found that a *Sustainable Planet Project* based on natural play had stimulated children's curiosity about the environment and led to the development of an embedded environmental awareness and social responsibility.

THEORY FOCUS

Biophilia: the attraction to nature

Evolutionary psychologists consider that humans have an innate, hereditary, emotional attachment to the natural environment. Urbanisation is a relatively new phenomenon and it is argued (Wilson, 2002) that we are programmed to align with the natural world. Studies have consistently found people are more relaxed when in the natural environment, and that the subsequent reduction in stress outside aids creativity and decision making (White and Stoecklin,1998). This seems to be backed up by studies which find that natural environments are consistently children's most favoured areas (Coulter and Taylor, 2001).

Figure 8.1 Boys as part of the natural environment

Biophilia = the innate tendency to be attracted by other life forms and to affiliate with natural living systems (Wilson, 2002, page 214).

Bounded places for relaxation

Although we have thought about stimulation and social and interactive aspects of play, *affordances*, *loose parts* and the theatre for fantasy play, we should also be aware that children need to retreat from social interaction and environmental stimuli. If they have been deeply involved in play, children will need *down time* to rest and reflect. Indoor and outdoor spaces should have areas for children to enter and relax in when they need *time out* from the stimulation of an active environment. Several authors have indicated that children are more likely to show aggressive or insecure behaviour if they lack opportunity for such withdrawal (Coulter and Taylor, 2001; Smith, Cowie and Blades, 2003). Again, dens and areas for sitting may meet this need.

Special play needs

Throughout this book I have purposely not particularly considered special play needs, as I believe that most play opportunities can be made accessible with a little thought. I also dislike stereotypical overviews identifying specific play responses for a labelled need. I believe that children have individual needs and it is important not to start with preconceptions when working with children. The greatest play asset to a disabled child is an open-minded and creative adult and a little forward planning.

We may here instead consider briefly the idea of children who may be restricted in play, or may need play as therapy. Consider children who experience a spell in hospital. We have hardly considered play as therapy in this book, but it is one arm of play that should not be forgotten. Through therapeutic play facilitated by a skilled practitioner (a hospital play therapist) children can act out in a concrete way what may happen, they can express fears and emotions, experience distraction from pain, and communicate post operational needs and concerns, trying to come to terms with loss or *while away* waiting time. *Play is used in hospitals to deal with the potentially damaging effects of anxiety and stress in child patients and to prepare children for medical procedures* (Coulter and Taylor, 2001, page vii). It can also be used to offer power (playing at being doctor), express needs, and communicate post operation when language may be difficult (Huddlestone, 1992). It can be used to help to deal with feelings of trauma and anger (Klein, 1979; Axline, 1964). Finally, play in a hospital situation can provide an element of normality, or diversion. We have already seen how moments of *flow* (Csikszentmihalyi, 1979, 2002) can move a child into a state of concentration, in which bodily needs may be temporarily forgotten. I present this context in recognition that all is not necessarily *rosy* for children's play in every situation, and there are contexts in which, although restricted, children will still play, and learn and develop through doing so. Perhaps you can think of some other such restrictive situations in which play may be valuable?

The global context for play

We now leap from the microcosm of a child in setting to the macrosystem (Bronfen-brenner, 2005) of global issues and world ideologies. Globalisation has obvious implications for play resources and has led to a commercialisation of play with per-haps the best example being the Barbie® fashion doll that aligns itself with Disney® and the latest film characters targeted at children. Much has been written about the stereotypes they promote and preserve, and the jury is out on the harm and the benefits. Although I can recognise some benefits in such resources which enable children to act out stories for greater understanding, I am also concerned at the stereotypes they portray.

We also have a development of new technologies, meaning that information and communication can pass so much more swiftly between countries. Children are much more technologically aware, certainly in the western world, but also with the spread of the mobile phone, across the globe. Online video clips show how children are used to test new technology and I am amazed at how competent some of today's digitally reared children are with the new technology and its built in affordances at a very young age. The world is moving fast to a new place, but this is not without some concerns.

There are global issues of sustainability and preservation of the natural environment, global warming and the potential for human destruction. The global context is an influence on how children will play and what they will play with, but also whether their play will help them to create the appropriate culture of the future. As Davis (2008) argues, the early years are the most significant growth period in a child's life. Experiences during this phase will *drive biological, psychological and social responses throughout the entire human lifespan. The implications for early learning about and for sustainability are obvious* (Davis, 2008, page i).

In 2004 an international conference on Education for Sustainable Development was held in Goteborg, Sweden, and led to the publication of a discussion paper on sus-tainability for early childhood. The recommendations of this paper were grounded on notions that children are competent, active agents in their own lives and are affected by, and capable of engaging with complex environmental and social issues (Davis, 2008). The recommendations were for a strengthening of education for sustainable development in the early years curriculum, and for children to be given the tools to create the future they will need. Further recommendations were for children to access lifelong learning, learning for change and networking, in arenas and partnerships (Siraj-Blatchford, Caroline Smith and Pramling-Samuelsson, 2010). Some of the ideas that have been presented in this chapter do align with these recommendations, in arenas for play, space for social discussion, and emphasis on recognising biophilia and engaging with the environment. Education for sustainable development has not appeared in the new EYFS so it is for practitioners to choose to include the practice. We know that children who engage in childhood nature play experience an additional dimension of awareness that they continue to value into adulthood (Vadala, 2007). Perhaps in this case we *should* be concerned for children as 'becomings' and build in simple steps to embed understandings of sustainability so that children have an informed voice in their future?

SUMMARY

There are so many contexts for children's play that there is not space to explore them all in one single chapter. Here we have briefly explored play in parks, play dens indoors, the environment for play outdoors, restrictive play spaces, and the global context. I have tried to address a range of ages and offered key concepts of affordances, loose parts and biophilia to help you to consider the flexibility of your environment for play, and the intention of your play space to stimulate play responses. A regular consideration of affordances, loose parts, and the play space will encourage audit and re-organisation. This will in turn encourage ongoing interaction with the resources, the acting out of cognitive ideas, the use of social spaces for communication, skills development and creative responses; learning from playing in the environmental context. The carefully planned, but flexible, environment can indeed be the third teacher, allowing the human teacher to spend more time observing to follow the child's lead. Finally we considered the macro context of play and sustainability.

FURTHER READING

Bilton, H (2010) *Outdoor Learning in the Early Years: management and innovation (3rd edition).* Abingdon: Routledge.

A very practical book that presents a range of ideas relating to how to set up, plan and manage outdoor play.

Broadhead, P and Burt, A (2012) Understanding Young Children's Learning through play: *Building Playful Pedagogies.* London: Routledge.

WEBSITES

http://playpods.co.uk/

Scrapstore Play Pods® website has a video clip of a play pod in action. Although being used by school aged children it really gives a good illustration of loose parts in action. Scrap comes out of a container and is used creatively by children demonstrating a range of play behaviours before playtime is over and they return to class.

www.playengland.org.uk/

The Play England website has a number of useful publications including those relating to the design of outdoor play areas and risk benefit analysis.

http://unesdoc.unesco.org/images/0015/001593/159355e.pdf
This takes you to the UNESCO document that discusses the contribution of early childhood education for a sustainable society.

Part 3

Children's rights and the ownership of play

9 The ownership of play: Play space, play cues and play actions

Through reading this chapter you will:

- reflect on who controls play and what that might mean;
- find out about the notion of children's rights in the play context;
- learn about Hart's Ladder of Participation;
- consider how you can further develop children's rights, responsibility and accountability in play;
- consider the adult role as *responder* rather than leader of the play process.

Referring back to our original concepts of play and freedom of choice this chapter will further develop our understanding of children's perspectives on their play and ownership of play activity.

Introduction

Children have an innate drive to play and this can take many forms. There is also a range of contexts for play, from local street play and play in wild places to constrained playful learning in an educational setting. Play is often problematical to adults as it has no consistently perceived purpose or outcome; being a process-led activity, or even a 'way of being' or feeling. It is perhaps for this reason that it is often in danger of being misunderstood and manipulated or controlled by those who are not doing the playing. The social policy writer, Hendricks (1995) suggests that play is often manipulated by adults to turn it into an educational experience, to justify it through a focus on the future adult. The language of the EYFS implies that it is to be made *purposeful* for learning. Even in this book we are seeking to explore the *purpose* of play as if it must have a reason to exist. Yet the very definition of play indicates self-determination, choice and autonomy, freedom and random selection of activity. The process of play relies on chance, serendipity, the way that the materials 'call' to the player. Perhaps play should not be shaped at all by adult-directed outcomes? In this chapter we will consider children's 'right' to play, how they perceive that right, and how play may be restricted by adults and their social expectations. In Chapter 10 we will consider the role of the adult.

The right to play

Else acknowledges that all children have a *drive to play* for some unknown biological reason, about which we can merely guess (Else, 2009). All children also have the *right* to play. In 1989, governments worldwide began to promise all children the same rights by adopting the United Nations Convention on the Rights of the Child (UNCRC). These rights, which include a right to play, are based on research on and discussions into what a child needs to survive, grow, participate in society and fulfil their potential. Applying to all children, the UNCRC is based on concepts of respect for the dignity and worth of each individual, regardless of background or wealth. It applies equally to every child under 18 years of age, regardless of who they are, or where they are from.

All United Nations member states except for the United States of America and Somalia have formally approved the Convention. The United Kingdom signed it on 19 April 1990 and ratified it on 16 December 1991. It came into force in the UK on 15 January 1992 (United Nations Children's Fund (Unicef), accessed online March, 2012). It is particularly Article 31 of the convention that relates to children's rights to play and recreation.

THEORY FOCUS

UNCRC and the right to play

Article 31 of the UNCRC is made up of two parts.

1. States parties recognize the right of the child to rest and leisure, to engage in play and recreational activities appropriate to the age of the child and to participate freely in cultural life and the arts.

2. States parties shall respect and promote the right of the child to participate fully in cultural and artistic life and shall encourage the provision of appropriate and equal opportunities for cultural, artistic, recreational and leisure activity.

The right to play is clearly stated, but alongside a right to participate in the cultural and artistic life and the arts. Play and cultural activities, creativity and the arts are aligned in this statement of right.

Janet Moyles (1994, 2005) highlighted the distinction between the child's right to recreation and the child's right to play, pointing out that these are often confused but we should remember that the child has the right to both.

Take a few moments to reflect and consider what may be the differences between *play* and *recreation*. Do you offer both in your setting?

The Oxford Dictionary Online defines the term 'recreation' as *an activity done for enjoyment when one is not working*. It comes from an old English word for renewal or regeneration and implies *time out* or relaxation. As such it may align with one purpose of play, but is obviously a different process to the purposeful creative play and play for cognitive development that we have explored.

Who owns play?

Gill (2007) considers that in general children are making plain their wish for greater freedom, autonomy and responsibility for their own safety in play. Perhaps children brought up with the UNCRC have more awareness of their rights and that their views should be taken into account when deciding their experiences? If so, the framework should lead to a gradual improvement in participatory practice over the years to come.

Children may be more readily making their wishes known, but is this impacting on the ownership of play within early childhood settings? I suspect that the response is mixed, in some cases it will be, but in others the adult will still be in charge of the outcome.

In a classroom or early years setting in which activities addressing the six areas of learning are laid out by the practitioner, adults, not the children, have chosen the outcomes they expect to see. The *ownership* of the play activity is clearly with the adult. The practitioner gives instruction before the activity starts. Children may take a playful attitude to the activity, but it has insufficient flexibility to become play in the deepest sense. The children do not hold the power in the relationship. The more the children begin to take over the activity, mixing up the materials in a creative way the more the play begins to become theirs.

Taking children out to a planned session in Forest School may be adult-led activity, carefully planned for hunting and gathering of seasonal colours and textures, fire play and physical development through a planned course. Again it is potentially merely structured playful learning until the children decide to take it over, or are given *free time* when they can take over the leadership of their own play interests and let their compound flexibility run wild.

Just as play was difficult to define, so the ownership of it is equally as slippery. Else acknowledges that there are many actions that may not start out as play, but which become playful as people engage and begin to be playful: *With the best intentions we may try to lead the play but if the children do not want to play there is little we can do about it* (Else, 2009, page 13).

In contrast, if children are already playing there is plenty that can be done to stop, redirect or curtail the play, such as calling time on it, asking questions about it, making suggestions without being invited to, and persisting in these suggestions. Furthermore, for some children, particularly younger children, play is restricted by a number of external factors that impinge upon their free time. A combination of school, homework, family visits, housework and after-school interest clubs mean *some children lead such busy lifestyles that finding the time to play, as much as they would like to, is often difficult* (Kapasi and Gleave, 2009, page 7). Adults also have the potential to restrict play behaviours by making them too structured. One study found that where children had had access to the natural environment they disliked it in later life when they recalled regimented experiences associated with it (Vadala *et al.*, 2007).

What do children think about play?

I am not sure that children often think about play. The majority of time they will be doing it, rather than thinking about it. However, research with children aged from four to 12 into their views on play identified three core characteristics that offer the most enjoyable experiences:

- friends to play with;

- time to play;

- freedom to play without structure (Kapasi and Gleave, 2009).

In this section I will draw quite heavily on this research as children were asked directly for their views.

Other findings from this research indicated that play was used as a controlling mechanism, as adults used such phrases as: *'If you don't do your homework you get less golden time'* [free time awarded to children for good behaviour] or *'You have to miss a playtime'*. This tendency to reduce playtime as a punishment could reinforce the idea that time for play is a reward rather than a right to which children are entitled.

Many children's days were highly structured which allowed less time for self-directed play. Children were taken from activity to activity in a busy schedule and restricted from planning their own exploratory or even therapeutic play activities.

All of the children favoured a mixture of informal play and organised activity, which ties in with the 'Effective Provision of Pre-school Education' (EPPE) research (2003). This research indicated that the most effective learning approach was a combination of both adult- and child-led activities. Children express that they need new ideas and stimulation in order to build on in their play.

Even short bursts of *free time* were important for children: *'My favourite time to play is at school because we can make up new games and let other people join in who are alone.'* (Kapasi and Gleave, 2009, page 15). Playing with others at school offered the opportunity for children to be inventive about their play and try out new games. They could be spontaneous when playing and it was clear that being with friends and exploring social relationships including empathy was an essential component of play.

Children also spoke of how play boosts their concentration and that the chance to let off steam in the playground could lead to improved behaviour in the classroom.

> *'It stops more fights if you get more play.'*
> *'Some children learn how to socialise when they play with other kids.'*
> *'It helps you concentrate in school.'*
> *'We need fresh oxygen from the playground.'*
> (Children talking, reported by Kapasi and Gleave, 2009, page 15)

This short list below from Kapasi and Gleave's findings indicates a range of benefits from play. Children valued play for its contribution to their inner spirit and emotional expression, health, rest and recreation, and creative imagination.

- 'If [children] don't play it makes them yuk and boring.'
- 'There might as well be no colour if you can't play!'
- 'It means being able to shout without getting told off!'
- 'Cos you need fresh air – if you don't have fresh air you might die well I would anyways – it's important to get air.'
- 'When you play you can let your imagination unfold.'
- 'Play does help your imagination run away.'

(Selection from Kapasi and Gleave, page 18)

The children in this study were old enough to answer when asked directly what they liked and disliked about play. There are many ways in which you can obtain children's views when they are too young to tell you verbally. Clark and Moss (2001, 2005) highlight how a *mosaic approach* can be used with young children, drawing on a range of perspectives including video observation, participatory activities and shared discussion between colleagues on the *findings*. These approaches are further developed in a book by Harcourt, Perry and Waller (2011) in which young children are clearly participants in assessing the environments of their settings, in some cases by actually being wired with a portable camera on their head! Observing babies and very young children very carefully will give insight into their likes and dislikes about their play opportunities and areas. Picture cards can also be used to discuss resources.

From observation through consultation to participation

Observing what children do and where they go in order to find out more about their views on play is one step towards realising both children's right to access play and also in their having a say in what happens to them (UNCRC Article 12). If play is about children being intrinsically motivated to follow their own interests and initiatives then they must be empowered to follow that motivation and to shape their environments as they grow accordingly. However, empowerment of children in society is in its infancy; we are not used to considering that children can be citizens, competent and able to make rational decisions about their needs for the future (Blatchford et al., 2010). In order to move beyond observation and adult decision to real participation by children in shaping their play opportunities, we adults have to be aware of what we are doing. We need to reflect on what we see, and perhaps seek templates from other cultural experiences to make this major shift in perspective. Many people look to Reggio Emilia with its 'One Hundred Languages of Children' approach as a prompt to consider how children can express themselves and be heard (Edwards et al., 2011) through art, actions, and an approach which asks children at the beginning of the day and plans with them rather than for them. *The full empowerment of children is really in its infancy in society, so achieving even a modest level of active participation is a major stepping-stone* (Siraj-Blatchford, Smith and Pramling-Samuellson, 2010, page 31).

Dialogue and the ladder of participation

There is a shortage of written material about children's views on the thing they do most in their childhood: *play*. Children are very often photographed and used to illustrate concern by adults for their needs, but are perhaps the least listened-to members of society (UNICEF/Hart, 1992). In recognition of the need to be aware of the potential tokenism in the way we work with children Roger Hart has adapted a *ladder of participation* from Arnstein (1969) to help us to specifically think about children's participation opportunities in projects. It is a model which is still useful and has been adapted many times to think about how children can be included in decisions that affect them, from local setting-based provision to government policy.

THEORY FOCUS

Hart's ladder of participation

Look at Hart's ladder of participation (Figure 9.1) and read this list from bottom to top as you rise up the ladder's rungs.

- *Child-initiated, shared decisions with adults:*
  The project is initiated by children and adults are invited in to participate in the decision-making process. The power in the project remains with the children.

- *Child-initiated and directed:*
  Children identify a need and start their own projects, they can direct their own actions to move the project forward as they choose. There is an implication of no adults on this rung.

- *Adult-initiated, shared decisions made with children:*
  The adults have the idea and begin the project, but children are empowered to make decisions and take responsibility for areas of work.

- *Consulted but informed:*
  The project is designed and run by adults, but children understand the process and their opinions are treated seriously.

- *Assigned but informed:*
  Children are told all about an adult-initiated project and then asked if they would like a role in helping it to happen, perhaps doing practical tasks. It is important in this rung that children are not coerced but volunteer to assist.

- *Tokenism:*
  A pretence of child participation such as in interview panels. What you say you listen to is not quite the same as really happens. The intention is there, but not followed through.

- *Decoration:*
  Children are used to market adult ideas.

- *Manipulation:*
  The use of children to support adult ideas, but with pretence of consultation.

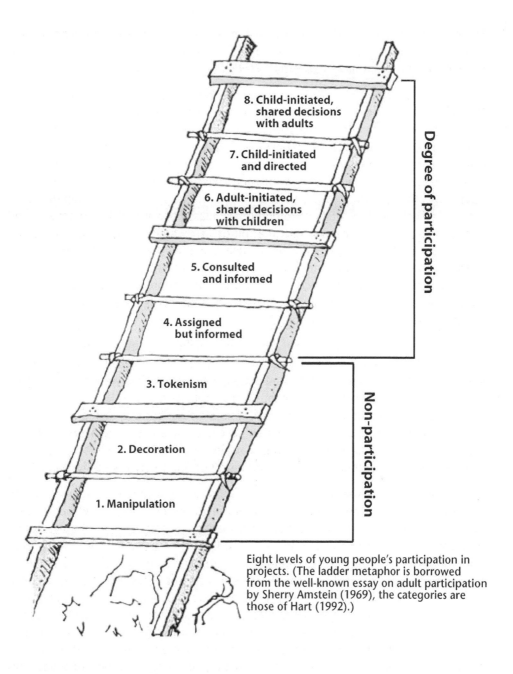

8. Child-initiated, shared decisions with adults

7. Child-initiated and directed

6. Adult-initiated, shared decisions with children

5. Consulted and informed

4. Assigned but informed

3. Tokenism

2. Decoration

1. Manipulation

Degree of participation

Non-participation

Eight levels of young people's participation in projects. (The ladder metaphor is borrowed from the well-known essay on adult participation by Sherry Arnstein (1969), the categories are those of Hart (1992).)

Reproduced with kind permission from Roger Hart from the original published in Children's Participation: From Tokenism to Citizenship. Florence, Italy: UNICEF Innocenti Research Centre, 1992

Figure 9.1 Hart's ladder of participation

There are eight rungs to Hart's ladder – and the level of participation increases the higher up the ladder you climb. The bottom three rungs are non-participatory; they do not include children in an empowering way.

1. The first or bottom rung *Manipulation* is the lowest end of the participation scale. Here children are coerced into acting in support of adult ideas. Hart cites the use of children to wave placards in protest as an example – children are good for the photo opportunity, but do not understand why they are really there. Hart cites another example of manipulation as asking children to draw their ideal playground to support a new playground design. The drawings are collected in and somehow assessed by adults to come up with a *children's design*. This at first sounds reasonable, but then we may reflect that the adults were potentially biased towards a design anyway and may well have selected the drawings that match. The children have no further say on the real detail of the design, and have no idea how their designs were used. Children at the point of manipulation are not given feedback or asked to assist with the next stage, but their ideas are selected to endorse adult-approved actions. In play the construction of pre-planned artwork such as Christmas cards is also a form of *manipulation* rather than participatory play.

2. The second rung up is *Decoration*. This rung is higher than manipulation as it does not pretend to be including children; rather it is merely a marketing tool. Children wear the T-shirt to support an adult-led action or event. Children wearing a nursery T-shirt are not only easily identified by the staff on trips out, but are also marketing the nursery. The use of cute photographs of children after a positive Ofsted inspection is often within this category. Where children have been taken out to join a *teddy bear's picnic* organised by a local authority this may also be *decoration*, endorsing a selected event intended for another purpose (fundraising or adult networking, for example).

3. The third rung is *tokenism*. This is where it appears that children may be included, for example on interview panels for staff. But actually their views play such a small part in the selection process that their participation is merely a sham, a presentation of espoused ideas (the belief that we ought to include children) that are not put into practice (perhaps through lack of time or commitment). Approaches to play are often bordering on this type of tokenism. Practitioners say that they are offering child-led play, but then in practice are seen to be setting out the boundaries of that play such that they merely address the intended learning matters outcomes. Argyris and Schön (1978) write of the difference between our *espoused theory* – what we say we do – and our *theory in action* or what we really do. If we were only to *say* that we include children in our planning for play (intending truly to do so), but did not follow this through with action in our practice, this would be tokenism.

We now reach the rung at which Hart considers children are genuinely playing a participatory role. He clearly indicates that it is not necessary to think that we should always be operating at the highest rungs of the ladder, but that different children, in different contexts and at different stages of development will be participating at different levels of the ladder. They will also move from one to the other of these rungs according to their understanding, context and conditions.

4. The a*ssigned but informed* rung is one where children are given clear jobs to do and are told about the reasons for those jobs. They are actively playing a meaningful part in the running of the organisation or event, but are not in a decision-making position beyond the choice to participate or not. So children may volunteer to help set out a play area (or clear away) but with clear adult guidance and full information as to why their help is needed. They are not in a position to substantially shape the area but are working voluntarily within others' boundaries. Children helping to dig and establish a new outdoor area may be *assigned but informed*.

5. *Consulted but informed* children play a real role in decisions made by an organisation or setting, but as consultants, selected for a fixed purpose/timeframe. The project may be designed and run by adults, but children understand the process and their opinions are treated seriously. Hart cites an example of children testing and offering advice to shape future children's television programmes. In play terms, children may discuss the redevelopment of the outdoor area, they may draw improvements, but this time their drawings are really considered, and the children are talked to about their meaning, receiving feedback on what happened. They may alternatively be consulted using pictorial catalogues, to identify what resources or toys they would like from a financial grant. They will be capable of discussing and selecting according to their perceived needs, but this is a fixed timescale activity and the adults then move the project forwards. A *mosaic approach* (Clark and Moss, 2001) is often implemented as consultation with children, but they are informed about the purpose and the relevance of the work to the whole setting environment.

6. *Adult-initiated, shared decisions* are situations where adults generate project ideas and then work to facilitate children's real involvement in decision making on an equal basis to implement the project. Much play activity in early years settings may be at this point on the rung. Adults have a concept of what will happen, and lay out the play resources and environment accordingly. Children within the play space are free to make decisions and shape the environment. The creative dens of the last chapter may well fall into this category as children are able to choose how to use the space that the adults have created, including breaking the boundaries of the space.

7. *Child-initiated and directed* activities are those that children really are in control of. Hart gives small-scale examples of children managing and directing their own play on an earth bank, making dams for water. The adults managed the parents' expectations, facilitating the maintenance of the play arena, but remained back to allow children to own the play and take it to their own conclusions. This is an example of a child-initiated and directed process activity. There are few truly child-initiated and directed social projects in early childhood, but perhaps there are ways that we can allow the space for more to occur – if we truly believe that children do have self-efficacy and are competent players in the socio-political world.

8. Finally we come to the top rung, *child-initiated, shared with adults*. Here children initiate an activity, but are so embedded in a supportive social structure that they are able to invite the adults to join them in the decision making on an equal footing, without fear of the project being taken over. As with the other models above, this

could be seen in relation to children's play within a setting, or a larger social *project* of some form.

An example at the local level within the setting might be where a child may come in with a new interest in the weather, perhaps from experimenting in catching rain in a pot at home. The child may wish to set up a *weather station* and have some broad idea but not know how to move it forward. They may ask other children or an adult to join them to help with ideas. The project is still in the child's hands, but the adult (or informed other) may offer ideas and resources without taking over the decisions. Decisions could be made jointly, or received from the adults and considered by the children to be accepted or rejected.

It is interesting that the higher up the ladder we go, the harder it is to find projects that show true participation in the community or wider social environment. Some examples may be community gardens that are designed and created by children.

ACTIVITY 1

Harry Shier (2001), a play training specialist now working with children's participation projects, has simplified this participation ladder down to only five rungs. I have added a ground level perception (level 0) which reflects that some adults do not recognise the need to listen to children.

5. *Children share power and responsibility for decision making.*

4. *Children are involved in decision-making processes.*

3. *Children's views are taken into account.*

2. *Children are supported in expressing their views.*

1. *Children are listened to.*

0. *Children are considered too young to be listened to.*

Where would you put yourself on this ladder? Do you really take children's views into account when initiating new changes in their play spaces?

One example that I came across of children being actively involved in the decision-making process for their setting was one of de-cluttering. In a joint recognition that the pre-school room was too cluttered, the practitioners removed all resources and children had to decide on a daily basis what they wanted back. Knowing that not everything could come back into the room, they made careful selections relating to those things that they used most, those they did not want any more, and any new items that they needed. As this was initially adult initiated, this would be at level 4 of Shier's ladder.

The ladders of participation are useful tools to help us to reflect on our roles in supporting the empowerment of children in making decisions that affect them.

Creation of play space, play cues and play actions

Power and participation issues apply to all adult and child interactions in play as well as to *projects* and new initiatives. Although children have the right to play, not all play in every circumstance is entirely appropriate or beneficial to the child. Recall the exasperation of Quintilian (cited by Frost, 2010) who valued the lively mind resulting from play but requested *only let there be moderation*. Else (2009) recognises that although children will begin playing with whatever will come to hand, adults will sometimes find their play *inconvenient* or *just plain wrong*. Sometimes play does not fit the social templates that we work with in our particular cultures. In England, playing at the table in a restaurant is largely frowned upon, particularly if it is being practised by a small child who likes to throw food around. Some researchers have also raised a concern that, although generally the value of play is now recognised, there is a need to ensure that children succeed in a society with educational values largely created by the generation before them; and with particular expected learning outcomes (such as those seen in the EYFS (2008). Adults, with greater experience, must sometimes make the decisions to encourage or curtail the right to play. This is OK in measured response; even children will curtail each others' play if they consider it inappropriate at that point.

In order to understand how the dialogic *power* and *release of power* mechanisms work we should consider the play process. This is largely a process of play cues and play returns that operates within this imaginal or real *play space* created between people, or between a person and the environment.

Throughout this book I have indicated the potential *spaces* in which play can occur; the space between parent and very young baby; the space that is between assimilation of ideas and adaptation of conceptual understanding; the space between society and individual will; the space between school or setting and home; the space created within a space to ensure an *arena* for play or relaxation from play.

The creation of the play space can be a matter of communication between two people. Drawing on Else (2009) and Else and Sturrock (2007), I shall here try to explain the play process as I interpret it.

1. A child responds to a trigger of some form prompting a desire to play. The trigger may be an object affording something of interest to the child, it may be a story being told, or it may be another child doing something.

2. The child then reveals the *play face* and an obvious intention to play. Between people, or child to child, this may be a moment of eye contact and a nod or similar action.

3. The second child or participating adult then gives a play response (a similar nod and smile) and the play *space* is created between them.

4. The play space may be reduced by the two participants moving together, or increased by their moving apart but by still communicating playfully with related signals the space is maintained.

5. Play cues may be given to other people to enter the play space to increase the numbers playing. Alternatively children's responses may reject the requests of others as they present their *cues*.

6. Children and participants in the play space may now be playing simultaneously with parallel cycles, with interlinked play cycles, or disjointedly, each having their own play cycle in operation.

7. When the play has come to saturation for any one child they will usually signal the end; a frustrated cry or head turn in a small infant; a toddler may throw down the toys; and an older child may just walk out of the frame, or even say *'I'm off'*.

8. The child then either engages in another form of activity than play (such as eating or sleeping) or wanders until another play trigger stimulates a response and so the cycle begins again.

We are reminded by Else that in breaking down the play cycle in this way we should not assume that children are explicitly conscious of the process – rather that the playing child exists in a world of the moment, making links and explorations. There appears to be a rhythm to this process and elements of creation and destruction, joining and unjoining. It is for us to guess and support, not to categorise and restrict by labelling and analysing time frames.

THEORY FOCUS

The play cycle

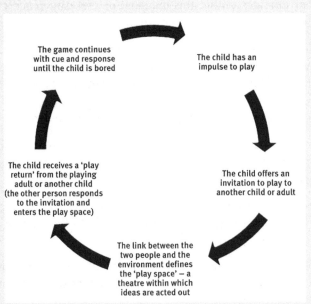

The game continues with cue and response until the child is bored

The child has an impulse to play

The child receives a 'play return' from the playing adult or another child (the other person responds to the invitation and enters the play space)

The child offers an invitation to play to another child or adult

The link between the two people and the environment defines the 'play space' – a theatre within which ideas are acted out

Figure 9.2 The play cycle

Just as other children can enter, exit or restrict the play cycle by their response to the cues, so adults can either respond positively to play cues, or restrict the play by changing the play frame, issuing cues in a different manner or overriding them with instruction.

We should recognise that children are best placed to lead their play. Just as children are able to push themselves to go further and try harder, they can also choose when to play, who to play with and when not to take part. Garvey (1977, page 32) argued that play behaviours are *revocable*, that is, that children can stop their play abruptly, they can change the names of characters, they can swap roles, and the rules change. Play is both real and not real, it is social, and pretend; it is risky, but also without risk; what is created can be destroyed and this is true of the play cycle too.

SUMMARY

In this chapter we have acknowledged that children have the right to play and have considered how we might support their participatory rights in their play activity. The ladder of participation models may be useful to consider how much power and control children really do have over their play experiences. We also considered if there may be times when adults do need to set boundaries and constrain activities to templates.

We briefly considered a range of children's statements about play. The lack of evidence of younger children's own words about their play indicates that there is a need for more work in this area. It is necessary to capture children's own experiences and the value of their play, rather than view adult interpretations of these. There is developing work in this area (Harcourt, Perry and Waller, 2011) which will undoubtedly give greater insight in future.

We have identified that children will respond to the environment and choose the play activities that they best need for their own reasons as play has its own dynamic with play affordances, cues, frames and responses inviting others to join in that play cycle, before the frame breaks. A child has the right to be able to pursue that play, and not have the frame broken or adulterated (Else, 2009) by inappropriate adult responses of overt questioning, or control of the activity. In the next chapter we will consider further the adult role in managing the balance of play and not-play, frame and not-frame, cues and responses.

Clerk, A and Moss, P (2001) *Listening to Young Children: The Moses Approach*. London: NCB/JRF.
Outlines a framework for listening to young children's perspectives in their daily lives and actions.

Else, P (2009) *The Value of Play*. London: Continuum.
A clear book which explains further the concepts of play space, play cues and play returns.
UNICEF/Hart, R (1992) *Children's Participation: From Tokenism to Citizenship*. Florence, Italy: UNICEF Innocenti Research Centre accessible online from UNICEF – in this document Hart presents and discusses his ladder of participation.

www.crin.org/
Children's Rights International Network
Another interesting site that offers discussion and resources relating to children's rights in the UK and globally. Some of the resources found on this site are offered by Save the Children such as:

www.crin.org/docs/resources/publications/hrbap/SCUK_participation.pdf
A very useful document concerned with involving children in research and evaluation which also critiques Hart's ladder of participation.

www.equalityhumanrights.com/
Website of UK Equality and Human Rights Commission
Search for play and you will get some play based scenarios highlighting inclusion discriminatory practices. There is a section on education and its links with equality in future.

www.unicef.org.uk/UNICEFs-Work/Our-mission/UN-Convention/
The Web page for the United Nations Convention on the Rights of the Child (UNCRC). Gives clear information about when it was first approved and ratified. There is a summary sheet of the 45 Articles of the Convention. You can also find a child friendly version on this site.

10 Developing a pedagogy for play

Through reading this chapter, you will:

- explore the concept of pedagogy and adult practice in support of play for learning in registered settings;

- reflect on the spectrum of adult-initiated learning and child initiated play;

- learn about some possible conceptual frameworks relating to pedagogy;

- review some comparative pedagogic practices;

- consider the strengths and weaknesses of your own approach.

Introduction

The intention of this chapter is to address the adult role in supporting children's play in the particular context of registered early years settings and early education. I shall for the moment broadly call this adult facilitative approach in support of play for learning 'pedagogy'. This chapter will reveal that understanding of the adult role and the use of the term pedagogy in relation to play is an area of some debate and confusion. It will explore some of the pedagogic debates and models in a search of a position which allows both play and learning to flourish with adult support.

Pedagogy is a relational and situated activity, that is, the nature of it depends on the people interacting and the specific place in which it occurs. An individual practitioner's approach, with his personal pedagogy, is likely to draw on or respond to his own values and concepts of play, the context in which he works, including the children, and the purpose of his intended interventions. You are encouraged, as you read this chapter, to consider the range of philosophies, concepts and models presented and relate these to your own practice context in order to identify your personal approach to practice.

What is pedagogy?

Pedagogy is a term that is open to interpretation. The term 'pedagogy' is derived from the Greek word *paid*, meaning child, plus *agogos*, meaning leading. Thus, pedagogy has been both defined as the way adults can lead and support a developing child; and the art and science of teaching children. The term has both historical connotations linked to teaching and more recent international connotations of support for social and socio-cultural development (social pedagogy).

The words play and pedagogy do not seem to go together very well. If I consider the concept of play I reach for the words spontaneous, child-led, intrinsically motivated, non-work. On considering the term 'pedagogy' I initially think of teaching and the provision of an environment and strategies to promote learning; concepts which immediately seem the opposite to play. Because I am aware of more recent research I can pause again and can also think of the social pedagogues of Denmark or Reggio Emilia who seek to support the child holistically as a free and competent individual. It is this recent perception of pedagogy which offers a bridge between the two words.

ACTIVITY 1

Take time here to consider the two terms 'pedagogy' and 'play'. Try to give each a meaning in your own words. If you are confused about the term pedagogy at this point don't worry, many practitioners are (McInnes et al., 2011; Moss, 2000).

Play is:

Pedagogy is:

Is there a link between the two definitions?

This chapter will help to support your ideas of pedagogy and play. Come back and revisit these definitions some time later and see if your ideas have changed.

In the traditional pedagogic model (Knowles, 1984) the child is prepared to receive knowledge and the teacher has full responsibility for making decisions about what will be learned, how it will be learned, and when it will be learned. Such teacher-directed instruction places the child in a submissive role and carries power-based assumptions. Children need only know only what the teacher teaches them and a 'blank sheet' or *tabula rasa* is assumed in the child. The adult knows best and this model does not align with play as a concept of intrinsic motivation, freedom and choice.

More recent understandings offer a model of facilitating learning in which play is a powerful process, entered into by competent children who are developing new understandings for the future. The traditional interpretation of pedagogy given above is in stark contrast to the philosophical concept presented by Danish social pedagogues in the quotation below. In this alternative model of intervention, children are supported by adults who recognise their prior learning and competence: *As a discipline, pedagogy is closely related to philosophy. The ideal is a free and competent individual. Values and opportunities are discussed in relation to this ideal and connected to issues relating to individual needs and requirements…and to questions of social condition and opportunity* (Jensen and Hansen, 2003, page 7).

This model is one in which, as Moss and Petrie (2002) explain, *the pedagogue sets out to address the whole child, the child with body, mind, emotions, creativity, history and social identity* (page 143).

The intention is to promote freedom and competence, opportunity and creativity. Such pedagogues not only seek to understand and address the whole child but also work to discuss and debate their pedagogic philosophy and approach. So in the Jensen and Hansen model, practitioners work as a team or *community of common practice* (Wenger, 1991). It is possible to see how this holistic but flexible approach aligns much more readily with concepts of play as a freely chosen, self-directed activity into which individuals bring their own interests, flexibility of thinking and creativity. Danish early childhood pedagogues are not constrained by concepts of preparation for school. Brooker (2011) reminds us that in Denmark, Sweden and other Nordic countries, play is given priority over the curriculum until approximately six years of age and a whole day's nursery activity could be freely chosen play with no curriculum constraints at all.

ACTIVITY 2

In exploring the meaning of pedagogy I have in this section presented a range of positions relating to curriculum and perspectives. The continuum below offers a simplistic indication of the spectrum of pedagogic approaches that may be seen in an early childhood setting, progressing from child-led pure play at one end to adult-led teaching at the other.

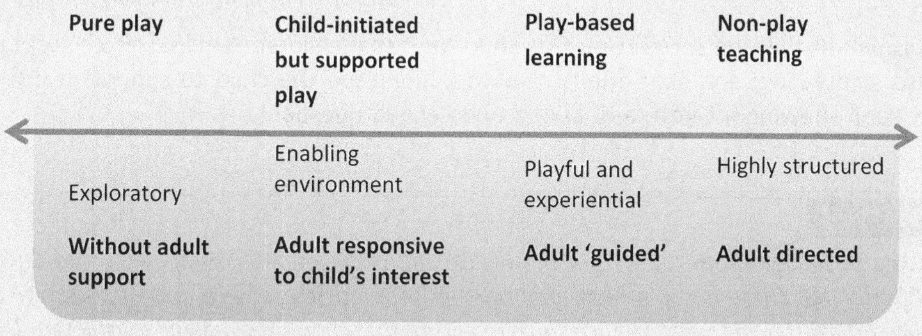

Pure play	Child-initiated but supported play	Play-based learning	Non-play teaching
Exploratory	Enabling environment	Playful and experiential	Highly structured
Without adult support	Adult responsive to child's interest	Adult 'guided'	Adult directed

Figure 10.1 The play continuum

Where would you place Knowles' perspective of pedagogy?
Where might Denmark sit?
Where on the spectrum is your own practice?

Does your pedagogic practice perhaps embrace a range of positions on the continuum with different approaches at different times?

Researching effective early years pedagogy

Play is a relatively new field for academic study. There are no clear and commonly understood definitions of play in early childhood, and as a result there is a lack of thorough research relating to the impact of play on learning. Many ideological positions persist without real evidence, as yet. The idea of play as an evolutionary activity,

UNIVERSITY OF WINCHESTER
LIBRARY

for example, requires a long-term study for evidence. It makes sense when considered in the light of what is known about animal play, but cannot be proven.

In contrast to the lack of research into the impacts of play on learning there are studies which have researched effective pedagogic practice over a long period of time (longitudinal research), and these support the use of both play and adult-led activity to support engagement in learning. The Effective Provision of Pre-school Education (EPPE) research (Siraj-Blatchford *et al.*, 2007) and Researching Effective Pedagogy in the Early Years (REPEY) (Siraj-Blatchford *et al.*, 2002) both identified benefits in offering play within a balance of adult-led and child-led activity. The researchers identified that the most effective pre-school provisions supporting learning:

- *provided children with a mixture of adult-initiated group work and learning through freely chosen play;*
- *viewed cognitive and social development as complementary;*
- *provided adult-to-child interactions that involved sustained shared thinking and open-ended questioning that recognised and extended children's learning…*

(Siraj-Blatchford *et al.*, 2007, page 1)

This tells us that the social context is important; that children require free choice, but also stimulation; and that adults can work alongside the child to support learning through showing interest, and asking open-ended questions.

ACTIVITY 3

A key pedagogical indicator from the REPEY and EPPE research (Siraj-Blatchford et al., 2007) is that there is something important in offering free choice and opportunity to play. Adults should therefore take steps to ensure that choice is available to children. This could also be choice to participate, choice to withdraw from an activity, or choice to do something different from that which the adult intends.

How do you support free choice in your setting?

A second pedagogic pointer is the consideration of a balance of adult- to child-led activity. Some settings are highly adult led, after-school clubs may choose to be almost entirely child led, and some schools I know aim for an 80% child-led to 20% adult-led approach to enable children to explore their own schema.

What proportion of activities in a week in your setting is adult led?

What proportion of activities are child led?

Why not compare these figures with colleagues in other rooms or different settings and think about why the different patterns occur.
Is there scope for increasing the child-led 'play' element in your setting?

The EPPE and REPEY reports link social development, play and cognition and offer advice on adult practice. The language of these influential reports can be found in the UK curricula today with an emphasis on adult-led and child-initiated provision combining release of power to the child within a structure of planned, purposeful play. The EPPE research is ongoing, now tracking children through school, and may offer information in the long run on the learning impacts of early play-based experiences.

The need to explore and explain pedagogy and play

In 2003 the BERA Early Years Special Interest Group recognised that play was fairly well established as the *bedrock of early childhood* (BERA EYSIG, 2003, page 14). Play is therefore becoming embedded in early years curricula across the world as formal 'teaching' is widely rejected in favour of informal, holistic, child-centred and play-based approaches (Woodhead, 2006). However, the BERA special interest group also found that *an agreed pedagogy of play is less well articulated* (2003, page 14). Not only is the concept of pedagogy not well understood by early childhood practitioners but definitions of play and concepts of adult support of play for learning leave many confused (Wood and Attfield, 2005; Broadhead and Burt, 2011). In order to explore play and pedagogy we need to consider a range of perspectives and positions, reflecting on these to inform our own.

ACTIVITY 4

The BERA research (2003) highlighted that practitioners find it difficult to articulate their own pedagogic practice bringing together play and learning. Current authors have found the same issues still exist (Rogers, 2011; McInnes, 2011). This activity encourages you to think about how you support play for learning.

You may find it helpful to answer the following questions:

* *How do I support children's learning through play?*
* *What approaches do I tend to take when supporting play?*

Could you now describe something of your own pedagogic practice?

* *What do you think are the influences on your own pedagogic approach?*
* *Are you aware of your own strengths and aptitudes in practice?*

You may wish to take time to explore these further.

Play, pedagogy and the new Early Years Foundation Stage 2012

The new English Statutory Framework for the Early Years Foundation Stage (EYFS 2012) (DfE, 2012) which now introduces seven areas of learning, indicates that:

> Each area of learning and development must be implemented through planned, purposeful play and through a mix of adult-led and child-initiated activity. Play is essential for children's development, building their confidence as they learn to explore, to think about problems, and relate to others. Children learn by leading their own play, and by taking part in play which is guided by adults.
>
> (EYFS, 2012, page 6)

This document gives clear indication that support for play is an aspect of pedagogic practice but articulation of desirable pedagogic practice to support this playful activity is not contained within the statutory document. It is for the practitioner to make ongoing judgements on the nature of their own involvement. The framework does adopt a stage development approach with a new emphasis on *school readiness*, indicating there should be a progressive adult intervention with age: *As children grow older, and as their development allows, it is expected that the balance will gradually shift towards more activities led by adults, to help children prepare for more formal learning, ready for Year 1* (EYFS, 2012, page 4).

So in the English Foundation Stage it is clearly expressed that the play-based activity is tailored to preparation for school.

THEORY FOCUS

Seven areas of learning of the new EYFS

The new EYFS 2012 (DfE 2012) promotes seven areas of learning in a significant change to the old Early Years Foundation Stage (DCSF, 2008). These key areas of learning, we are advised, must 'shape' educational programmes in early childhood settings in England and are considered to be inter-connected. Three are particularly highlighted as crucial to ignite *children's curiosity and enthusiasm for learning, and for building their capacity to learn, form relationships and thrive* (EYFS, 2012, page 4). These are:

* communication and language;

* physical development;

* personal, social and emotional development.

This approach indicates a shift from a content-based approach to a recognition of the key developmental competencies of communication, health and social and emotional well-being as conditions essential for successful learning.

THEORY FOCUS *continued*

In addition to these three prime areas, there are four specific areas of greater content:

- *literacy;*
- *mathematics;*
- *understanding the world;*
- *expressive arts and design* (DfE, 2012).

Play is mentioned throughout the Statutory Framework and related documents, but the new EYFS 2012 still leaves us with a confused pedagogic understanding, very much implying that the situated response is open to individual interpretation.

Tensions in the terms

Play is often identified as the opposite to work activity and, therefore, is at odds with the idea of pedagogy – which is often defined as teaching and applied to classroom management. Rogers (2011) expresses concern at a *pedagogisation of play* which increasingly reduces play to become an instrument for learning. This fails to recognise play as the freely chosen, transformative, life-enhancing phenomenon in which children are operating at the boundaries of understanding.

Settings can actually constrain play, as adults may expect that children will:

- 'play properly';
- recognise play as a reward for hard work;
- experience play 'directed' to expected learning;
- meet adult-predicted outcomes through play.

Those who support play in the purest concept of it may argue that there should be no adults present when children are playing and that you cannot plan for play: *Practitioners cannot plan children's play, because this would work against the choice and control that are central features of play* (DCSF, 2009, page 11).

The UK curriculum continues to prompt practitioners to offer planned and purposeful play, facilitated by adults. There are real tensions in the language and concepts of play in a learning setting and, as a result, ideas of how adults should be, behave or work with children who are 'at play'.

Several authors (Broadhead, 2010; Katz, 1992) have argued that there are three main perspectives underpinning pedagogic practices:

1. *Top down* is a perspective in which information in relation to the curriculum comes down from central government to be relayed by the practitioner to the child. This is a technical transmission model in which power resides in the adult.

2. *Bottom up* is a perspective which uses as its basis for assessment the question: *what does it feel like to be a child in this environment?* (Katz, 1992, page 99). This model supports child led-play and exploration. It seeks to identify what the child is really doing in the setting, and what learning arises from their chosen play activity. Although there is much praise for the bottom-up approach, in that it is holistic and integrates several aspects of child development, there is also criticism that the value of play for learning has not been fully established, and that learning is less easily monitored.

3. *Co-construction of understanding.* Some practitioners and theorists express concern that there is a danger that play without targets will not necessarily achieve socially and culturally desirable learning outcomes (Wood, 2011; Broadhead, 2011). They remind us that children do have to take their place in a merit-focused society and therefore may need some direction and support to succeed. However, this third model recognises that child and adult can work together in a relational way, influencing each other. Power at times resides with the adult and at others with the child. Rogers describes this as an approach in which *meanings are negotiated in the context of play* (Rogers, 2011, page 6). The traditional idea of pedagogy is taken apart and re-conceptualised, such that traditional power relationships in the classroom are altered.

THEORY FOCUS

Defining play for learning

Moyles (2010, page 22) usefully indicates three perspectives of play that relate to bottom up and top down pedagogic practices in supporting learning. I summarise her explanation below:

1. *Pure play* – is play under the control of children, initiated and led by them, sustained and developed by them for their purposes. This form of play most highly aligns with children's intuitive ways of being, is open ended and highly creative. It may be difficult to attain such play in a managed setting. An adult's role here will be: to ensure an appropriate environment and resources; to observe progress and only join in if invited.

2. *Playful learning* – relates to learning experiences which may be adult- or child-inspired, but which engage the child in playful ways. These experiences are close to those of intuitive play, but have a clear learning outcome and may not be perceived by the child as pure play. The child is engaged in playful modes of learning. The adult's role is varied, but sensitive to the child's needs perhaps involving planning, modelling, enhancing vocabulary, observing and assessing learning achievement and future need.

3. *Playful teaching* – focuses on the adult role of teaching, but in an approach which utilises the children's innate disposition towards play in the design of learning activities. The adult role is to ensure that the tasks presented to children are as open ended as possible and that they are *planned and presented in a way that is meaningful and enjoyable to the children* (page 23).

Perspectives on pedagogic practice

Moss (2000) points out how different pedagogic approaches draw on those key philosophical concepts of the child that we have already come across in this book:

- the child as empty vessel and knowledge receptor;

- the child as innocent;

- the child of nature;

- the scientific child viewed through the lens of developmental psychology;

- the child as co-constructor of knowledge in relation with other children and adults (adapted from Moss, 2000, page 10).

He cites two opposing approaches: Lilian Katz, writing in 1993 about American models of early childhood provision, and Loris Malaguzzi, writing slightly earlier about the Reggio Emilia pedagogic philosophy. Katz was concerned that early childhood programmes are drawing more and more on production models seen in industry, in which planned input and resources lead to expected output or perceived success:

> *...early childhood programmes are increasingly in danger of being modelled on the corporate/industrial or factory model so pervasive in elementary and secondary levels of education... factories are designed to transform raw material into prespecified products by treating it to a sequence of prespecified standard processes.*
>
> (Katz, 1993, pages 33–34, cited in Moss, 2000, page10)

This idea of the early childhood institution and related pedagogic practice as a machine for production of appropriately educated citizens is so obviously contradictory to the slightly anarchic play work approach (found in adventure playgrounds and holiday clubs) which advocates for the rights of children as individuals, able to think for themselves, often with a clear, and challenging, voice. The factory model assumes children can be shaped into copies of successful adults. However, those adult templates may be out of date as the future will be different to the present of today's shapers of society. As a result of new understandings relating to education for a future we do not yet know, we have moved on from an industry-influenced approach, but ideas of resource input, standardisation and outcome measurement for school readiness still pervade the English Early Years Foundation Stage (DfE, 2012).

The Reggio Emilia approach of the town of that name in Northern Italy is concerned with social construction, the creation of community and the transformative development of new understandings arising from children's voices. Not constrained by a top-down curriculum, their philosophy is one in which the environment is the third pedagogue (the others being the teacher and parent). Spaces are created for dialogue and social interaction to allow for generation of new understandings. A far cry from the factory approach in which the outcome is predicted and expected, the philosophy is of a curriculum that is emergent. The pedagogic practice is also clearly articulated to allow for this. Children are both citizens and co-constructors of knowledge within a community and the adult role is to support this: *our image of the child is rich in potential, strong, powerful, competent and, most of all, connected to adults and other children* (the words of Malaguzzi, cited by Moss, 2000, page 10).

In this model the curriculum arises from the child's interests rather than being handed down by the adult. The pedagogic practice involves seeking new understandings and negotiating with the child what can be learnt from each new situation that unfolds. Malaguzzi spoke of *leaving room for learning*, observing, reflecting and questioning one's own assumptions.

> *...it is clear that openness to children's thinking and learning results in more effective teaching. The greater our awareness of pedagogical practices the greater our possibility to change through constructing a new space... it is, above all a question of getting insight into the possibility of seeing, talking and acting in a different way.*
>
> (Carla Rinaldi, 1994 cited by Scott, 2001 page 23)

Such an approach which prompts observation, insight and innovation, could well align with a play-based approach to learning and related pedagogic practice. Rinaldi exhorts practitioners to deconstruct their current practice and see things in a new light. They must let go of their expectations. However, the Reggio way is implemented by a whole community approach. To adjust pedagogic practice to a play-led approach of this kind requires that the practitioner *lets go* of the historic need to establish achievement of milestones determined by others according to developmental frameworks and prescribed curricula. Practitioners also need the support of others who work with them.

The New Zealand curriculum Te Whāriki (New Zealand Ministry of Education, 1996) also adopts a specific socio-cultural perspective. In this model the practitioner as pedagogue both recognises the child's social context but also seeks to acknowledge and promote the bi-cultural nature of New Zealand (with Maori and Western European cultures). An important aspect of this model is that it seeks to nurture learning dispositions, rather than curriculum content, indicated through the following five strands:

- well-being;
- belonging;
- contribution;
- communication;
- exploration.

There are, within each strand, developmental, cultural and learning goals. However, the practitioner's role is to support children to achieve these goals through the creation of an appropriately stimulating learning environment, offering activities that are culturally appropriate. While play is not given explicit priority, practitioners are encouraged to offer opportunities for spontaneous play to support learning that is meaningful to the child. Pedagogic practices adopted include:

- an emphasis on reciprocal and responsive relationships with adults aware of children's development and changing capabilities (page 20);

- a recognition that within minutes children can shift from independence to dependence according to changes in temperament, environment or adult expectation;

- adults that remain predictable and consistent in their approach so that the child knows they will get the support expected, even if their own mood swings are unpredictable;

- a key worker system with adults who are unconditionally responsive, loving and available when needed by children;

- adults actively encouraging independence;

- adults and environments offering challenges, resources and support to explore ever widening interests;

- adults encouraging sustained conversation, query and complexity including social concepts of fairness, difference and similarity;

- adults able to manage the organisational and structural aspects of early years provision such as resources, scheduling, policy and procedure management, liaison with parents and other partners. There is emphasis here on stability and structure providing a secure framework within which children can explore through self-initiated active learning.

It is interesting that the Te Whāriki documentation (New Zealand Ministry of Education, 1996) indicates that planning is not there to push the process forward, but *should help adults who work in early childhood education to understand what young children are learning, how the learning happens, and the role that both adults and other children play in such learning* (page 28).

Taguchi (2010) offers another perspective which argues for a balance of planning and free choice:

> *...we need to make plans for our learning endeavours with the children. Plan ahead, but also always be on the edge and be prepared to immediately diverge from, or let go of that plan when necessary. We must often simply stand back and wait to see what might happen next... This is why slowing down and delaying our movements in the pedagogical space is very important from time to time* (page 116).

These pedagogic practices are not about 'teaching' but about facilitating environments within which children can flourish, play and explore.

THEORY FOCUS

Sustained shared thinking

The EPPE and REPEY reports referred to a process of adult and child interaction *sustained shared thinking* and the Te Whāriki documents refer to engaging in *sustained conversation* to stimulate query and explore complexity. So what is sustained shared thinking?

It is an episode in which two or more individuals work together to solve a problem using intellectual skills and understanding. Sustained shared thinking requires open questioning and may clarify a concept, evaluate activities, extend a narrative or achieve some other outcome. The word 'shared' is important as both the child and adult must contribute to the thinking which develops and extends existing understanding (Siraj-Blatchford *et al.*, 2002). Sustained shared thinking may be adult initiated or child initiated, but should then be led by the child. An example of sustained shared thinking from my experience was offered by a sudden snowstorm which prompted the children in nursery to all rush to the window. Staff keen to support children's learning asked if the children wanted to go outside. Together they explored the issues of cold and wet, the clothes to wear and what parents would want. The practitioners observed how the children responded to the snow when outside and then helped them to catch the snow, make snowballs, sculpt and so on.

Pedagogic practices to support sustained shared thinking include:

- the adult tuning in to the child, observing and listening carefully to what the child is doing;
- showing genuine interest, establishing the relationship through eye contact, focused attention, smiling, nodding and affirming the value of the child's actions. Respect is shown for the children's own decisions and choices and they may ask 'Tell me what you are doing' or 'I really want to know more about this';
- adults maybe repeating what the child has done, or thinks can happen. The purpose of this can be affirmation or summary. Practitioners may say things like 'So you think that will happen?' or 'So you have decided to put that on there?';
- making suggestions, but drawing on your own experiences, for example, 'When I cook I like to do it this way', which still leaves the choice and power of exploration in the child's hands;
- offering alternative viewpoints, for example: 'Perhaps your parents would not want us to go outside and get all wet?' or 'Why can't we make snow women as well as snow men?';
- offering reciprocal responses to show that practitioner and child are *in it together: for example, 'It is a good job you showed me how to do that; it was melting fast'*;
- modelling thinking: 'Now let me think about this for a minute; perhaps we need to ask advice on how to do this?'.

Sustained shared thinking can last for minutes or for days and weeks. A child with a special interest in something can continue to return to it again and again.

THEORY FOCUS *continued*

I once witnessed a long period of sustained shared thinking involving a child interested in the weather. The interest started with considering clouds, then weather maps on TV and in the newspapers; it was supported by the practitioner sensitively extending his interest with questioning and research. They established a weather centre to catch rain and check wind speed in the nursery garden. The practitioner brought in weather reports and news items such as tornados in America. The child came with new information from museum trips and photographs he had taken of clouds. In this way the child's interest and growing knowledge was sustained for weeks following an initial tentative interest.

Was this play? The child freely chose their area of interest. They were deeply involved and became engrossed in the subject. When bored they chose to leave it, to return the next day when feeling fresh again. Perhaps it was play?

Pedagogy, play and the curriculum

The four different curricula for the early years in the UK all espouse play and play-based learning for young children. Each has different pedagogic perspectives and all also prescribe significant elements of curriculum content. Settings are monitored to expected outcomes based on these. We know in relation to performance indicators that people will focus on what they are being measured to, and in so doing neglect other key areas of work (Pollitt, 2008). It is the prescription and monitoring of learning outcomes that conflict with the language of play and almost inevitably shift the practitioners' pedagogic response to one of planning to ensure they address the curriculum requirements rather than supporting play from a child-led focus. As a result *the pedagogy of play is directed to meeting adult imposed targets* (Brooker, 2010, page 162).

Another aspect of good pedagogic practice is awareness and understanding of child development to inform appropriate responses and observe progress. The four curricula all draw on the tradition of Piaget and a developmental perspective of children which emphasises stages of young children's physical, psychosocial and cognitive growth during early childhood. Because of the monitoring requirement practitioners tend to reach for the normative charts and measure children against these. Some theorists question this pedagogic practice of reliance on developmental stage theory, indicating that we should rather be concerned with children's engagement, participation and dispositions for learning:

> *The stage theorists are asking the wrong question! Respecting childhood competence is not about measuring the progress of their development, like you might measure the height of a growing tree in order to decide when it should be felled. The more useful question is 'How do children's competencies develop through appropriate levels of participation.'*

> (Woodhead, 2005, page 94)

Practitioners need to develop confidence to adhere to a play-based approach in which they *capture* progress rather than leading it. The Learning Journeys of Te Whāriki and Reggio Emilia are increasingly implemented in practice today and Chapter 4 of this book has attempted to address the pedagogic practice of good observation of children at play.

Looking beyond the EYFS

The English EYFS 2012 is not the only curriculum for the early years in the UK and although recently updated, it is still beneficial to consider this document and its particular perspective with some critical reflection. In England practitioners must adhere to it and use it to shape their practice, but there is potential for interpretation. The accompanying guidance does give additional pedagogic advice that supports play in settings.

Wales has adopted the language of a play-based approach in their curriculum documents for *the Welsh Foundation Phase* (Welsh Assembly, 2008) and more thoroughly articulates the relevant pedagogic approaches to play.

> *The purpose of play/active learning is that it motivates, stimulates and supports children in their development of skills, concepts, language acquisition/communication skills and concentration. In addition to consolidating learning, it also provides opportunities for children to develop positive attitudes, demonstrate awareness/use of recent learning, skills and competencies (page 8).*

Practitioners in Wales are expected to plan experiences and environments which stimulate play for learning. Pedagogic practices promoted include ensuring that:

- learning experiences are meaningful to children;
- exploratory play is offered which includes consolidation and practice, evaluation and review;
- opportunities should be made available for children to make choices;
- the environment is stimulating;
- there is a balance of practitioner-led and child-initiated activity;
- there are opportunities for both experiential learning and reflective discussion
- problem-based learning approaches are employed;
- there is emotional support for effort and perseverance, and praise both in child-led and adult-initiated activity;

The curriculum delivery is not all about adult-planned exploratory playful learning, as we are informed that children can at times be *led* in learning and at other times left alone to their own explorations.

The document also recognises that the most effective practice builds on shared aims and principles across the team, which results in consistent practice. Reflective practice as a team is therefore also essential to aid the judgement on approaches or responses and assessment matters.

ACTIVITY 5

Within the Welsh Foundation Phase document 'Learning and Teaching Pedagogy' you will find the following quote from a practitioner...

As we move towards a problem-solving approach to all learning and develop children's skills, we need to step back and really develop authentic relationships with the children in our care. Remember we are not working towards helping them achieve an end result but towards going on a learning journey with us. They need to be comfortable in the environment and have ownership of that environment. We need to be so aware of their emotional well-being, help them to express their emotions and feelings, and to develop a positive self-image and a willingness to persist at an activity...'We take children to the starting line – they take us to the finishing line.' It is not a race, it is a journey. It is a process. They need to learn and develop, and they need help and support along the way, but it is their finishing line.

(Welsh Assembly 2008, page 27)

Consider what this is saying philosophically about pedagogy. Is this approach adopting a top-down or bottom-up perspective?

How does it relate to your practice?

Does it allow for fun, freely chosen and personally directed play activity?

Is there anything that you can draw from this to inform your own practice?

Play frames, power and understanding

We have already considered power issues in the top-down or bottom-up models of pedagogic practice. Paulo Freire (1996) recognised the importance of power and adjustment of power in pedagogic practice to empower those who were currently powerless. All pedagogic practice relies on such relational activity: the power relationship between the child and adult. In *pure play* the power resides with the child. In *playful learning* a balance of power is sought, in learning through play the power resides with the teacher.

Drawing on a relational model, but clearly placing this in the context of play, McInnes *et al.* (2011) further explore the concept of *play frames and play cues* (page 122) to analyse pedagogic practice in relation to play for learning in two settings. Their research emphasises that it is the adult's concept of playful pedagogy and their articulation of this in their facilitation of play, that affects the way in which children may perceive an activity. Children, they argue, are very sophisticated in their understanding of play cues and play responses, identifying some things as play and others as 'not play'. Children also may consider a maths activity in one setting as play and not in another, it being rather classified as 'work' or 'learning'.

You may recall that the idea of play frames (Else, 2009) relates to the creation of relational play space between child and environment. A play cue is offered to the child by the environment, objects, or other children. These play cues can be accepted or rejected by a *play return* – an indication of intention to be involved, or not. The child can also offer play cues to the adults or other children nearby. So, a table laid with bright Lego bricks may offer a *cue* in its affordances to prompt a child to play, the child responds to this by picking up some blocks. Similarly a child playing with a ball who throws the ball to a nearby adult with the play face clearly on display is offering a cue to the adult to join in. The adult offers a play return by smiling and throwing the ball back.

McInnes *et al.* (2011) found that the play cues and the pedagogic approach of adults were important in 'framing' learning activity as play. They present a model in which adults can either adopt a strong play framing approach (taking control of the cues) or a weak play framing approach (in which the child is in control, offering cues to the adult). They found that it was the playful attitude to learning in the adults that promoted children's playful engagement in a learning environment. This became as important as who frames the activity. Emotionally sophisticated play cues were offered by some adults who intend to facilitate planned learning to children in a playful way. It is the child's response to the cue that creates a distinction between play and not play, not the adult's intention.

In one of the settings researched, practitioners had developed and articulated a clear understanding of play and their role in supporting play activity by children. Although they planned a range of both adult- and child-led activities, they participated along-side children in all activities, engaging in a way that offered children choice and control. In the other setting, however, they found that the practitioners did not have a clear understanding of play and were unsure of how they should approach their role. This team planned for adult-led and child-led activities, but generally only participated in the adult-led activities (with strong adult framing) and left child-led activities to children. As a result the children did not show the subtle distinction in reading cues that they had with the first setting, but used the presence of adults to determine whether an activity was play or not play.

This study implies that the insecure understanding of play by staff in the second setting was less successful in promoting play than the first setting. This was despite their attempts to offer free play. The successful approach of the first setting relied on a coherent practice that had been discussed, explored, was consistent, and had blurred the boundaries of adult presence in children's play. This resulted in a more sophisti-cated child understanding of the cues they were offered.

Although research was limited in sample, it problematises the play and not play continuum offered by many play work theorists (Hughes, 2001; Else, 2009). Play is not necessarily adult free, and perhaps adults can play. We can also draw on this piece of research to explore the bridge between play and pedagogic practice. I draw three clear pointers for consideration:

1. Is pedagogic practice which is founded on a clear understanding of play and learning (and that is articulated and practised as a team) more beneficial in prompting playful responses to learning?;

2. Where adults are regularly involved alongside children (whether at play or in more structured activity), could the boundary between children's perceptions of play versus learning be reduced?;

3. Is there a benefit in adults recognising and knowing how to offer play cues in an emotionally supportive way, prompting playful responses in children? Should there be more training for confident cueing?

Drawing on play work theory and the adult role

I have encouraged a consideration of play beyond its place in the early years curriculum. Let us now look to the Playwork sector for another set of pedagogic pointers. Playwork practice is based on a philosophy of empowerment. Drawing on a combination of political, socio-cultural and human rights perspectives the 'play space' is often offered for compensatory reasons to children otherwise deprived of play opportunity in some way. The Playwork world also draws on biological understandings of play for evolutionary adaptive purposes and has articulated a form of pedagogy relating to play frame management. It may be helpful to reflect on this here as an opening to consider personal pedagogic practice.

THEORY FOCUS

Approaches to pedagogy to support play

Bob Hughes (2002) with Play Wales has identified a number of *intervention modes* that could also be applied in the early years setting in relation to play. With the assumption that play should be *unadulterated*, child led and without expected outcome the *intervention modes* are offered as an advanced mechanism for effective practice. The nine given modes of adult intervention in play are:

1. Distance – the adult keeps his/her distance from children's play. Distant supervision is the preferred mode allowing the children to interact with the environment and peers in a play process not corrupted by adult agendas and interventions.

2. Perceived authentic – an approach in which the play worker navigates and engages with the play space in obvious comfort and enjoyment, interacting with children when initiated by them. The relaxed approach of the worker will be accepted by children as a perfectly acceptable element of the play environment.

---

continued

THEORY FOCUS *continued*

3. Without preconceptions – the play worker does not have any prior ideas about education or socialisation that they impose on the children at play. The environmental space is there only to facilitate and enable play.

4. Unadulterating – very much aligned with point 1. The adult recognises the advantages of child-led play and only engages in their play when invited.

5. Permissional – this mode recognises the anarchy of play and that children will challenge and overturn usual ways of behaving when they are at play. This mode of intervention gives permission for children to explore such behaviours without criticism. This may be difficult to achieve in some settings and may need to be bounded in some way.

6. De-centred – the play worker is not at the centre of what is going on, but observing from the sidelines. Recognising that sometimes situations need analysis and resolution, the adult is at a tangent so he or she has a broader perspective, a dispassionate overview, seeing the facts of conflicts and behaviour.

7. Perceived indifferent – in this mode the play worker may appear to be deliberately ignoring specifically targeted children to ensure that they do not feel pressure to conform and therefore have the freedom to work through their needs. In reality the worker is not indifferent, but actually very alert and aware of what is going on.

8. Without stereotypical play narratives, the adult does not predict the narrative that the child is developing.

9. Compensatory – Working with a moral intention to increase children's play experiences, this mode of intervention is about the practitioner being aware of the challenges of the play context. This mode adopts a philosophy which aims to compensate for any play deficits that have been identified in their environmental, resource and activity planning in future.

Consider how points 1 and 6 contrast with the research of McInnes *et al.* (2011) in which the adult can play *with* children. Which would you adopt?

SUMMARY

I have presented a range of approaches to pure play and playful pedagogic practice in this chapter and hope that you are sufficiently interested to pursue further research into these. Many authors have noted that learning for the twenty-first century is not so much about content, but about nurturing an ability to learn, and to maintain that interest in learning for life. Technology, for example, is moving so fast that we do not know what the next phase will bring. Perhaps play is evolutionary, offering the conditions to support cognitive plasticity, supporting children and adults' innovative thinking in response to the changed environment. If so it will be more and more required as a foundation for creativity in adulthood in a fastmoving society.

SUMMARY *continued*

We began this chapter by considering how play was not well articulated in the early years and how practitioners' pedagogy was not clearly understood or designed. We end with an understanding of the importance at a local level of a coherent articulation of play pedagogy among a team of workers. Such coherence will offer stability within which children can explore and learn. A playful pedagogy is about creating an enabling environment, balancing power, promoting independence, loosely planning, understanding how to cue, consciously letting go, and ultimately slowing down our factory-based tendencies to push for control of input and output (the product of a becoming adult).

To develop strong pedagogic practice settings should take time to discuss and debate their philosophy and design their related pedagogic practice in order to offer an articulated consistent response for stability. A team approach will more easily enable a shift to a more play-based focus in preparation not just for school, but to cope with what the twenty-first and twenty-second centuries will throw at future generations.

A play-based pedagogy is a risky business in a world of targets and comparative measures of achievement so here I make that plea to those already offering bottom-up, play-based approaches to continue to share practice. I exhort those who merely espouse ideas of play-based pedagogy to support each other and make the shift from stated philosophy to embedding this in practice.

Finally I should like to borrow from Goffee (2005) who argued that good leaders are themselves, but better and argue that good early childhood pedagogues are also themselves but better. In other words they do not try to be something they are not, but work to their strengths, are aware of their weaknesses, values and principles as influences on their practice and seek honesty in their work with children.

ACTIVITY 6

Use the table below to stimulate reflection on your own pedagogic practice and the strengths, weaknesses, aspirations and barriers you experience. First reflect on the three questions, then complete the table below.

What is my philosophy of play?

Do I support pure play, or offer playful learning or playful teaching?

What is my aspiration for children's play in my setting?

What are my strengths in supporting play for learning?

continued

ACTIVITY 6 *continued*

What are my strengths in supporting play for learning?	Do I have weaknesses in supporting play for learning that I would like to address?
What is my aspiration in relation to my pedagogy? What would I want it to look like in my setting?	What are the barriers that I will have to addresses to achieve my aspirations?

Table 10.1 Reflection on pedagogic practice

Can you set yourself a few targets to achieve over the next six months?

FURTHER READING

DfE (2012) *The Statutory Framework for the Early Years Foundation Stage*. London: DfE.

Accessible through **www.education.gov.uk/childrenandyoungpeople/earlylearningandchildcare/delivery/education/a0068102/early-years-foundation-stage-eyfs**

The Foundation Stage website – DfE endorsed website packed with useful information for pedagogues!
www.foundationyears.org.uk/

The Welsh Foundation Phase document 'Learning and Teaching pedagogy' Welsh assembly 2008 accessed at **http://wales.gov.uk/dcells/publications/policy_strategy_and_planning/early-wales/whatisfoundation/foundationphase/2274076/pedagogye.pdf;jsessionid=vHGVPQVcJ6Y08SM8RkRjSrPGLJGFpRFTfJZJR6dMxQyv7D9mMgGT!546169119?lang=en**

New Zealand **www.educate.ece.govt.nz/learning/curriculumAndLearning.aspx** (accessed online 03/04/12)

Website material – High Scope video Francesca and sustained shared thinking **www.youtube.com/watch?v=SmZsDfVTa8I** A video which reveals basic interpretations of sustained shared thinking, with useful voice-over explaining the practitioner's role and approach.

11 Conclusion: Play is for life, not just for nursery

In reading this chapter you will:

- be presented with some concluding thoughts relating to play;
- review some potential impacts of play beyond foundations for school-based learning;
- consider the relevance of play as a lifelong activity;
- reflect on your own playfulness and the constraint of this.

Finally, in this chapter readers will be asked to consider whether they are playful in their practice, and are asked to advocate for children's play.

Introduction

This chapter forms a brief summary of the exploration of play that we have undertaken in the chapters of this book. It also presents play and playfulness as behaviour that goes beyond childhood, becoming a lifelong process that bridges generations.

We began this book with an exploration of the elusive meaning of the term 'play' and as I end this book I find it still cannot be distilled into a bounded and easily defined concept. In one sense, 'play' really is only a generic term that covers all that children do that is not adult directed or emotionally constrained. Yet there is something more to this free behaviour than responds to mere scientific dissection, analysis and definition of the parts. The concepts included within the word 'play' really need the development of new vocabulary to encapsulate the many facets of it; turning and reworking them as new understandings emerge from our observations of what children intuitively do. Even the former easy distinction of play being something that happens without adult involvement now seems to have been overturned. We begin to understand that adults can beneficially play *with* children if they have an appropriate attitude (McInnes *et al.*, 2011). Despite this breakthrough in understanding, one difficulty in supporting play relates to the understanding that play is not actually an adult-planned activity that supports learning, but an attitude or way of being that can only be determined by the player. An individual child's sense of being 'at play' therefore relates to their concepts of freedom, self-efficacy, and opportunity for unfettered exploration. If adults wish to support play appropriately they must learn to relinquish control and adopt a more responsive stance following the child's lead, but offering support when requested.

Key themes arising from this book

In the first chapter I cited Moyles, who wrote that defining play is like *trying to seize bubbles, for every time there appears to be something to hold on to, its ephemeral nature disallows it being grasped!* (Moyles, 1994, page 4). The more I have explored play concepts to write this book, the more evident it is that there are layers of *play* and *not play*, and that the play experience, not just the analysis of it, can develop in an organic, *rhizomatic* way (Yeu, 2011) which confounds our adult desire to organise and categorise the phenomenon. It is perhaps for the child to tell us, in due course, the benefits of their early play?

Despite its complexity there are some key ideas that leap from our explorations over the past ten chapters:

1. *Play is a relational activity that is culturally situated.* Play is a behaviour which is influenced by and influences those around the player. It reflects the culture in which it happens at both a micro level and a macro level (local setting culture and the cultures of country or community). Children also create their own cultural spaces and childhood potentially has a culture of its own, distinct from the adjacent adult culture, but influenced by it.

2. *Play is a phenomenon that seems to operate at the boundaries of control.* Play is in that space between assimilation and accommodation of information; between attachment and independence (Bowlby, 1988; Ainsworth, 1969); between comfort and challenge; between order and chaos (Battram and Russell, 2002). It operates in the zone of proximal development, in transitional spaces, close to civilisation, but away from watchful eyes. Winnicott (2005) describes play as taking place in a transitional space between the inner and outer reality which enables creative action. In this risky space, objective reality is tempered by imagination leading to the creation of a *transitional reality* in which one can experiment with different ways of being and relating to others.

3. *Play offers opportunity to stimulate unusual connections of ideas in the brain.* Think here of compound flexibility (Piaget and Inhelder, 1969; Hughes, 2001). Through play children are not constrained by standard logic or expected outcome. Rational thought, creativity and make believe can join together, and somehow do so at high speed when released from constraint.

4. *We should expect an element of anarchy, contrariness and challenge in children at play.* They will overturn the norm, and push at the boundaries. They may sit when they should stand, loudly explore new language and use things in ways not intended. Such challenging play behaviour may merely be a form of self-assertion as a child makes a bid for independence from constraint and can be tolerated to a point as an aspect of play. The setting behaviour values should be in place and the

child gently reminded to return to these, so the child is allowed to challenge, but is reminded of the purpose of the constraints.

5. *Adults can create the conditions for children's play.* Adults can support a stimulating environment, adopting playful attitudes themselves, and understanding what is happening and where and when it is appropriate to intervene. Adults can advocate for play, as it is they who preserve and maintain the play spaces (whether time bound or physically framed).

6. *The conditions for play involve both security and challenge.* The adult role is to create the play arena or maintain the play frame, offering the resources and environmental affordances. Think of the attached child and their desire to enter the adjacent exploratory space close to an adult, or the establishment of boundaries of behaviour in others that allow a child to explore intricate activities without damage. The security that children require is not a constraining stability with over-concern for safety, but a stability that creates a steady space in which challenge can be faced knowing support is there if needed, and activities can be left safely to return to later.

7. *Play is about power and balance of compliance and independence.* Play is an exploration of compliance and independence, and as such involves power struggles, whether with peers, the freedom of the child from adult control, or managing the adult wishing to work alongside the child at play (a side-frame position). It could also relate to the child establishing control over the elements within their world. These are all issues of power and control, fundamental struggles that will continue throughout life.

ACTIVITY 1

Reflect here on the main points that you have gained from reading this book.

Perhaps it is a new definition of play?

Perhaps some other ideas have triggered a different response in your own practice awareness.

Are they different from mine?

How might you reflect them by amending your practice?

The above points were those that stood out to me, but perhaps you will have a different selection? Hopefully we are agreed that play is essential to the developing child. Just as pregnant women have *pica*, desiring certain foods to meet mineral needs, so children seem to instinctively seek the play form appropriate to the concerns they are working through. It is in play that children will explore social relationships, generate flexibility of mind, gain therapeutic respite or consider alternative perspectives of themselves. By playing they will also develop skills, dispositions and aptitudes that will support them in later childhood and to adulthood, not necessarily to a preconceived agenda.

Potential impacts of childhood play activity on adult behaviour

Because play is not a clearly defined activity, there are substantial difficulties in identifying the impacts of play. There is, as a result, a lack of understanding of the long-term benefits and changing nature of it within the life course. We now know play activity generates further individual responses to the environment and possibly evolutionary development. Remember Fraser Brown's (2003) *compound flexibility* – the flexibility of the speed of connections made by the mind in response to a stimulating and challenging environment. Through play the child has practised and prepared the compound workings of the mind to face future unknown challenges. The results of our individual intuitive behaviour in childhood are what make us unique and create new ways of doing things. Take for example the following tale.

Jonah Lehrer (2009) wrote of the human ability to make decisions. He cites a true tale of firefighters in Gulch Valley, America who, in the course of tackling an incident, are faced with a bush fire racing towards them at a pace faster than man can run. Despite their desperation, they do all turn and run. But one man is able to think so flexibly that he stops, burns a patch around him, and steps into it to survive (the fire goes around him as he has already used the fuel it needs). Most of his colleagues perish from trying to outrun the flames. What was it that made this one individual make that breakthrough (that has now become common practice for such firefighters)? Lehrer points out that it is a combination of the firefighter having experience to draw on, and a presence of mind to slow down and come to the rational decision that he could not outrun the fire and so would have to do something else. Was it perhaps also some early experience at play that had trained his brain to slow down, make judgements and draw on a range of experiences, enabling him to have an innovative, flexible thought pattern that would save his life in adulthood?

Play and physical attributes

The example of the quick-witted firefighter related to his cognitive skill. However, Plato had argued both for the physical benefit of play and that dispositions and aptitudes arise in childhood. I am surprised by how many tales of athletes relate that their childhood play experiences led them to develop their specific physical skills and interests. A recent article in the *Guardian* (McGrath, 2010) relating to England cricketer and world-class bowler, Stuart Broad, for example, notes how he was brought up in a cricketing family, and picked up a cricket ball in the garden when he was six. A key factor in his development, he recalls, was that he was able to have fun while playing the game. This enabled him to translate his experiences, adapt, and extend his coached technical ability. *Both my parents instilled an attitude of striving to be the best I can be but always ensuring that I had fun doing it... My mother always told me to 'have fun when playing'* (*Guardian*, November 27, 2010). The enjoyment factor led to flexibility and creativity.

Do adults play?

The word 'play' is rarely applied to adult activity except in sport or drama. Yet we do speak of creativity, social activity, recreation, playing sports, and we also dress up to go out (playing with identity?). Adults play but call it something else. Perhaps we are engaging in loose parts play when we reorganise our rooms and gardens? Pellegrini argues that play is essential for all human development, even into adulthood – enabling children and adults to be *adaptive to the niches that life presents* (Pellegrini, 2011, page 21).

ACTIVITY 2

McInnes et al. (2011) suggest it is the playful attitude of the practitioner that indicates play to the child.

Take time here to consider the ways in which you are playful as an adult.

Do you perhaps play with or alongside the children at work?

How do you relax outside of work?

Do you play a sport, or do creative activities?

Reflect on how these make you feel.

Do they offer a release from pressure as both Spencer (2000) and Schwartz et al. (2010) suggest?

Consider how you might increase your playfulness.

Schwartz, Gomes and McCarthy (2010) highlight how as adults we need to play, or at least need time for recreation away from targeted work for optimal performance. They drew on research into musicians' performance and recognised that long periods of practice alone did not lead to high performance, but if practice were broken into time slots of a maximum of 90 minutes, interspersed with relaxing activities in between, performance was enhanced. This aligns with Spencer's (2000) surplus energy theory, in which play is a period of rest and recuperation after a period of intensive action. It also indicates a rhythm in life's patterns of work, play and rest.

Creativity and possibility thinking

In Chapter 7 we drew on the work of Anna Craft (2001) to explore the link between creativity and play and the generation of children's abstract thinking. She argued that play leads to *possibility thinking* stimulating divergent thought through removal of the expected outcome. Increasingly play is being introduced into businesses and management activities to inject energy and such creativity. Jaqueline Miller writes that *games and music can help people to reactivate the intelligence centres of the brain... getting back to the 'inner child' can greatly help to put more joy into life, and especially work* (Miller, 1997, page 255). Akerstrom Andersen (2009) cites Huizinga in stating that *some of the great business concerns deliberately instil the play spirit into their workers so as to step up production* (page 1). There are now many books and articles written about the use of play and experiential *playful* techniques in support of team and individual development in adult contexts.

Social skills, resilience and power management

Play in early childhood is also about learning about self and others, how we relate to each other, how to support and how to manipulate or resist manipulation. In play with others we find out how to make friends and fall in and out of favour with each other (and vice versa), how to tease and joke, and who holds the power. In a great turn of phrase, Ailwood reminds us that *early years settings are sites of human interaction where relationships are played out within particular conditions of possibility* (Ailwood 2011, page 29). If, as she suggests, children are able to deal with this complexity and manage their activities within the social structures and institutions in which they find themselves, then this must also surely offer templates of understanding on which we draw later as adults, negotiating power, space, and boundary. Yeu (2011, page 136) writes of how children will *mock educational canons,* and in so doing, *twist, crack and rupture the taken-for-granted views* of both a nominally play-based approach and related power. Play becomes an area for social experimentation and testing in which children step in and out of layers of meaning making, in so doing they are able to enter the process of *self-transformation into more relational beings well attuned to the other* (page 137). Surely again these are skills for life? Social play has been taken up in management-training techniques of role-play and active experiential learning, recognising that complex social relationships can be worked out through playful activity.

Play and the development of culture

No longer currently in vogue beyond its role in education, play was not so long ago recognised by the Government for its impact on culture and the future economy. In 1998, the then Secretary of State for Culture Media and Sport had highlighted a perceived economic importance of play, commenting that *play is not only important to the quality of life of children. It is of great importance to the creative industries, the economy and to the country's future* (cited by National Playing Fields Association, 2000, p4). At the most fundamental level the claim was that 'play' can have an economic impact by contributing to the development of citizenship, culture and the creative industries. Play England today acknowledges a link between play and culture, but from the child's perspective of re-enacting culturally specific themes (as discussed in Chapter 6). In later childhood and early adulthood it is likely that choices made in relation to cultural activity will influence the future shape of culture, and that choices made in childhood shape the way for these cultural activities.

Adult responsibility to advocate for play

There is an assumption by some writers that those people are happiest who can most rely on their own resources and resilience. In 1984 the Opies wrote:

> *If children's games are tamed and made part of school curricula, if wastelands are turned into playing fields for the benefit of those who conform and ape their elders, if children are given the idea that they cannot enjoy themselves without being provided with the 'proper' equipment, we need blame only ourselves when we produce a generation who have lost their dignity, who are ever dissatisfied and who descend for their sport to the easy excitement of rioting, or pilfering, or vandalism.*
>
> (Opie and Opie, 1984, page 16)

These words, written almost half a century ago, have resonance today echoing those of the media especially in the light of the urban riots in the United Kingdom in 2011. In a different plea for play, Broadhead and Burt (2012) cite research which indicates that:

> *Direct teaching and rote learning in early childhood fail to ensure lasting school success even when they produce temporary test results, because they provide an inadequate base for the higher order thinking skills that are needed in later schooling and in adult life. These skills have their foundation in play – in initiative taking, problem solving and innovating within the constraints of reality...*
>
> (Broadhead and Burt, 2012, page 21)

It is our role to promote play, perhaps using the Charter for Children's Play (given in the further reading below). Why not consider it as you develop your team's playful pedagogy, and promote the right to play to others. It is essential that these rights are truly protected to ensure that children develop creativity, flexibility and innovation appropriate for an unknown future.

SUMMARY

Advocating for play (as an essential early childhood experience) may seem less important than issues of economy, global peace and sustainability. But to reduce the importance of play below such adult agendas is both short sighted and essentially ignores children's rights.

Over the long term, progress on all these issues depends critically upon the children of the future growing up as engaged, self-confident, responsible, resilient citizens, who both feel they have some control over their destinies and are alive to the consequences of their actions. This will only happen if their childhoods include some simple ingredients of frequent, unregulated, self-directed contact with people and places beyond the immediate spheres of family and school, and the chance to learn from their mistakes.

(Gill, 2007, page 84)

---

continued

SUMMARY *continued*

I would like to add that in order to address those big issues for society in future, children now (who will themselves become adults) need to feel secure and confident in their innovations and creativity, with confidence to maintain a smiling spirit and resilience in the face of future concerns. Schwartz et al. (2010) have informed us that a playful attitude not only enhances creative performance and increases efficiency, but also allows for time to play throughout life. This benefits physical and mental health. Life in the 'flow' zone is more rewarding (Csikszentmihalyi, 2002) and adults who play will be more able to model play to children.

Childhood is transient, and as many parents of older children will be only too aware, passes in a flash, but the memories and neural pathways laid down then are there for very much longer. Let us work to maintain our own and our children's playful spirit for whatever life experience may bring!

If play is a preparation for maturity *(Groos, 1896)*, then what are the mature doing when they play?
Are they preparing for death?

(Sutton-Smith, 1979, page 47)

WEBSITES

Play England (2009) *Charter for Children's Play.* London: Play England. **www.playengland.org.uk/ media/71062/charter-for-childrens-play.pdf**

Look at the Pearson teacher of the year site. **www.teachingawards.com/winners/2011/UK_Panel/ 53595**

Consider whether the winners carried forward playfulness into their practice.

Look to other sources for stimulation – sites such as TED (Technology, Entertainment, Design) offer innovative ideas through regular podcasts and videos. **www.ted.com/search?q=Early+Education** is the link to the early education thread on the site.

Time line

5000BC	Early toys found in China dating from this era.
2400BC	Greek wine vases depict children playing with toys.
2000BC	Oldest toy found in Britain – a small carved animal placed in a child's grave at Stonehenge.
375–360BC	Plato states in the Republic that learning should be *put before children as play.* He recognises that play has importance for social and physical development.
384–322BC	Aristotle, a student of Plato, links play to *catharsis* or the release of complex concerns by bringing them to the surface.
43–410AD	Romans invade and stay in Britain. Roman toys found in recent times include dolls, five-stones and model animals.
400–1066AD	Anglo-Saxon period children have a range of home-made toys, games, model animals, spinning tops, dolls and small-sized tools. Time for play is limited as children worked.
1000AD	Chinese painting depicts 100 children at play, dressing up and taking part in physical games.
1066–1154	Normans invade Britain and there is a rise in church influence on morality and the restriction of play.
1154–1485	Middle Ages – a lack of evidence of play.
1497	Erasmus argues for enjoyment to be applied to study.
1560	Pieter Bruegel the Elder paints *Children's Games*. The painting shows children at play in Flanders, including games of piggy-back, marbles, dressing up, chase.
1592–1670	Comenius, a philosopher, states that children should learn through enjoyable first-hand experiences.
1632–1704	John Locke writes several pieces on education. Considered to be the first 'empiricist', he believes children to be a 'blank slate' or *tabula rasa* waiting to take on new information through the senses. He promotes that learning should be fun.
1712–1778	Jean Jacques Rousseau publishes 'Emile – On Education' in 1762. He argues that children are naturally inclined to be active explorers and social beings, instinctively and actively learning for future survival. He asserts that children learn more from the playground than the classroom.

1724–1804	Immanuel Kant argues for a balanced approach in which children are born with some cognitive understanding and potential. He believes this is developed through the child's informed interaction with their environment and other people – foundations of constructivist approach.
1746–1827	Johann Pestalozzi establishes a school in 1805 based on Rousseau's ideas, linking education to nature rather than nurture. Pestalozzi stresses the importance of suitable learning environments and play as spontaneity and self-activity.
1771–1858	Robert Owen sets up the first infants' school and nursery in Scotland in 1816, placing it adjacent to the mills for women workers. The intention is to care for and to educate the new population for social benefit. Play is important.
1759–1805	Friedrich von Schiller, philosopher and poet, describes play and the *play drive* as the expression of exuberant energy and the origin of all art.
1782–1852	Friedrich Froebel opens the first *Kindergarten* in 1837 – and suggests that educational play is important in young children's development to help the unfolding child to absorb knowledge and develop imagination and language. He establishes set resources, *gifts* and *occupations* (planned tasks).
1859	Charles Darwin's *Origin of the Species* is published, influencing interest in evolution and study of animals in context.
1820–1895	Herbert Spencer presents the *surplus energy* theory in which play is presented as a means to 'let off steam'. He draws analogies from industrial processes and considers that children with abundant energy also need pressure-release mechanisms.
1849–1936	Ivan Pavlov carries out his famed behaviourist work with animals (and conditioned reflex work). This is later applied to humans by the behaviourists.
1854–1938	Sigmund Freud reintroduces the ideas of catharsis (*see* Aristotle). Play helps to release negative feelings resulting from traumatic events. Play and dreams are windows to the subconscious.
1861–1925	Rudolf Steiner is concerned with spirituality and supporting the essential nature of the child. He proposes that the role of the adult, the environment and natural resources are important in developing *a free human being*.
1861–1946	Karl Groos, a German psychologist, writes *The Play of Animals* in 1898, arguing that play is essential for survival in later life. He uses observation to inform his ideas.

1860–1931	Margaret McMillan, with her sister Rachel McMillan, campaigns for health and education reforms for poor children. Her writings indicate a value placed on play and active learning. She opens an open-air nursery and training school in Peckham in 1914.
1870–1952	Maria Montessori develops the Montessori learning method. She opens her first *casa bambini* (children's house) in 1907. She advocates for choice in children's learning and provides real-life learning experiences in a planned and structured environment which develops the *inner lives* of children through sensory and scientific experiences.
1872–1945	Johan Huizinga writes of play as a *culture creating force*, but one that *must be pure and free.* He advocates for play as part of the generation of new society. He was killed by the German forces just before the end of World War Two.
1884–1924	G Stanley Hall proposes in 1906 that *recapitulation* play helps children to work through primitive instincts and with it the development of the species – echoing human development towards civilisation through activities such as hunting, gathering and den building.
1896–1934	Lev Vygotsky researches play and the psychology of development. He is interested in the value of play in its social context: a key theory is the *zone of proximal development.* He states that *in play a child is always above his average age.* His works are not widely translated until the 1960s.
1896–1980	Jean Piaget identifies play as a vital part of developing mental frameworks (*schemas*) which support cognitive development through the process of assimilation and accommodation. He considers child development in stages and also recognises an emotional impact of *disequilibriation*.
1885–1948	Susan Isaacs, a psychologist, joins an experimental school, the Malting House. Here she observes children at play, taking careful notes. She declares play to be a child's *life's work* in 1929. Isaacs and Piaget communicate about play and psychological development.
b.1902	Mildred Parten publishes her developmental *Play Types* relating to social play development from unoccupied to co-operative, in 1933.
1919	First Waldorf School (later to become Steiner Waldorf schools) opens in Stuttgart (funded by the Waldorf Astoria Company) with an intention to address class exclusion and support a better social state for the working class. Emphasis on play as the spiritual, creative movement and learning by 'doing'.

1895–1982	Anna Freud contributes to the field of psychoanalysis. With Melanie Klein (1882–1960), she draws on the work of her father (see Sigmund Freud) to develop the use of play as therapy, to *play out* the troubled feelings in children.
1904–1990	B F Skinner develops the behaviourist approach of *operant conditioning* – with children being encouraged to do something for tangible reward.
1915–present	Jerome K Bruner, a strong advocate of play, sees children as active learners. He draws on Vygotsky's social constructivist ideas to describe *scaffolding*. He stresses the importance of learning through first-hand experience and play.
1924–1929	Malting House experimental school runs in Cambridge. Susan Isaacs takes careful observations of children at play. As a result of her studies, the practices of this school remain influential today.
1925	National Playing Fields Association is established *to ensure that everyone should have access to free, local outdoor space for play and recreation and sport.*
b.1925	Albert Bandura draws on the work of Skinner and develops the behaviourist approach of *social learning theory* (ie that children are influenced by the behaviour modelled by others).
1943	First adventure playground opens in Copenhagen, Denmark, called *Skrammellegepladsen* or junk playground.
1948	First UK 'adventure playground' opens in Camberwell, London. Such playgrounds are described as places where *most of the site can be used by the children for games of their own invention* (adventureplay.org.uk).
1961	Pre-School Playgroups Association is set up to offer childcare to working mothers through a co-operative approach.
1963	National Bureau for Co-operation in Child-Care (NBCCC), which later becomes the National Children's Bureau, is established, maintaining a focus on play.
1963	Reggio Emilia education system begins in Italy. First pre-schools using the *Reggio Approach* (developed after World War Two) are opened in the Italian town of the same name.
1967	Plowden Report, the first review of Primary Education since 1931, states that play is the central activity in nursery schools and infant schools. This highly influential education report recognises that play is important for children's learning and development and prompted a renewed interest in play as learning through the 1970s.

1969	Piaget and Inhelder write their cognitive development response to behaviourism and conditioned learning. Play features strongly in the text.
1969	Iona and Peter Opie publish their research into children's games around Britain collected in the 1960s.
1970	National Children's Bureau emerges from the NBCCC and develops a remit to support play, later hosting the Children's Play Council.
1971	Simon Nicholson writes of the theory of *loose parts* in which *in an environment the degree of inventiveness is proportional to the number of variables*. This theme is picked up by the play movement.
1970s	Vivian Gussin Paley writes of the importance of play to learning in the USA. Her research raises the profile of play and embeds inclusion.
1979	Lillian Katz introduces the concept of dispositions for learning.
1979	Johnson and Johnson Paediatric Round Table discussion on play in which Sutton-Smith, Hutt, Csikszentmihalyi and other play researchers publicly discuss play theory. This is subsequently published as an influential document for the field.
1988	The National Curriculum is introduced for all children over five.
1989	Children Act comes into being, an overarching act relating to children's well-being. This gives local authorities the duty to provide day care and play provisions for children under eight. Also brings in inspection requirement.
1991	Tina Bruce writes of play as a process, not product and uses the term *free-flow play*.
1991	United Nations Convention on the Rights of the Child (UNCRC) is ratified by the UK Government recognising, among a range of rights, all children's right to play.
1992	Office for Standards in Education, Children's Services and Skills (Ofsted) is established and has the duty to inspect children's play provisions where registered.
1995	Pre-school Learning Alliance is the new name for the former Pre-school Playgroup Association.
1996	Ferre Laevers introduces the Leuven involvement scale and emotional importance of children being *at home* in a setting as prior condition for learning and involvement.
1997	Effective Provision of Pre-School Education (EPPE) and aligned Researching Effective Pedagogy in the Early Years (REPEY)

	research commences, following the development of 3,000 children across England.
1998	Perry Else and Gordon Sturrock explore psychological concepts of ludic play, play cues and play responses.
1999	Sure Start, a New Labour Government initiative, is introduced to support children and families, reduce poverty and offer opportunity. Family play sessions feature among a number of other initiatives in the Sure Start Centres.
2000	*Best Play* is published, stating what play provision should do for children.
2000	Curriculum Guidance for the Foundation Stage embeds play within early years provision and support for learning. There is widespread concern that it actually restricts play in introducing a curriculum for the under fives.
2001	Bob Hughes writes *Evolutionary Playwork and Reflective Analytic Practice* in which he claims that children at play demonstrate *recapitulation*, the exploration of stages of evolution through play.
2002	Welsh Assembly Government Play Policy is released.
2003	Every Child Matters is issued as a green paper. It considers childhood as holistic with five overarching *outcomes* essential for all children (stay safe; be healthy; enjoy and achieve; economic well-being; make a positive contribution).
2003	Initial EPPE and REPEY reports released. Siraj-Blatchford *et al.* identify that practitioners have a narrow concept of play, largely relating to imagination/role play and the outdoors.
2003	Birth to Three Matters is issued. This is a highly praised pack to support learning in children aged 0–3. The document is thoroughly researched and uses play approaches.
2003	Fraser Brown writes of play and *compound flexibility*.
2003	Chris Athey writes of research exploring children's *schemas*.
2003	Scottish Curriculum for Excellence is released.
2004	Getting Serious About Play: A Review of Children's Play is produced by a panel chaired by Frank Dobson MP. This triggers funding for play projects in England.
2007	Play England is established from the Children's Play Council as part of a Big Lottery Fund project to promote children's play across England.

2007	English Early Years Foundation Stage (EYFS), a framework and statutory guidance for early years education and care is issued.
2008	The First National UK Play Strategy is released.
2008	Scottish Government creates a policy framework for play.
2008	EYFS is amended slightly and re-released.
2008	The Welsh Foundation Phase curriculum, a play-based approach to learning for the under-eights, is introduced by the Welsh Government.
2010	Scottish Curriculum for Excellence is amended and re-released and focuses on an *active learning* approach from three years, with play as an integral part.
2010	MP Frank Field's report into poverty and children's life chances highlights access to play opportunities as a predictor of children's successful life chances.
2011	Dame Clare Tickell review of the EYFS is issued.
April 2012	New EYFS is issued. The main Statutory Framework document has limited reference to play, but support documents promote learning through play.

References

Abbott, L (2001) Perceptions of play, a question of priorities?, in Abbott, L and Nutbrown, C (2001) *Experiencing Reggio Emilia: Implications for pre-school provision.* London: Routledge.

Abbott, L and Nutbrown, C (eds) (2001) *Experiencing Reggio Emilia: Implications for pre-school provision.* London: Routledge.

Abbott, L et al. (2005) *Birth to Three Matters.* Nottingham: DfES Publications. Available at **www.education.gov.uk/publications/standard/publicationdetail/page1/birth** (accessed 24/06/12).

Ailwood, J (2011) It's about power, researching play, pedagogy and participation in the early years of school, in Rogers, S (2011) *Rethinking Play and Pedagogy in Early Childhood Education.* London: Routledge.

Ainsworth, MD (1969) Object relations, dependency and attachment; a theoretical view of the infant mother relationship. *Child Development* 40(4): 969–1045.

Aitken, KJ and Trevarthen, C (1997) Self/other organization in human psychological development. *Development and Psychopathology,* 9: 653–677.

Albon, D (2010) Reflecting on children playing for real and really playing in the early years, in Moyles J *Thinking About Play: Developing a Reflective Approach.* Maidenhead: McGraw-Hill/Open University Press.

Andersen, NA (2009) *Power at Play, the Relationship between Play, Work and Governance.* Basingstoke: Palgrave Macmillan.

Anning, A, Chesworth, E and Spurling, L (2005) *The Quality of Early Learning, Play and Childcare Services in Sure Start Local Programmes.* Nottingham: DfES Publications. **www.ness.bbk.ac.uk/implementation/documents/1187.pdf** (accessed 11/02/11).

Appleby, K (2011) Playing and learning: ways of being in action, in Canning, N (ed) (2011) *Play and Practice in the Early Years Foundation Stage.* London: Sage.

Appleby, K and Andrews, M (2011) Reflective practice is key to quality improvement, in Reed, M and Canning, N (eds) *Implementing Quality Improvement and Change in the Early Years.* London: Sage.

Argyris, C and Schön, D (1978) *Organisational Learning.* Reading, MA: Addison Wesley.

Ariès, P (1962) *Centuries of Childhood.* London: Jonathan Cape.

Arnold, C (2003) *Observing Harry: Child Development and Learning 2–5.* London: Sage Publications.

Arnold, C and the Pen Green Team (2010) *Understanding Schemas and Emotions in Early Childhood.* London: Sage.

Athey, C (2004) *Extending Thought in Young Children.* London: Paul Chapman Publishing.

Axline, V (1964) *Dibs-In Search of Self.* London: Penguin.

Ball, D, Gill, T and Spiegal, B (2008) *Managing Risk in Play Provision: Implementation Guide.* Nottingham: DCSF Publications.

Barber, N (1991) Play and energy regulation in mammals. *Quarterly Review of Biology,* 66: 129–147.

Battram, A and Russell, W (2002) The Edge of Recalcitrance: Playwork, Order and Chaos. Presentation first given at the Spirit of Adventure Conference, Cardiff, May.

BERA (British Educational Research Association) Early Years Special Interest Group (EYSIG) (2003) *Early Years Research Pedagogy, Curriculum and Adult Roles, Training and Professionalism*. Southwell: BERA.

BERA (British Educational Research Association) (2011) *Ethical Guidelines for Educational Research*. Southwell: BERA.

Berlyne, D (1969) Novelty and curiosity as determiners of exploratory behaviour. *British Journal of Medical Psychology*, 41(5): 68–80.

Bilton, H (2010) *Outdoor Learning in the Early Years: management and innovation*. 3rd edition. Abingdon: Routledge.

Bion, W (1962) *Learning from Experience*. London: Heinemann.

Bjorklund, D and Gardiner, A (2011) Object play and tool use: developmental and evolutionary perspectives, in Pellegrini, AD (ed) *The Oxford Handbook of the Development of Play*. New York: Oxford University Press.

Bowlby, J (1965) *Childcare and the Growth of Love*. Second edition with two new chapters by Ainsworth, MD. Harmondsworth: Penguin.

Bowlby, J (1988) *A Secure Base*. London: Routledge.

Boyd, W (1956) *Emile for Today: the Emile of Jean Jacques Rousseau selected, translated and interpreted*. London: Heinemann.

Bozena, M (2007) Exploratory play and cognitive activity, in Jambor, T and Van Gils, J (eds) *Several Perspectives on Children's Play: Scientific Reflections for Practitioners*. London: Garant.

Broadhead, P and Burt, A (2012) *Understanding Young Children's Learning Through Play: Building Playful Pedagogies*. London: Routledge.

Broadhead, P, Howard, J and Wood, E (eds) (2010) *Play and Learning in the Early Years*. London: Sage.

Brock, A, Dodds, S, Jarvis, P and Olusoga, Y (2009) *Perspectives on Play: Learning for Life*. Harlow: Pearson Education.

Brooker, L (2011) Taking play seriously, in Rogers, S *Rethinking Play and Pedagogy in Early Childhood Education*. London: Routledge.

Brooker, L and Edwards, S (eds) (2010) *Engaging Play*. Maidenhead: McGraw-Hill.

Bronfenbrenner, U (1979) *The Ecology of Human Development*. Cambridge: Harvard Publishing.

Bronfenbrenner, U (2005) *Making Human Beings Human: Bio-ecological Perspectives on Human Development*. London: Sage.

Brown, F (2003) *Playwork: Theory and Practice*. Buckingham: Open University Press.

Bruce, T (1991) *Time to Play in Early Childhood Education*. London: Hodder and Stoughton.

Bruce, T (2004) *Early Childhood Education*. London: Hodder & Stoughton.

Bruce, T and Meggitt, M (2005) *Child Care and Education*. 3rd edition. London: Hodder and Stoughton.

Bruner, JS (1976) Nature and uses of immaturity, in Bruner, J, Jolly, A and Sylva, K (eds) 1985) *Play: Its Role in Development and Evolution*. Harmondsworth: Penguin.

Bruner, JS, Jolly, A and Sylva, K (eds) (1985) *Play: Its Role in Development and Evolution*. Harmondsworth: Penguin.

Canning, N (ed) (2011) *Play and Practice in the Early Years Foundation Stage*. London: Sage.

Canning, N (2012) Exploring the Concept of Quality Play, in Reed, M and Canning, N (eds) (2012) *Implementing Quality Improvement and Change in the Early Years*. London: Sage.

Carle, E (2003) *The Very Hungry Caterpillar*. London: Puffin.

Carr, M (2001) *Assessment in Early Childhood Settings: Learning Stories*. London: Sage.

Carr, M and Claxton, G (2002) Tracking the development of learning dispositions. *Assessment in Education: Principles, Policy & Practice*, 9(1): 9–37.

Casey, T (2007) *Environments for Outdoor Play: A Practical Guide to Making Spaces for Children*. London: Paul Chapman Publishing.

Christensen, P and James, A (2008) *Research with Children, Perspectives and Practices*. 2nd edition. London: Routledge.

Clark, A and Moss, P (2001) *Listening to Young Children: The Mosaic Approach*. London: National Children's Bureau (NCB).

Cooperrider, DL and Whitney D (2005) *Appreciative Inquiry, a Positive Revolution in Change*. San Francisco: Berrett Koehler Publishing Inc.

Coulter, F and Taylor, J (2001) *Realising the Potential of Cultural Services: The Case for Play*. London: LGA Publications.

Craft, A (2001) Little c creativity, in Craft, A, Jeffrey, B, Leibling, M, *Creativity in Education*. London: Continuum.

Craft, A, Cremin, T, Burnard, P and Chappell, K (2007). Developing creative learning through possibility thinking with children aged 3–7, in Craft, A, Cremin, T and Burnard, P (eds) *Creative Learning 3–11 and How We Document It*. London: Trentham.

Csikszentmihalyi, M (1979) The concept of flow, in Sutton-Smith, B (1979) *Play and Learning: The Johnson and Johnson Pediatric Round Table III*. New York: Gardner Press.

Csikszentmihalyi (2002) *Flow: The Psychology of Happiness*. London: Random House/Rider.

Cunningham, H (2005) *Children and Childhood in Western Society Since 1500*. Harlow: Pearson Education.

Curtis, A (1994) Play in different cultures and different childhoods, in Moyles, J (2000) *The Excellence of Play*. Buckingham: Open University Press.

Dahlberg, G, Moss, P and Pence, A (1999) *Beyond Quality in Early Childhood Education and Care: Post-modern Perspectives*. London: Routledge.

Danish Federation of Early Childhood Teachers and Educators (BUPL) (2006) *The Work of the Pedagogue: Roles and Tasks*. www.bupl.dk/iwfile/BALG-7X4GBX/$file/The%20work%20of%20the%20pedagogue.pdf (accessed 24/06/12).

Darling, J (1994) *Child Centred Education and Its Critics*. London: Sage.

David, T, Goouch, K, Powell, S and Abbott, L (2003) *Birth to Three Matters: A Review of the Literature*. London: HMSO. Available at https://www.education.gov.uk/publications/standard/publicationDetail/Page1/RR444 (accessed 24/06/12).

Davis, JM (2008) What might education for sustainability look like in early childhood? A case for participatory, whole-of-settings approaches, in Pramling-Samuelsson, I and Kaga, Y, *The Contribution of Early Childhood Education to a Sustainable Society*. Paris: Unesco, pp18–24.

Department for Children Schools and Families (DCSF) (2003) *Every Child Matters*. London: DCSF Publications.

Department for Children, Schools and Families (DCSF) (2007) *Staying Safe: A consultation document*. London: Department for Children, Schools and Families.

Department for Children, Schools and Families (DCSF) (2008a) *The Early Years Foundation Stage*. Nottingham: DCSF Publications.

Department for Children, Schools and Families (DCSF) (2008b) *It's Child's Play: Early Years Foundation Stage*. Nottingham: DCSF Publications.

Department for Children, Schools and Families (DCSF) (2009) *Learning, Playing and Interacting: Good Practice in the Early Years Foundation Stage*. Nottingham: DCSF Publications.

Department for Education (DfE) (2012a) *Statutory Framework for the Early Years Foundation Stage*. London: DfE Publications. Available at **https://www.education.gov.uk/publications/standard/publicationDetail/Page1/DFE-00023-2012** (accessed 24/06/12).

DfE/British Association for Early Childhood Education (2012b) *Development Matters in the Early Years Foundation Stage (EYF 2012)*. London: DfE.

DfES (1967) *The Plowden Report – Children and their Primary Schools: A Report of the Central Advisory Council for Education (England)*. London: HMSO. Accessed at **www.educationengland.org.uk/documents/plowden** (accessed 24/06/12).

DfES (2005) *Birth to Three Matters*. London: DfES.

Dewey, J (1991) *How We Think*. London: Prometheus Books.

Donnachie, I (2003) 'Education in Robert Owen's New Society: The New Lanark Institute and Schools', *The Encyclopaedia of Informal Education*. Available at **www.infed.org/thinkers/et-owen.htm** (accessed 24/06/12).

Drummond, MJ (2003) *Assessing Children's Learning*. 2nd edition. London: David Fulton.

Eaude, T (2011) *Thinking Through Pedagogy for Primary and Early Years*. Exeter: Learning Matters.

Edgington, M (2004) *The Foundation Stage Teacher in Action*. London: Sage.

Edwards, C, Gandini, L and Foreman, G (2011) *The Hundred Languages of Children: The Reggio Emilia Experience in Transformation*. Santa Barbara, CA: Praeger.

Else, P and Sturrock, G (2007) *Therapeutic Playwork Reader One, 1995–2000*. Eastleigh: Common Threads.

Else, P (2008) Playing: The space between, in Brown, F and Taylor, C (2008) *Foundations of Playwork*. Maidenhead: OUP/McGraw-Hill.

Else, Perry (2009) *Value of Play*. Continuum International Publishing Group.

Field, J (2008) *Social Capital: Key ideas*. London: Routledge.

Fox, W (2008) *A Theory of General Ethics*. London: MIT Press.

Freire, P (1996) *Pedagogy of the Oppressed* translated by Myra Bergman Ramos. London: Penguin.

Froebel, F (1887/2010) *The Education of Man*. Charleston, SC: Forgotten Books/Classic Reprint.

Frost, J (2010) *A History of Children's Play and Play Environments: Toward a Contemporary Child-Saving Movement*. London: Routledge.

Gardner, H (2011) *The Unschooled Mind (Twentieth Anniversary Edition)*. New York: Basic Books.

Garvey, C (1991) *Play*. 2nd edition. London: Fontana.

Gibson, JJ (1996) *The Ecological Approach to Visual Perception*. New Jersey: Lawrence Earlbaum.

Gill, T (2007) *No Fear: Growing up in a Risk Averse Society*. London: Calouste Gulbenkian Foundation.

Gill, T (2010) It is Time to Puncture the Zero Risk Myth. Online National College of School Leadership (NCSL). **www.nationalcollege.org.uk/index/leadershiplibrary/ldr-magazine/back-ldr-issues/ldr-june-2010/ldr-jun-10-viewpoint.htm** (accessed 15/09/2010).

Goffee, R (2005) Managing Authenticity: The Paradox of Great Leadership. *Harvard Business Review* online December 2005. **http://hbsp.harvard.edu/hbrsa/en/issue/0512/a** (accessed 28/2/2012).

Goldschmied, E and Jackson, S (1994) *People under Three: young children in day care*. London: Routledge.

Goldschmied, E and Jackson, S (2003) *People under Three: young children in day care*. 2nd edition. London: Routledge.

Goleman, D (1996) *Emotional Intelligence: Why it Can Matter More Than IQ*. London: Bloomsbury.

Greishaber, S and McArdle, F (2010) *The Trouble with Play*. Maidenhead: Open University Press.

Groos, K (1896) The play of animals: Play and instinct, in Bruner, JS, Jolly, A and Sylva, K (1985) *Play: Its Role in Development and Evolution*. Harmondsworth: Penguin.

Guldberg, H (2009) *Reclaiming Childhood: Freedom and Play in an Age of Fear*. London: Routledge.

Hall (1906) *Youth*. New York: David Appleton & Co.

Hanawalt, B (1993) *Growing Up in Medieval London: the Experience of Childhood in History*. Abingdon: Oxford University Press.

Harcourt, D, Perry, B and Waller, T (2011) *Researching Young Children's Perspectives: Debating the ethics and dilemmas of educational research with children*. London: Routledge.

Hargreaves, L (1996) Seeing clearly: Observation in the primary classroom, in Moyles, J *Beginning Teaching: Beginning Learning*. Buckingham: Open University Press.

Heaslip, P (1994) Making Play Work in the Classroom, in Moyles, J (ed) *The Excellence of Play*. Buckingham: OUP.

Hendricks, H (2010) The child as a social actor in historical sources, in Christensen, P and James, A (2008) *Research with Children, Perspectives and Practices*. 2nd edition. London: Routledge.

Hewes, J (2007) The value of play in early learning: Towards a pedagogy , in Jambor, T and Van Gils, J (eds) *Several Perspectives on Children's Play: Scientific Reflections for Practitioners*. London: Garant.

Hobart, C and Frankel, J (2004) *Practical Guide to Child Observations and Assessments*. 3rd edition. Cheltenham: Stanley Thornes.

Holland, P (2003) *We Don't Play With Guns Here*. Buckingham: Open University Press.

Huddlestone, A (1992) Play as Preparation. *Nursery World*, October: 11.

Hughes, A (2010) *Developing Play for the Under 3s: the Treasure Basket and Heuristic Play*. London: David Fulton.

Hughes, B (1996) *A Taxonomy of Play Types*. London: NPFA.

Hughes, B (2001) *Evolutionary Playwork and Reflective Analytic Practice*. London: Routledge.

Hughes, B (2002) *A Playworker's Taxonomy of Play Types*. 2nd edition. Ely: PlayEducation Ltd.

Hughes, B (2007) Do locomotor play levels change following environmental modification?, in Jambor, T and van Gils, J (eds) (2007) *Several Perspectives on Children's Play: Scientific Reflections for Practitioners*. London: Garant.

Hughes, FP (2010) *Children, Play and Development*. 4th edition. London: Sage.

Huizinga, J (1976) Play and contest as civilizing functions, in Bruner, J, Jolly, A and Sylva, K, *Play: Its Role in Development and Evolution*. Harmondsworth: Penguin, pp675–687.

Hutt, C (1979) Exploration and play in Sutton-Smith, B (ed) *Play and Learning: The Johnson and Johnson Pediatric Round Table*. New York: Gardner Press, pp175–194.

Isaacs, S (1929) *The Nursery Years: The Mind of the Child from Birth to Six Years*. London: Routledge and Kegan Paul.

Isaacs, S (1930) *Intellectual Growth in Young Children: with an Appendix on Children's 'Why' Questions by Nathan Isaacs*. London: Routledge and Sons Ltd.

James, A, Jenks, C and Prout, A (1998) *Theorising Childhood*. Cambridge: Polity Press.

Jenkinson, S (2001) *The Genius of Play*. Stroud: Hawthorn Press.

Jensen, JJ and Hansen, HK (2003) The Danish pedagogues – a worker for all ages. *Children in Europe*, 5: 6–9.

Johnston, J and Nahmad-Williams, J (2009) *Early Childhood Studies, Principles and Practice*. Harlow: Pearson Education.

Joint National Committee on Training for Playwork (JNCTP)/Cole-Hamilton, I and Gill, T (2002) *Making the Case for Play: Building Policies and Strategies for School-aged Children*. London: National Children's Bureau.

Kaarby, KME and Osnes, H (2007) Natural playgrounds: Opportunities for play and learning. *Journal of the European Teacher Education Network*, 3: 49–59.

Kalliala, M (2006) *Play Culture in a Changing World*. Maidenhead: Open University Press.

Kant, I (1781/2004) *A Critique of Pure Reason*. New York: Dover Publications.

Kapasi, H and Gleave, J (2009) *Because it's Freedom: Children's views on their time to play*. London: Play England.

Karmiloff-Smith, A (1995) *Baby It's You*. London: Ebury Press.

Karmiloff, K and Karmiloff-Smith, A (2001) *Pathways to language: from fetus to adolescent*. Massachusetts: Harvard University Press.

Katz, LG (1992) *What Should Young Children Be Learning*? Urbana, IL: ERIC Digest.

Kellmer-Pringle, M (1986) *The Needs of Children*. 3rd edition. London: Routledge.

Klein, M (1979) *The Psycho-Analysis of Children*. London: Vintage.

Knowles, M (1984) *Andragogy in Action: Applying Modern Principles of Adult Learning*. London: Jossey Bass.

Konner, M (1991) *Childhood: A Multicultural View*. London: Little, Brown and Company.

Kottak, K (2011) *Window on Humanity: a concise introduction to general anthropology*. London: McGraw-Hill.

Laevers, F (1993) Deep level learning: an exemplary application on the area of physical knowledge. *European Early Childhood Education Research Journal*, 1(1).

Laevers, F (2000) Forward to basics: Deep level learning and the experiential approach. *Early Years: an International Journal of Research and Development*, 20(2) Spring.

Langston, A and Abbott, L (2010) Birth to three in Bruce, T (ed) *Early Childhood: A Guide for Students*. London: Sage.

Lave, J and Wenger, E (1991) *Situated Learning: legitimate peripheral participation*. Cambridge: Cambridge University Press.

Leach, J and Moon, B (2008) *The Power of Pedagogy*. London: Sage.

Learning and Teaching Scotland (LtS) (2006) Occasional Paper 2, *Lets Talk About Listening to Children*. Stirling: LtS.

Lehrer, J (2009) *The Decisive Moment: How the Brain Makes Up its Mind*. London: Canongate.

Lewin, K (1942) Frontiers in group dynamics: Concept, method and reality in social sciences: Social equilibria and social change. *Human Relations* (1947) 1(1): 5–41.

Lewis, M (1979) The social determination of play, in Sutton-Smith, B (1979) *Play And Learning: The Johnson and Johnson Pediatric Round Table III*. New York: Gardner Press.

Lilliard, PP (1982) *Montessori: a Modern Approach*. London: Arrow.

Lindon, J (2005) *Understanding Child Development: Linking Theory and Practice*. London: Hodder Arnold.

Locke, J (1689/1979) *An Essay Concerning Human Understanding: With a Foreword by Peter H Nidditch*. Oxford: Oxford University Press.

Locke, J (1699) *Some Thoughts Concerning Education*. 4th Edition. London: A & J Churchill. Available through Early English Books Online at **http://eebo.chadwyck.com/home** (accessed 15/12/2011).

Louv, R (2005) *The Last Child in the Woods: Saving our children from nature deficit disorder*. New York: Workman.

Macintyre, C (2012) *Enhancing Learning Through Play: A Developmental Perspective for Early Years Settings*. 2nd edition. London: David Fulton.

MacNaughton, G (2005) *Doing Foucault in Early Childhood Studies: Applying Post structural Ideas*. London: Routledge.

McCall, R (1979) Stages in play development between zero and two years of age in Sutton-Smith, B (1979) *Play And Learning: The Johnson and Johnson Pediatric Round Table III*. New York: Gardner Press.

McGrath, N (2010) *My Family Values: Stuart Broad*. Guardian, 27 November.

McInnes, K, Howard, J, Miles, G and Crowley, K (2011) Differences in practitioners' understanding of play and how this influences pedagogy and children's perceptions of play. *Early Years,* 31(2): July, 121–133.

Malaguzzi, L (1996) The right to environment, in Filippini, T and Vecchi, V (eds) *The Hundred Languages of Children: The Exhibit*. Reggio Emilia: Reggio Children.

Manning Morton, J and Thorp, M (2004) *Key Times for Play*. Buckingham: Open University Press.

Miller, J (1997) All work and no play may be harming your business. *Management Development Review*, 10(6–7).

Mitchell, E and Mason, B (1948) *The Theory of Play*. New York: Barnes.

Moss, P (2000) *Workforce Issues in Early Childhood Education and Care for consultative meeting on International Developments in Early Childhood Education and Care*. The Institute for Child and Family Policy Columbia University, New York Thomas Coram Research Unit: Institute of Education University of London.

Moss, P and Petrie, P (2002) *From Children's Services to Children's Spaces: Public Policy, Children and Childhood.* London: Routledge.

Moyles, J (1994) *The Excellence of Play*. Buckingham: Open University Press.

Moyles, J (2005) *The Excellence of Play*. 2nd edition. Buckingham: Open University Press.

Moyles, J (2010) *The Excellence of Play*. 3rd edition. Maidenhead: Open University Press.

Moyles, J (ed) (2010a) *Thinking About Play: Developing a Reflective Approach*. Maidenhead: McGraw Hill/Open University Press.

Murphy, C (1991) *Emil Molt and the Beginnings of the Waldorf School Movement*. Edinburgh: Floris Books.

National Playing Fields Association (NPFA) (2000) *Best Play: What Play Provision Should Do For Children*. London: NPFA/Children's Play Council/Playlink.

New Zealand Ministry of Education (1996)*Te Whāriki: Early Childhood Curriculum* Wellington NZ: Learning Media. Accessed at **www.educate.ece.govt.nz/learning/curriculumAndLearning/TeWhariki.aspx** (accessed 24/06/12).

Nicholson, S (1971) The Theory of Loose Parts – How not to cheat children. *Landscape Architecture Quarterly*, 62(1) October.

Nunnally, J and Lemond L (1973) Exploratory behavior and human development, in Reese, HW (ed) *Advances in Child Development and Behavior,* vol. 8. New York: Academic Press.

Nutbrown, C (2006) *Key Concepts in Early Childhood Education and Care*. London: Sage.

Nutbrown, C, Clough, P and Selbie, P (2008) *Early Childhood Education: History, Philosophy and Experience*. London: Sage.

OED (2001) *Concise Oxford English Dictionary by Catherine Soanes*. Oxford: Oxford University Press.

Ofsted (2011) *Regulating Play-Based Provision*. Manchester: Ofsted/Open Government Publications.

O'Kane, C (2008) The development of participatory techniques: facilitating children's views about decisions which affect them, in Christensen, P and James, A *Research with Children: Perspectives and Practices*. 2nd edition. London: Routledge.

Opie, I and Opie, P (1984) *Children's Games in Street and Playground*. Oxford: Oxford University Press.

Owen, J (2008) Britain's Oldest Toy Found Buried with Stonehenge Baby? National Geographic News, 21 October. Accessed at **http://news.nationalgeographic.com/news/2008/10/081021-stonehenge-toy.html** (accessed 24/06/12).

Palaiologou, I (2008) *Childhood Observation*. Exeter: Learning Matters.

Paley, VG (1990) *The Boy who Would be a Helicopter: the Uses of Storytelling in the Classroom*. USA: Harvard University Press.

Papatheodorou, T (2010) Being, belonging and becoming: some worldviews of early childhood in contemporary curricula. Forum on Public Policy Online, ISSN 1556-763X, 2010, Volume 2010, Issue 2, 18 accessed at **http://forumonpublicpolicy.com/spring2010.vol2010/spring2010archive/papatheodorou.pdf** (accessed 24/06/12).

Papatheodorou, T and Luff, P with Gill, J (2011) *Child Observation for Learning and Research*. Harlow: Pearson Longman.

Parten, M (1932) Social participation among preschool children. *Journal of Abnormal and Social Psychology*, 28: 136–147.

Passmore (2010) *Excellence in Coaching: The Industry Guide*. London: Kogan Page.

Pellegrini, AD (1991) *Applied Child Study: A Developmental Approach.* Hove and London: Lawrence Earlbaum Associates.

Pellegrini, AD (1996) *Observing Children in Their Natural Worlds: a Methodological Primer.* New Jersey: Lawrence Erlbaum Associates Inc.

Pellegrini, AD (2009) *The Role of Play in Human Development.* New York: Oxford University Press.

Pellegrini, AD (ed) (2011) *The Oxford Handbook of The Development of Play.* New York: Oxford University Press.

Pellegrini, AD and Galda, L (1982) The effects of thematic-fantasy play on the development of children's story comprehension. *American Educational Research Journal*, 19(3): 443–452.

Pellegrini, AD and Smith, PK (1998) Physical activity play: The nature and function of a neglected aspect of play. *Child Development*, 68: 577–598.

Pestalozzi, JH (1894) *How Gertrude Teaches her Children*, translated by Lucy, E. Holland and Frances C. Turner. London: Swan Sonnenschein.

Petrie, P (1994) *Play and Care Out of School.* London: HMSO.

Piaget, J (1951) Mastery Play, in Bruner, JS, Jolly, A and Sylva, K (eds) (1976) *Play: Its Role in Development and Evolution.* Harmondsworth: Penguin.

Piaget, J and Inhelder, B (1969) *The Psychology of the Child: Translated from the French by Helen Weaver.* New York: Basic Books.

Plato (360BC/1974) *The Republic: Translated with an introduction by Desmond Lee.* 2nd edition. London: Penguin.

Play England (2009) *Charter for Children's Play.* London: Play England. **www.playengland.org.uk/media/ 71062/charter-for-childrens-play.pdf** (accessed 24/06/12).

Play England (2011) *A World Without Play: an Expert View.* London: Play England.

Play Wales (2002) *The First Claim – Desirable Processes: A Framework for Advanced Playwork Quality Assessment.*

Pollitt, C (2008) *Time, Policy, Management; Governing with the Past.* Oxford: OUP.

Portchmouth, J (1969) *Creative Crafts for Today.* London: Studio Vista.

Pramling-Samuelsson, I and Fleer, M (2009) *Play and Learning in Early Childhood Settings: International Perspectives.* New York: Springer.

Pre-School Learning Alliance (PLA) (2012) *Our History.* Accessed at **https://www.pre-school.org.uk/about-us/ history** London: PLA (accessed 24/06/12).

Qualification and Curriculum Authority (QCA) (2002) *Designing and Timetabling the Primary Curriculum.* London: QCA.

Qvortrup, J (2000) Macroanalysis of childhood, in Christensen, P and James, A (2000) *Research with Children: Perspectives and Practices.* London: Falmer Press.

Robinson, M (2011) *Understanding Behaviour and Development in Early Childhood: A Guide to Theory and Practice.* Abingdon: Routledge.

Robson, S and Smedley, S (1996) *Education in Early Childhood.* London: Fulton.

Rogers, S (2011) Play and pedagogy: A conflict of interests? in Rogers, S *Rethinking Play and Pedagogy in Early Childhood Education.* London: Routledge.

Rogoff, B (2003) *The Cultural Nature of Human Development.* Oxford: Oxford University Press.

Rousseau, JJ (1762/1964) *The First and Second Discourses edited by Roger D Masters.* New York: St Martin's Press.

Russell, W (2005) *Reframing Playwork: Reframing Challenging Behaviour.* Nottingham: Nottingham City Council. Available at **www.fairplayforchildren.org/pdf/1280153308.pdf** (accessed 12/02/2012).

Santer, J, Griffiths, C and Goodall, D (2007) *Free Play in Early Childhood: a literature review.* London: PlayEngland/National Children's Bureau. **www.playengland.org.uk/media/120426/free-play-in-early-childhood.pdf** (accessed 24/06/12).

Schaefer, CE (2011) *The Foundations of Play Therapy.* London: Wiley.

Schiller, P (1944) Innate motor action as a basis of learning: Manipulative problems in the chimpanzee, in Bruner, JS, Jolly, A and Sylva, K (eds) (1985) *PLAY: Its Role in Development and Evolution.* Harmondsworth: Penguin.

Schwartz, T, Gomes, J, McCarthy, C (2010) *The Way we're Working isn't Working: the Four Forgotten Needs that Energise Great Performance.* New York: Simon and Schuster.

Scott, W (2001) Listening and Learning, in Abbott, L and Nutbrown, C *Experiencing Reggio Emilia: Implications for Pre-school Provision.* London: Routledge.

Scottish Executive (2007) *A Curriculum for Excellence Building the Curriculum (2) Active Learning in the Early Years.* Edinburgh, Scottish Executive. **www.ltscotland.org.uk/images/Building_the_Curriculum_2_tcm4-408069.pdf** (accessed 24/06/12).

Segal, H (1981) *Melanie Klein.* Harmondsworth: Penguin.

Shackell, A, Butler, N, Doyle, P and Ball, D (2008) *Design for Play: A guide to creating successful play spaces.* London: Play England.

Shier, H (2001) *A Child's Journey into the Future, or Sailing the Seven C's.* Paper based on keynote address at the Network of Community Activities' biannual conference, Manly NSW, Australia, May 2001. Available at **www.harryshier. comxa.com/** (accessed 24/06/12).

Shier, H (2006) Pathways to Participation Revisited. *Middle Schooling Review (New Zealand),* 2:14–19. Available at **www.harryshier.comxa.com/** (accessed 24/06/12).

Silber, K (1965) *Pestalozzi. The Man and his Work.* 2nd edition. London: Routledge and Kegan Paul.

Singer, D and Singer, P (2001) *Make-believe: Games and Activities for Imaginative Play – A Book for Parents, Teachers and the Young Children in Their Lives.* Washington USA: Magination Press.

Siraj-Blatchford, I (1994) *Praxis Makes Perfect: Critical Educational Research for Social Justice.* Ticknell, Derbyshire: Education Now Books.

Siraj-Blatchford, I (2010) A focus on pedagogy: Case studies of effective practice, in *Early Childhood Matters. Evidence from the Effective Pre-school and Primary Education Project,* Sylva, K, Melhuish, E, Sammons, P, Siraj–Blatchford, I and Taggart, B (eds) pp149–65. London: Routledge.

Siraj-Blatchford, I, Mattock, S, Gilden, R and Bell, D (2003) *Researching Effective Pedagogy in the Early Years: Research Brief No 356.* Nottingham: DfES Publications.

Siraj-Blatchford, I, Sylva, K,. Taggart, B, Melhuish, E and Sammons, P (2007) *The Effective Provision of Pre-School Education (EPPE) Project, Intensive Case Studies of Practice across the English Foundation Stage.* Presented at the Vision Into Practice Conference Dublin February 2007.

Siraj-Blatchford, J, Caroline-Smith, K and Pramling-Samuelsson, I (2010) *Education for Sustainable Development in the Early Years.* Stockholm: OMEP.

Skinner, BF (1971) *Beyond Freedom and Dignity.* New York: Bantam Books.

Smidt, S (2005) *The Developing Child in the 21st Century.* Abingdon: Routledge.

Smidt, S (2011) *Playing to Learn: The Role of Play in The Early Years.* London: Routledge.

Smilansky, S and Shefatya, L (1990) *Facilitating Play: a Medium for Promoting Cognitive, Socio-emotional and Academic Development in Young Children.*

Smith, LB and Thelen, E (2003) Development as a dynamic system. *Trends in Cognitive Sciences,* 7(8) August: 343–348.

Smith, MK (1997) Johann Heinrich Pestalozzi YMCA: Infed. **www.infed.org/thinkers/et-pest.htm** (accessed 30/01/12).

Smith, PK and Hagan, T (1980) Effects of deprivation on exercise play in nursery school children. *Animal Behaviour,* 28: 922–928.

Smith, PK, Cowie, H and Blades, M (2003) *Understanding Children's Development.* 4th edition. Oxford: Blackwell.

Smith, PK (2011) Observational methods in studying play (Chapter 12), in Pellegrini, A, *The Oxford Handbook of Developmental Play.* New York: Oxford University Press, pp138–149.

Spencer, H (2000) *First Principles.* London: Elibron Classics.

SPRITO (1992) *National Occupational Standards in Playwork.* London: Sport and Recreation Industry Training Organisation.

Steiner, R (1924) Lecture Three, Stuttgart, Morning, April 10, in Steiner, R (1997) *The Essentials of Education.* New York: Anthroposophic Press.

Steiner Waldorf Schools Fellowship pages online (2011) **www.steinerwaldorf.org.uk/** (accessed 24/06/12).

Stephen, C, Ellis, J and Martlew, J (2009) *Turned on to learning 2: Active Learning* Stirling Institute of Education Research Briefing Paper, 8 January.

Stephen, C (2005) *Early Years Education: Perspectives from a Review of the International Literature.* Edinburgh: Information and Analytical Services Division, Scottish Executive Education Department.

Stephen, C (2010) Pedagogy: the silent partner in early years learning. *Early Years,* 30(1) March: 15–28.

Stern, D (1977) *The First Relationship.* Cambridge, MA: Harvard University Press.

Sutton-Smith, B (ed) (1979) *Play and Learning; the Johnson and Johnson Pediatric Round Table III.* New York: Gardner Press.

Sutton-Smith, B (2011) The antipathies of play, in Pellegrini, AD (ed) *The Oxford Handbook of the Development of Play.* New York: Oxford University Press, pp110–115.

Sylva, K and Pugh, G (2005) Transforming the early years in education. *Oxford Review of Education,* 31(1): 11–27.

Taguchi, HL (2010) *Going Beyond the Theory Practice Divide in Early Childhood Education: Introducing an Intra-active Pedagogy.* London: Routledge.

Tannock, M (2011) Observing young children's rough and tumble play. *Australasian Journal of Early Childhood,* 6(32).

Thelen, E (1980) Determinants of amounts of stereotypical behaviour in normal human infants. *Ethology and Sociobiology,* I(2): 141–150.

Thomas, Dylan, *Reminiscences of Childhood,* broadcast on BBC Radio 1943.

Thomson, P and Sefton-Green, J (2011) *Researching Creative Learning: Methods and Issues*. London: Routledge.

Thorne, K (2007) *Essential Creativity in the Classroom: Inspiring Kids*. London: Routledge.

Tickell, Dame C (2011) *The Early Years: Foundations for life, health and learning: An Independent Report on the Early Years Foundation Stage to Her Majesty's Government*. London: DfE.

Tishman, S Jay, E and Perkins D (1992) *Teaching Thinking Dispositions: From Transmission to Enculturation*. Cambridge MA: Harvard University. **http://learnweb.harvard.edu/alps/thinking/docs/article2.html** (accessed 16/03/2012).

Tovey, H (2007) *Playing Outdoors: Spaces and Places, Risk and Challenge*. Maidenhead: Open University Press.

Tovey, H (2010) Playing on the edge: Perceptions of risk and danger in outdoor play, in Broadhead, P, Howard, J and Wood, E (eds) *Play and Learning in the Early Years*. London: Sage.

Trevarthen, C (2001) Intrinsic motives for companionship in understanding: Their origin, development and significance for infant mental health. *Infant Mental Health Journal*, Jan-Apr, 22(1/2): 95–131.

Trevarthen, C (2005) First things first: infants make good use of the sympathetic rhythm of imitation, without reason or language. *Journal of Child Psychotherapy*, 31(1): 9–113.

Ugaste, Professor A (2007) The cultural-historical appproach to play in the kindergarten context, in Jambor, T and Van Gils, J (eds) *Several Perspectives on Children's Play: Scientific Reflections for Practitioners*. London: Garant.

United Nations (1989) *United Nations Convention on the Rights of the Child*. Accessed at **www2.ohchr.org/english/law/crc.htm** (accessed 24/06/12).

UNICEF/Hart, R (1992) *Children's Participation: From Tokenism to Citizenship*. Florence, Italy: UNICEF Innocenti Research Centre.

Vadala, CE, Bixler, RD and James, J (2007) Childhood play and environmental interests: Panacea or snake oil? *The Journal of Environmental Education*, 39(1): 3–18 **http://dx.doi.org/10.3200/JOEE.39.1.3-18** (accessed 12/01/2012).

van der Kooij (2007) Play in retro-and perspective, in Jambor, T and van Gils, J (eds) (2007) *Several Perspectives on Children's Play: Scientific Reflections for Practitioners*. London: Garant.

Vygotsky, L (1933) Play and its role in the mental development of the child. *Voprosy Psikhologii*, 1966, No. 6 translated by Catherine Mulholland, available through Psychology and Marxism Internet Archive (marxists.org) 2002 **www.marxists.org/archive/vygotsky/works/1933/play.htm** (accessed 30/01/2012).

Vygotsky, L (1966) Play and its role in the mental development of the child. *Soviet Psychology*, 5(3) 6–18. Publisher: ME Sharpe

Waller, T (2007) The Trampoline Tree and the Swamp Monster with 18 heads: outdoor play in the Foundation Stage and Foundation Phase, Education 3-13. *International Journal of Primary, Elementary and Early Years Education*, 35(4): 393–407.

Waller, T (2008) Don't Come Too Close To My Octopus Tree: Recording and Evaluating Young Children's Perspectives on Outdoor Learning. *Children, Youth and Environments* 16(2): 2006.

Walsh, D (2005) Developmental theory and early childhood education: necessary but not sufficient, in Yelland, N (2005) *Critical Issues in Early Childhood Education*. Maidenhead: McGraw-Hill, pp41–48.

Wegerif, R (2010) *Teaching for Thinking and Creativity in Primary Education*. London: McGraw-Hill.

Welsh Assembly Government DCELLS (2008a) *Foundation Phase Framework for Children's Learning for 3 to 7-year-olds in Wales.* Cardiff: Welsh Assembly.

Welsh Assembly Government DCELLS (2008b) *Learning and Teaching Pedagogy.* Cardiff: Welsh Assembly Government.

White, R and Stoecklin, V (1998) Children's Outdoor Play and Learning Environments: Returning to Nature. *Early Childhood News,* March/April. **www.whitehutchinson.com/children/articles/outdoor.shtml** (accessed 12/02/2012).

Wilson, E (2002) *Biophilia.* London: Littlebrown/Harvard University Press.

Wilson, P (2009) *The Playwork Primer.* Maryland: Alliance for Childhood. Accessed at **www.ultimateblockparty.com/download/Playwork_Primer.pdf** (accessed 24/06/12).

Winnicott, DW (2005) *Playing and Reality.* London: Routledge Classics.

Wood, E (2010a) Developing integrated pedagogical approaches to play and learning, in Broadhead, P, Howard, J and Wood, E (eds) *Play and Learning in the Early Years.* London: Sage.

Wood, E (2010b) Reconceptualising the play-pedagogy relationship: from control to complexity, in Brooker, L and Edwards, S (eds) *Engaging Play.* London: McGraw-Hill.

Wood, E and Attfield, J (2005) *Play, Learning and the Early Childhood Curriculum.* London: Sage.

Woodhead, M (2006) Changing perspectives on early childhood: theory, research and policy. *International Journal of Equity and Innovation in Early Childhood,* 4(2): 1–43.

Woodhead, M and Faulkner, D (2008) Subjects, objects or participants? Dilemmas of psychological research with children, in Christensen, P and James, A (2008) *Research with Children, Perspectives and Practices.* 2nd edition. London: Routledge, pp10–35.

Wyse, D and Dowson, P (2009) *The Really Useful Creativity Book.* London: Routledge.

Yeu, Hae-Ryung (2011) Deconstructing the metaphysics of play theories: towards a pedagogy of play aesthetics, in Rogers, S *Rethinking Play and Pedagogy in Early Childhood Education.* London: Routledge.

Index

Added to a page number 'f' denotes a figure and 't' denotes a table.

UNIVERSITY OF WINCHESTER
LIBRARY